EQUATORIAL CROSSINGS

*Two Ordinary People,
One Extraordinary Journey*

DAVE SHREFFLER

Copyright © 2003 by Dave Shreffler

Maps & Illustrations by Ann Soule
Foreword by Chris Duff
Book design by Laurel Black and Cyn Gabriel
All photographs by the author, except as noted.

All rights reserved. No part of this book may be used, reproduced, or transmitted in any manner or by any means whatsoever without written permission from the author, except in the case of brief quotations embodied in critical articles or reviews.

All photographs are copyrighted to the photographers credited.

Front cover photo: Tondongi Reef, a gem amidst Sulawesi's Togian Islands.

Back cover photos: the outback of Australia's Northern Territory (upper left); Monro Beach, South Island, New Zealand (center left); sailing along the southeast coast of Sulawesi (lower left); powdered *tika* face pigments, near Pashupatinath Temple, Nepal (center); the "all-seeing" eyes of Buddha, Kathmandu, Nepal (upper right); Trekking toward Cho Oyu, Nepal - Tibet border (center right); sorting maize, near Hwedza, Zimbabwe (lower right).

Library of Congress Control Number: 2003091864
ISBN 0-9729608-4-8

Printed in the United States of America

Trevelrie Publishing
3890 Lost Mountain Road
Sequim, WA 98382-7925

For Waverly Soule Shreffler:
you're so much more than the sum of us.

Contents

	Acknowledgements	xi
	Foreword	xiii
	Prologue	1
1	No Small Promise	9
2	One Way Ticket	13
3	Into the Outback	19
4	Sea Cadence	33
5	Coral Sea Odyssey	49
6	Tale of the Turnbull	59
7	Sailing to Kaleleng	67
8	The Flight of the Kinglet	85
9	A Prayer for the Living	95
10	Role Reversal	103
14	From West to East	117
12	Solu Khumbu Sojourn	123
13	The Friendship Highway	143
14	Beyond Lhasa	157
15	The Power of Compassion	171
16	Jupiter's Moons	179
17	Trevelrie	199
	Epilogue	205

to USA
10/15/96

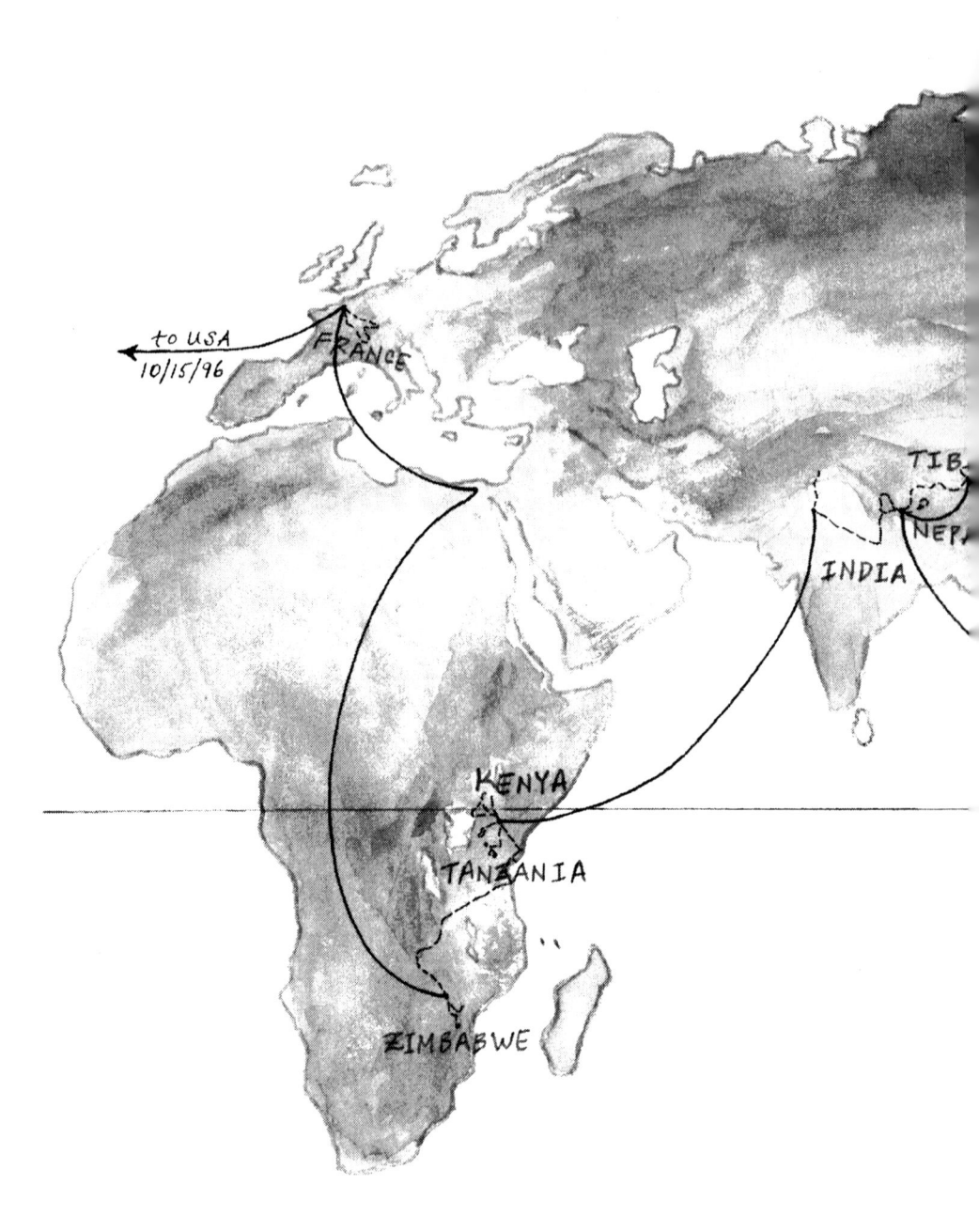

FRANCE

TIB.
NEP.
INDIA

KENYA
TANZANIA

ZIMBABWE

Equatorial Crossings

— Air route
--- Overland route

from USA 10/6/95

Sulawesi

Equator

INDONESIA

AUSTRALIA

NEW ZEALAND

Acknowledgements

A significant part of the wonder of travel is meeting new people. During our adventures, the generosity we received from complete strangers was truly amazing. This book is my way of saying a heartfelt "thanks" to all the people around the world who fed us, gave us shelter, and shared the beauty of their respective cultures. Luckily, the simple language of a smile is universal, because English is not.

Upon our return home, I began writing as a way of condensing my ramblings in five trip journals into something more readable. I thought that I was undertaking this writing journey for me, but with the birth of our beautiful daughter, Waverly, I realized that I was really writing for her. So, thank you Waverly for unknowingly giving me the motivation to continue when quitting would have been considerably easier, and for your patience as I spent countless hours "working on the book" when I could have been playing with you. I hope the wait was worth it. *Equatorial Crossings* is my gift to you.

Completing this book was far from a solo journey. I could not have finished *Equatorial Crossings* without the help and guidance of trusted friends and family. I am especially indebted to many fellow writers: Chris Duff for tirelessly supporting me in every step of this miraculous journey of self-discovery called writing—you were my tether through uncharted waters; Tim McNulty for seeing the forest in my seedlings and helping me to believe I had a book inside me; Kate Reavey for encouraging me, with love, patience, and careful editing, to write and rewrite and rewrite again; Blythe Barbo for suggesting several invaluable revisions to "Flight of the Kinglet" and "The Power of Compassion;" David James Duncan for sending me a postcard that inspired me to persevere and to strive for every sentence "to give a little gift to the reader: a twist, a fresh metaphor, a note that bends like a blues guitarist's string;" and Bill McKibben for reviewing a draft of the book and shedding some light on the puzzling world of publishing. Thank you all for believing in me.

Kudos to Laurel Black and Cyn Gabriel for your expert help with typesetting, layout, and the book design, and for your cheerful perseverance through multiple "proofs" of the book. Thanks also to: Randy Johnson for your graphics expertise and painstaking assistance with the color photo insert; Hall and Pete Stuart-Lovell for allowing me to use your computer for graphics layout; and Jane Hall for providing me with professional contacts and many helpful pointers about the printing of this book.

Our journey would not have happened without the unwavering support of my mom, Dorothy Shreffler, and Ann's mom, Hildy Pehrson. You breathed life into our childhood dreams and you continue to nurture our adult passions. Although our deceased dads, Don Shreffler and Ed Soule, were not witnesses to our world journey, they certainly are a major part of who we are and why we travel.

I am also grateful to Dorothy, Hildy, Betsy Crandell, Richard Davis, and Mike Grossmann for enriching our travels by joining us on various adventures; Lynda and Bill Driskell for sending an unforgettable care package with photos, new underwear, and homemade fudge; the Swingle family for taking care of our dog, Buddy, and the Lost Mountain Loft, while we traveled; and the countless friends and family who somehow tracked us down via *poste restante* and shared news from home, grounding us when we felt adrift. Your support made our journey possible and your love guided us home.

Most of all, I am indebted to my life partner, Ann, for opening her soul and dancing with me along the path of discovery. We are kindred spirits on the ultimate adventure.

Foreword

If I had the skill of a painter, and were to attempt to capture the textures, the colors, and the passion of life's journey on canvas, I imagine there would be a mural filled with mountains, rivers, people, foreign lands, laughter, sunshine, heartbreak, and full moons hanging in clear skies. If I were a painter, I would not be afraid to use bold strokes of certainty, brilliant colors that spoke of free-reining joy and subtle colors that hinted at times of introspection and inner growth. This mural, if there were to be one, would tell a story both universal and personal, a mural for all people to find themselves within its three dimensional depths, its colors of sky and earth, and its collage of life's choices. At the bottom of this mural there would be a small space left blank for the signature of the one who finds their life, or a part of their life, within the borders of the painting.

When we paint a picture, inscribe the first letters of a poem, or squeeze our sweat and blood onto the pages of a book, we lend to the observer a glimpse into our lives that we believe and hope will strike tones of familiarity and connection. The painting, the poetry, and the prose are gifts for the eyes, the ears, and the heart. They are gifts presented so as to perhaps give us reason to pause and reflect on the beauty of life.

The creation of any art form is similar to life. There are decisions we make, colors we choose to paint our individual murals with, and risks we take in writing our personal stories. The value of life perhaps is to see it as a work of art in progress, one where we make conscious decisions and can pause long enough along the path to look at the canvas we are creating and hopefully be pleased with what we see before us.

The canvas you are now holding, *Equatorial Crossings*, is a very intimate account of Dave and Ann's journey of world travel and self-discovery. The gift of this book is its honest sharing of doubts, difficulties, small triumphs, and global wonder as Dave brings to life the textures and colors of a mural he and Ann co-created. Dave and Ann's choice to travel the world for a year and to give serious thought to the questions of life's journey was a conscious effort at living life to the fullest. In the writing of that journey—in the miles, the people, and the adventures they sought or were challenged with—I see a couple evolving and growing deeper in their relationship to each other and to the world.

In *Equatorial Crossings*, Dave shares with readers his struggle to find personal balance in today's complex world. After reading this narrative, I have a different perspective of Dave and Ann as I ski with them in the back country of Olympic National Park, or sea kayak with them on Washington State's beautiful Strait of Juan de Fuca. I see them not only as friends, but also as fellow travelers affected by the cultures and people they interacted with during their global travel. Across the entrance of their home is a string of faded and fluttering Tibetan prayer flags. The flags are a visible reminder of what Dave and Ann have brought back from their travels — a connection to the emotions and the people living together on this small planet.

Equatorial Crossings is a bridge spanning a year of travel that brought Dave and Ann in contact with cultures and customs, challenges and rewards, issues of poverty and spiritual wealth, and answers to some of the questions which they had set out to find. If we are given but one life to live, then perhaps the choices we make could be guided by the same qualities of compassion and humility that Dave and Ann found along their paths of travel. As I read of their journey, I was reminded of why I, too, have chosen a life of travel. It is the serendipity, the adventure, and the belief that life's mural is truly painted with the colors and textures we choose.

Life is about using all the colors — the bold ones and the subtle ones combined — to paint a picture that we can recognize as unique and personal. As you read *Equatorial Crossings*, imagine that you are Dave or Ann, and that in front of you is a broad canvas upon which you are about to leave your mark of life. And when your mural is finished, leave a small space at the bottom as Dave has done and sign it as a way of saying you participated fully in the gift of life.

Chris Duff

November 2002

Prologue: Icy Wildness

The camp was made on a rocky bench near the front of the Pacific Glacier, and the canoe was carried beyond the reach of the bergs and the bergwaves . . . Climbing higher for a still broader outlook, I made notes and sketched, improving the precious time while sunshine streamed through the luminous fringes of the clouds and fell on the green waters of the fiord, the glittering bergs, the crystal bluffs of the vast glacier, the intensely white, far-spreading fields of ice, and the ineffably chaste and spiritual heights of the Fairweather Range, which were now hidden, now partly revealed, the whole making a picture of icy wildness unspeakably pure and sublime.

-John Muir, *Travels in Alaska*

"What are you, nuts?" the weary immigration officer blurted out as we crossed the border from the Yukon Territory into Alaska. There was no hint of disdain in his voice, just simple disbelief. The golden leaves of the quaking aspens and the crisp autumn mornings should have alerted us to the prospect of an early winter, but we were too love struck to take much notice of changing colors or morning frosts. It was mid-August 1990. Ann had just completed her Master's thesis and we were fleeing north, up the Alcan Highway, to celebrate her success and our recent engagement with a three-month journey from Seattle to Alaska and back.

Finally reunited, after our pursuit of graduate degrees and gainful employment pried us apart, we bounced along in a state of carefree bliss. Captivated by the boundless enthusiasm of our favorite comic strip characters, Calvin and Hobbes, we adopted their "Yukon Ho!" rallying cry and flew north in a 4-wheel drive pickup— our version of Calvin's magic, flying sled. We organized our kayaking, fishing, hiking, and camping gear in plastic milk crates beneath a sheet of 1/2-inch plywood perched on pine slats—the bed we shared with my dog, Buddy, or, more accurately, the bed he allowed us to share with him. In the remaining nooks and crannies, we cached a two month supply of dehydrated food, comprised of supposedly "non-perishable" military rations that my grandparents had stockpiled in their basement in case "the big bomb" hit: delicacies like vegetable protein pellets that were a dead ringer for rabbit turds; mystery meat labeled "beef steak"; and fossilized wood chips masquerading as "chunked turkey." On top of the canopy, we lashed our recently acquired 22-foot, canary yellow, double kayak, which we christened, *Ilulaq*, an Aleutian Eskimo word meaning "to dwell harmoniously together."

❊•❊

From our treeless aerie on a bluff overlooking Tarr Inlet, the two immense tidewater glaciers below signaled how far we had paddled since our beginning in the dripping moss-forest near the Glacier National Park headquarters. Margerie Glacier was a sculptor's masterpiece, an intricate statue of icy-blue pinnacles, fissured seracs, and cavernous couloirs: a study of scale and perspective, a meeting of ice and sea. In contrast, Grand Pacific Glacier was an imposing, raw swath of snow, ice, rock, and morainal rubble that tumbled from a wall of ominous clouds, twisted, then jolted to the water like a newly-graded highway framed within the world's largest bulldozer tracks.

Bathed in the bluish light of the full moon, Glacier Bay's frozen wilderness sparkled all around us. Ann and I were visitors in a place where tidewater glaciers, grizzlies, and wolves are the totems of wildness. Paddling up-bay was like rolling back time, cresting the recent wake of the receding glaciers and gliding down the backside into newly formed landscapes—landscapes one park ranger called the "chaotic rock-and-rubble aftermath of a glacial romp."

As we lay nested in the warmth of our joined down sleeping bags, we mutually confessed that our journals were filled with hopes for the future, centering on marriage. I laughed, "If we can survive the sight and smell of each other in this same polypropylene long underwear for another three weeks of paddling, we can survive anything."

Gazing at the profusion of stars, we reflected on our travels, our stories punctuated by white thunder, the booming symphony of Grand Pacific and Margerie, as they crackled, growled, and calved cruise ship-sized blocks of ice—

newborn icebergs—into the sea below us. Earlier in the day, as we entered Tarr Inlet, an Olympic torch-shaped iceberg had inspired us to hum the Olympic theme song in salute to this flame of ice. One week into our journey, we had already glimpsed the magic of Glacier Bay: the variety and richness of habitats exposed by the 25-foot tidal range; the flutter of a thousand pairs of scoter wings as they frothed the water, struggling into flight; and the distant blows and synchronized poetry of two breaching humpback whales, astounding then sounding. We had cherished the setting sun over Muir's "ineffably chaste" snowy spires of the Fairweather range, the highest, Mt. Fairweather, soaring to 15,320 feet. And we would recount for years to come the primal experience of floating motionless within a raft of 50 loons as they serenaded us with their mournful song.

By my calculations, our bluff-top campsite was 15 miles from "the rocky bench near the front of the Pacific Glacier" where John Muir had camped in 1879. Such a rapid rate of glacial recession—15 miles in 111 years—is known nowhere else in the world. We were 65 miles from the nearest aggregation of people and infrastructure that could be called civilization, and glad of it. We had ample food, shelter, water, stunning views, and each other. At the base of the bluff, we tethered Ilulaq to a car-sized boulder five feet above the high tide mark. Our two 5-gallon metal bear canisters—miniature versions of 40-gallon oil drums—we securely stowed several feet higher than the kayak. Snuggled in our tent, the night sky stretched to forever, and so, seemingly, did our passion.

Early the next morning, the call of nature forced me from our down cocoon. I agreed to go cook breakfast on the beach, while Ann broke camp. As I descended the bluff through the slippery Sitka alders to find some toilet paper, I could see everything was exactly how we left it the previous night. Everything, that is, except the kayak.

"Whose lame idea of a practical joke is this?" I muttered aloud, briefly imagining that some fun-loving, fellow kayakers had hidden our boat. But a quick survey of the area turned up nothing and no one.

The sea had claimed Ilulaq.

I stared in disbelief at the ice-choked inlet, then hopped from boulder to boulder, glassing every bit of coastline with our compact binoculars, which suddenly seemed foolishly inadequate. Flashing through my head were images of our kayak sinking or splintering into fiberglass shreds in the maw of jagged ice—the horror of the moment magnified by the realization that our life jackets, spray skirts, and dry bags with all our clothes and film were stashed inside the boat. Ilulaq was gone.

I took a deep, slow breath and tried to think positive, rational thoughts. Ann was still at the campsite, several hundred feet above me on the bluff, and out of hearing distance if I were to shout. I again scanned every visible portion of water and coastline. Nothing. I could postpone the inevitable no longer. I had to go break the unbelievable news to Ann.

"Ann," I exclaimed as I poked my head inside the tent, "the kayak is gone!" Thinking this was yet another one of my practical jokes, she chuckled, then resumed cramming the sleeping bag into a stuff sack. But her smile quickly faded when she looked up into my icy eyes. The magnitude of my words sunk in.

"How?" she asked the tent walls. "How is that possible?"

Together we walked along the rim of the bluff, hoping we might somehow spot Ilulaq pinned against the shore by the pan ice. Two hundred feet below us, sparkling icebergs bobbed like ice cubes in a glass of flat champagne. Gone was the effervescence of the previous night. We stood in silence, immersed in a world of chilling blues. Blue glaciers. Blue icebergs. Blue-green water. Blue-gray sky. Our bright yellow kayak was gone.

Fog was advancing our way, and the already poor visibility was rapidly diminishing. Ann remembered that the sightseeing boat, *Spirit of Adventure*, regularly motored into the East Arm of the Bay. But did it enter Tarr Inlet? Thoughts of signaling the boat raced through my mind. But signal them how? Our flares were tucked away in the pockets of our life jackets, and our whistles hung from the zipper pulls. A signal mirror was useless without sun. A rock cairn would go unnoticed in this metamorphic jumble of glacial tailings. The beams of our miniature headlamps would never be seen in daylight across miles of open water.

"We could jump around naked, swinging our clothes over our heads and shouting," Ann suggested, eliciting a forced grin from me.

Admittedly, I found the prospect of Ann dancing around naked enticing, but my immediate focus was on our missing kayak. The best bet seemed to be a large, smoky fire. We had our stove, matches, extra white gas, and now a plan of action. We rifled through the tent for the sightseeing boat brochures the ranger had given us at Bartlett Cove. There were no scheduled cruises into Tarr Inlet.

Prologue: Icy Wildness

At Ann's prompting, we agreed to search the shoreline to the east of us, around the next bend. Bolstering each other's spirits, we made a checklist of what we had with us and what was in Ilulaq. We found small comfort in the knowledge that we had at least a two week food supply, the tent and sleeping bags, and a flowing stream nearby. I thought to myself, as I stopped to grab a paddle, we aren't just "up a creek without a paddle" — we're up a bay without a boat.

We stashed all the remaining gear, except the bear canisters, in the tent, zipped it shut, and secured the corners with boulders we could barely heft. At water's edge, we found no clues to Ilulaq's disappearance — no sign of the bow line, the kayak, or anything stored in or on her. The extreme, full-moon tide must have crept up the beach higher than we predicted it would; this was the only hypothesis our scientific minds could accept.

I suddenly felt small and very conspicuous in this landscape of sea, ice, and rock. My emotions lay naked — exposed, like the rocks I stood on, by the retreating sea. The same sea that for days had buoyed our spirits now stranded us like flotsam.

We plodded east, agonizing over each slow step on the slick layer of glacial silt that covered the exposed intertidal. We walked side by side, heads down, for what seemed like miles, without seeing or saying anything.

Ann eventually broke the troubled silence, "What did happen? Did the knot fail? Did the rope break? A rogue wave?"

She was verbalizing my exact thoughts. The night had been calm and windless. There hadn't been any storms or cruise ships to create abnormally large waves. We had hauled the boat out miles from the snout of Grand Pacific glacier. It would have taken a berg wave of incomprehensible size to wash away Ilulaq.

Periodically, we stopped to scan the icy bay with binoculars. If the tide had claimed our boat, it seemed more likely that she would be floating in the middle of the inlet, amidst all the icebergs, rather than washed up on shore. I paused to examine a strand of frayed rope; it hadn't come from Ilulaq. Frayed myself, I scanned the shoreline to the east one last time.

"There, LOOK!" I bellowed.

In the distance, high in the intertidal, we could make out a sliver of pink, similar to the bright pink buoy tied to our crab pot that was lashed to the deck of Ilulaq. My pace quickened along with my heartbeat. I broke away from Ann, excited to see more.

"Oh please let the buoy still be attached to the boat," I mumbled, scuttling over the next 100 yards as rapidly as my slick, rubber calf-boots would allow.

I shouted back to Ann, "I see yellow; I SEE HER!"

I broke into a run, yelling over my shoulder as I got closer, "There's the spare paddle and the fishing pole."

A glacial epoch later, I stood next to Ilulaq, panting. Everything was still inside. The two containers of exposed film I had set in my seat the previous night remained exactly where I had left them. There wasn't a drop of water in the boat. Ilulaq rested parallel to the shoreline, perfectly balanced on two boulders—one under the tip of the stern with the rudder hanging over the edge, one under the bow, with no points of contact in between. Her tether snaked through upslope rocks. The loop and knot were still intact, confirming our hypothesis that the full-moon tide had jostled the rope up and over the boulder anchor. I hugged Ilulaq like the lost child she was, examining her bruised nose as Ann sat down trembling. Emotion swept over us, as we realized that our serious predicament had turned into a story of good fortune.

We hugged and cried in disbelief. "What charmed lives we lead," I blubbered.

"I can't believe it; I just can't believe it," Ann sighed, unable to take her eyes off the kayak.

Ever the photographer, I decided another millisecond couldn't pass without a picture of Ilulaq posed on her precarious perch. I scurried back to camp to get the camera and our paddles, and counted my steps as I retraced the shoreline distance of just over one-half mile that our wayward daughter had wandered.

Ann joked that, "Ilulaq must be going through puberty; she thought she could sneak out the back door unnoticed while we were sleeping."

We paddled her safely back to camp and grounded her. Only this time we tied her to a boulder five vertical feet higher than the previous night. Ann proclaimed, "Good moods are mandatory for the remainder of the trip, in honor of our good fortune." We spent the remainder of the day counting our blessings and planning our wedding.

The next morning we awoke to a watercolor mural of lavender sky, pure white clouds, glacial hues of blue that exist nowhere else in nature, and a sparkling sheet of pan ice frosting the inlet around dollops of translucent icebergs. The wall of clouds looming above the glaciers had parted, unveiling the magnificent Fairweather

Prologue: Icy Wildness

Mountains from which these rivers of ice flowed. The ground had frozen in places overnight and we welcomed the comfort of sun-warmed fleece. We packed the boat leisurely, quietly, stopping often to gaze at the splendor surrounding us. Margerie and Grand Pacific hailed us with a sun-spangled banner of glacial blues.

Ann's paddle glided over and dipped the mirror surface of Tarr Inlet in a contemplative rhythm, as we joined the outgoing icebergs on the ebbing tide. Her head, cocked slightly to the right, formed her hair braid into an *S*. Against our fiberglass hull, pan ice tinkled, reminiscent of the fairies' bells in the Nutcracker's *Dance of the Sugarplum Fairies*. I, too, became lost in thought.

We couldn't have chosen a more perfect name than Ilulaq for our kayak with a wandering spirit. Not only were Ann and I beginning to dwell harmoniously together with each other, but also with nature. The oneness I felt with this watery planet was manifested by my newfound joy of floating across it. "We're a part of this water," I marveled. "It guides our craft; we taste its spray; we revel in its beauty."

As we slalomed down bay through the last of the pan ice and bergs, I leaned forward and whispered to Ann's braid, "It's so great to be alive." She turned and smiled, "It's so great to be alive, and *together*." Stretching to the blue horizon was Muir's icy wildness, unspeakably pure and sublime.

1

No Small Promise

The dream of travel announces that each of us has the power to transform our lives in a fundamental way. It promises that if we pluck up our courage and agree to undertake the journey, the road upon which we travel will lead to self-discovery. It is no small promise.

-Joseph Dispenza, *The Way of the Traveler*

The earthy smells of autumn drifted through the cracked French doors, as we sat at our cluttered dining room table, going over lists one more time. We had created lists of "Trip Gear" and "Things to Investigate," and an "Action Plan" complete with a timeline and milestones. There was a list of what to give away before leaving, and another of what to store in our safety deposit box. One list, titled "Health Considerations," seemed strangely neglected in comparison to the many others, which were filled with checks, questions marks, scratched out pencil, and two colors of ink.

The most daunting list was one called, simply, "Finances"—our crude estimates of what it would cost us to travel to an undetermined number of countries for an undetermined period of time, possibly for up to one year. All these lists were neatly compiled in a composition notebook labeled, "WORLD TRIP," with a hand-drawn sketch of the globe squeezed into the "O" of "WORLD." In the back we taped a few precious family photos and lists of contacts around the world, given to us by friends and fellow travelers. This simple act was a poignant reminder that our journey was not destined to be ours alone. Our dreams had become the dreams of our families. Close friends shared in our hopes and fears. Repeatedly we heard how others would travel vicariously through us.

Equatorial Crossings

Our departure was only a few days away, and amidst the seeming order of our multiple lists, my mind was still cluttered with the minutiae of last-minute preparations. And then Murphy—of Murphy's Law—dropped in for an unexpected visit. On the evening before we were scheduled to leave for Australia, we returned home from one last visit with friends in Seattle to discover that a relative had plugged our downstairs toilet. Naturally, the toilet had overflowed, covering the bathroom floor in several inches of water and unsavory floating bits.

"What was the plug?" I asked the RotoRooter guy, as Ann and I stood outside watching him recoil 20 feet of vacuum hose.

"Bout a dozen cigarette butts and some shredded paper—looked to me like pages from a diary," he replied matter-of-factly, as if he'd seen this hundreds of times before.

"Diary pages?!" Ann repeated, bewildered. Under different circumstances, we might have allowed ourselves the time to ponder what tales those shredded pages held. Instead, our final hours ticked away as Ann packed boxes to go into storage, and I disinfected the floor, walls, and cabinetry of the bathroom on hands and knees. I stood to give my knees and back a break, and I noticed our *National Geographic* map-of-the-world shower curtain hanging inside the rim of the bathtub.

Several years earlier, we had hung this shower curtain as a fun reminder of the journey ahead. Countless times, I had traced a sudsy finger from country to country, imagining our adventures. When I was finished purging the bathroom, I found Ann upstairs, packing boxes in the kitchen.

"Should we take the shower curtain with us?" I said with a grin, catching her by surprise. "I don't see it on any of our lists."

She chuckled, and then replied, "Hey, are you really taking hiking boots, Tevas, and running shoes?"

"I can't decide ... probably not my running shoes."

"What did you find out about traveler's insurance?"

"I'm still waiting to hear back."

"Should we leave the renters written instructions about how to use the woodstove?"

"Yes, but I'm still undecided about our aging cedar hot tub."

And so the conversation went. Back and forth. Question and considered reply. Until Ann broke the monotony: "Remember in Baja, when I asked how you felt about taking a year off and traveling abroad?"

"How could I forget," I smiled. "That's when we conceived the pipe-dream account."

"That seems so long ago, now," Ann sighed, remembering the four years that had passed since our honeymoon sea kayaking expedition in Baja's Sea of Cortez.

"Yeah," I answered, walking out onto the deck. "So much has happened since then."

We gazed out at Blue Mountain and Klahhane Ridge, across a landscape of firs, hemlocks, and cedars, interspersed with an occasional blaze of gold—the unmistakable hue of big leaf maples in full fall glory. Ann came closer, encircling my waist with her arms and resting her head between my shoulder blades. The closeness felt good against the chill of the autumn evening.

The dream of world travel—launched five years earlier in the icy wildness of Glacier Bay, and shaped one year later on our Baja honeymoon—inspired our wanderlust. Yet, we had come to love the Olympic Peninsula. This was where we had chosen to establish our careers, invest in the community, and put down roots. Lost Mountain, the land beneath our feet, knew the labor of our hearts and soles. We could name every mountain peak in view, and most of the plants that graced our hillside. Our home watershed, the Dungeness River, had inspired me to fledgling lines of poetry:

> Gold and silver
> thread these hills
> Maples and Salmon
> Autumn's revelation,
> mine too.
>
> Fertile spawners heave upstream
> as spent leaves weave down
> the two bouquets converge, too briefly,
> a potpourri of land and sea
> circling in a frolic of shadow and light,
> a waltz of death and rebirth
>
>   gold...silver...gold
>   maples...salmon...maples
>
> Interwoven life histories
> stitched by coniferous needles and deciduous time
> a gift of memory and imagination.

Equatorial Crossings

So why were we leaving Lost Mountain and our newly built home? And why now, during the fall harvest and the salmons' homecoming?

Lured by the promise of unknown waters, we were leaving home right as salmon, drawn by the certainty of home waters, were returning. Like opposing tides, we ebbed seaward as salmon flooded landward. And there was urgency in both pulses—for salmon, the necessity of spawning; for us, the resonant plea of my recently widowed mom: "Go! Travel now while you're still young and healthy."

"What are you thinking about?" Ann asked, jolting me from my reverie, and us from our embrace.

"How 'grown up' this trip seems," I replied, "leaving home, arranging for a property manager, making a video tape of our possessions, writing our wills..."

"I know," she said softly, looking into my eyes. "I haven't said anything, but the whole will-writing experience really shook me; it's so strange to think about things like who should get my favorite earrings."

"Wasn't part of the idea behind this trip to simplify our lives?" I asked.

Ann responded, "Yeah, well, I don't think our lives will feel simplified until the plane takes off!"

There were so many seemingly unconnected events in our lives that had led us to this departure point—the divorce of dear friends, the joys of designing and building our Lost Mountain home together, agonizing discussions over whether or not to have children, and our ongoing search for more spiritually fulfilling lives. But no event had as profound an effect on our travel plans as the untimely death of my 61-year-old dad, one year earlier.

When Dad died suddenly of a heart attack, less than six months before he planned to retire, so did his dreams of traveling with Mom. At the time, I felt angry, confused, and cheated. I despaired. My dear mom, amidst her own grief, brought clarity and relevance to our loss:

> *Don't make the same mistake we did,*
> *pushing off all our dreams until retirement.*
> *Life is too unpredictable.*
> *Go!*
> *Travel now while you're still young and healthy.*
> *Go, and make memories!*

2

One Way Ticket

Wealth lies not in having great possessions, but in having few wants.
-Epicurus

*A*nn's girlfriends often tease her about leading a "charmed life" and wishing they could "cling to the tail of her comet." I knew exactly how it felt to do such clinging, having witnessed the way serendipity follows her. Good things just seem to happen to Ann, and so, as we began our travels, I was secretly hopeful that she would pull me further into her orbit, that her magnetism would somehow overwhelm my pragmatism.

I spent most of the 14-hour flight trying to grasp how it was possible to leave the Los Angeles airport on Friday, October 6th, 1995 and arrive in Sydney, Australia two days later on Sunday, October 8th. My scribbles and calculations covered the in-flight magazine, two airsickness bags, and several newspapers.

I asked Ann, "How much do you think it would cost to call 'time' from the airplane?" I didn't call, but instead reached the following well-reasoned conclusion: October 7th, 1995 never happened.

While the pink sun of dawn bobbed atop the South Pacific Ocean, Ann was busy chronicling the flurry of our pre-departure days in her first journal entry:

> *Only one skirt was coming – which?*
> *Only one journal needed – which to bring?*
> *I still wonder if I should have brought my running shoes*

and more underwear . . .

Too Late. Just have to see how the things I did bring work out!

She goes on to reflect on recent nightmares about insect larvae rooting around in her ear, and her backpack sinking into the ocean. All of this pre-trip anxiety led Ann to a conscious reminder that "keeping a positive attitude will allow full enjoyment, whereas my anxiety could rob me of the pleasure and full memories I want."

We arrived at 6:15 am Sydney time, dazed and stiff, and we scrambled all morning to find a room for less than $90 Australian per night. Eventually we wound up on the outskirts of Chinatown, a confluence of flashing neon lights and too many people. As I stood in a sweat-soaked T-shirt on the third flight of the George Hotel stairs, panting under the weight of my 35-lb pack and my half of our 65-lb collapsible double kayak, I recalled the sage advice of several friends who are experienced travelers: "Whatever you do, travel LIGHT!"

After stashing our load, we dragged our jet-lagged bodies out of the hotel. We meandered through Chinatown to Darling Harbour and caught a rocket ferry to the Circular Quay, where we were confronted by a confused sea of local commuters, tourists, street performers, and vendors. I soaked another T-shirt, and it was barely noon. The heat and the strange cacophony of ferries, street music, and the incessant hum of humanity drove me to the closest shade—a tourist map of the Quay—and I crumpled on a sightseeing brochure. Ann joined me after securing two overpriced, but ice-cold sodas.

Two freckle-faced Aussie girls sweetened the moment with their dueling violins. Yet, the exuberance of these young girls belied the nagging sense I had that their parents must insist on this daily grind. Food money? New shoes? Violin lessons? Nearby, a drunk soured the air with his didgeridoo rants. We might, under less sweat-soaked, jet-lagged, hungry, and disoriented conditions, have been able to ignore the disturbing music and relish the shade and cold drinks, but his relentless begging forced us to move on. Peeling away the sightseeing brochure that was cemented with sweat and dirt to the backs of my thighs, Ann asked, "Are you planning to keep this as a souvenir?"

The outgoing tide of humanity eventually swept us toward the Opera House, where we fulfilled our tourist obligation of posing on the steps and taking 24 consecutive pictures of Sydney's most famous landmark from every conceivable angle, and several inconceivable ones. Back at the Circular Quay, we spent 32 seconds meticulously selecting a bottle of 1991 Australian Shiraz to compliment our spicy Lebanese takeout. In the refuge of our hotel room, we capped our frenetic first day with a quiet meal and the wine, most of which spilled on the carpet as I grappled with the cork. Long before dark, we collapsed into bed and slept for nearly 12 continuous hours. I awoke only once, in the middle of the night. I rolled over and tiptoed to the window. As I pulled back the curtain, I noticed Ann's peaceful face awash in the red, neon glow of Chinatown, and I reveled in the realization that our pipe dream was suddenly very real.

The next morning, at a quaint, European-style cafe in Newtown, we met some Aussie mates of our friends Ann and Kevin back in Washington State. "G'day," said a lanky, smiling man, extending his hand. "You must be Dave and Ann."

"Yes," we replied in unison, "and you must be Dave and Gail."

"Did Ann and Kevin let you know we were coming?" I asked.

"Sure enough, they wrote us about you," Gail said, and then added a bit shyly, "We were expecting you to visit, we just didn't know when."

We walked inside and stared for awhile at the black chalkboard hanging above the counter. The list of specials was plenty enough to whet our appetites, but the smells of still-steaming scones sent us over the edge. While Gail and Dave nibbled on fruit and nut toast and sipped their tea, Ann and I inhaled eggs, potatoes, and scones smothered in various jams. It would be another month, and many bigger than necessary meals later, before moderation — gastronomic and economic — became part of our daily vocabulary.

After a delightful breakfast filled with pleasant, easy conversation, centering on our respective countries, family, and careers, Gail and Dave took us to their home in Merrickville. There we spent many more hours talking about our evolving travel plans and getting their tips on what to do and see in "Oz." The only segments of our Australian journey that we prearranged were the one-way flight from Los Angeles to Sydney, and a diving trip to the Coral Sea more than two months later. The world was suddenly ours to discover.

Gail and Dave generously offered to let us stay at their home, while we oriented ourselves and booked our bus tickets for Queensland and beyond. We accepted, promising "we'll only stay a day or two." Five days later, we were still discovering the charms of multi-cultural Sydney. Still "tourists" and not yet "travelers," we explored some of the many popular attractions. One sunny afternoon in Hyde Park, we watched men and women of all ages playing full-contact rugby on their lunch breaks in Hyde Park. I asked Ann, "Do you suppose it's socially acceptable to go back to work in rugby clothes?" She replied teasingly, "Or for tourists to walk around in sweaty T-shirts?"

Equatorial Crossings

That afternoon we toured the air-conditioned New South Wales Art Gallery. Four hours later, we emerged raving about an exhibit called "Yribana" featuring Aboriginal art from the Northern Territory. "Did you notice all the dramatic scenery in that video?" Ann asked. "Are you kidding," I replied. "I can't wait to see the 'top end'—those billabongs and rock escarpments are unimaginably huge."

We capped the day by wandering through a maze of narrow, cobbled streets to "The Rocks," Sydney's once squalid and now tastefully restored historic district. At a pub on Lower Fort Street, we scored our first "pint and a pie," a warm pint of beer served with a hot meat pie. The special of the day was kangaroo and rosella—shredded kangaroo meat in a red tomato sauce. Our attempts at conversation were completely drowned out by rugby and cricket matches, competing for attention on the pub's two TVs.

Part of our daily routine became sampling exotic fruits, local brews and wines, and some of the world's finest mango ice cream. I can't even remember how many days in a row we strolled through the Royal Botanical Gardens with an ice cream cone in hand. And the sunset view across crimson-dappled water to the Opera House and the Harbour Bridge from Mrs. Macquaries Point stands out as one of my indelible memories of Sydney.

We came and went from the Merrickville house as we pleased, and shared evening meals with Gail and Dave and their two teenage kids, Nami and Tim. I remember fondly the evening Gail and Dave made stir fry and fresh fruit salad, and we joined them for the first of many family meals. Dave described in detail his current work as a civil engineer on a massive casino project in Darling Harbour. He joked, in a voice laced with cynicism, "Building a casino has been my lifelong dream."

Gail, an accomplished potter, talked demurely about her art. She specializes in a technique known as soda-glaze ceramics, which she has perfected in her backyard studio overlooking the Cook River. Tim, and Nami to a lesser degree, plied us with questions about life in the U.S., especially pop music, professional sports, and the latest fashions. The disappointment in their faces was obvious, when we tried diplomatically to explain that we had last purchased a compact disc three years before, the closest professional sports team to our home was a two hour drive and thirty minute ferry ride away, and the latest fashion in Sequim was Carhartt jeans and T-shirts. Later that night, I asked Ann in private, "Do you think they're disappointed we're not from L.A.?"

One morning, while the family was away, we unloaded our gear and spread everything out to reassess our load: pleasure books (3 each), travel guides (2), tent, stove, cooking pot and accessories, sleeping bag (one for both of us that zipped onto a sheet, which I had sewn to fit snugly over our joined Thermarest sleeping pads), clothes, toiletries, a 3-lb first aid kit, a two-person collapsible kayak, life jackets, fishing line and lures, spray skirts, paddles, a Frisbee, and more. Our "necessities" completely filled their front porch, and we couldn't suppress our laughter at our attachment to STUFF.

Unable to venture too far out of our comfort zone yet, we repacked everything except two novels, and then baked cookies, washed clothes, and read the local newspaper. We chased the dogs, Quincy, a cocker-spaniel mix, and Misty, a heeler, who escaped daily over the low brick wall in the front yard. And Merrickville began to feel a lot like home; even the dogs and two parakeets seemed to accept us as new additions to the household.

A week after arriving in Sydney, we finally left behind the comforts of our adopted home. At the Greyhound bus terminal, we hugged Gail and Dave and smiled as they shook their heads in disbelief at our heaps of gear. The latest addition was a soda-glazed sugar bowl that we bought from Gail's studio.

We leapfrogged our way up the east coast, hopping on and off buses in Byron Bay, Airlie Beach, Townsville, and Cairns, all the while musing that our collapsible sea kayak really travels better across water than land. But we remained determined to reach our original destination, the Northern Territory, and that wasn't going to happen via water.

So, our grand adventure began with a one-way ticket to Australia and no itinerary, warm wishes from new friends, recharged bodies, and ample good-natured heckling from Aussie bus drivers, fellow travelers, and innocent bystanders.

"Good god, mate, are ya packin' a circus tent in there?"

"What's all that stuff weigh?"

And my favorite jab, from an Aussie child to his mam — "Are all Americans crazy?"

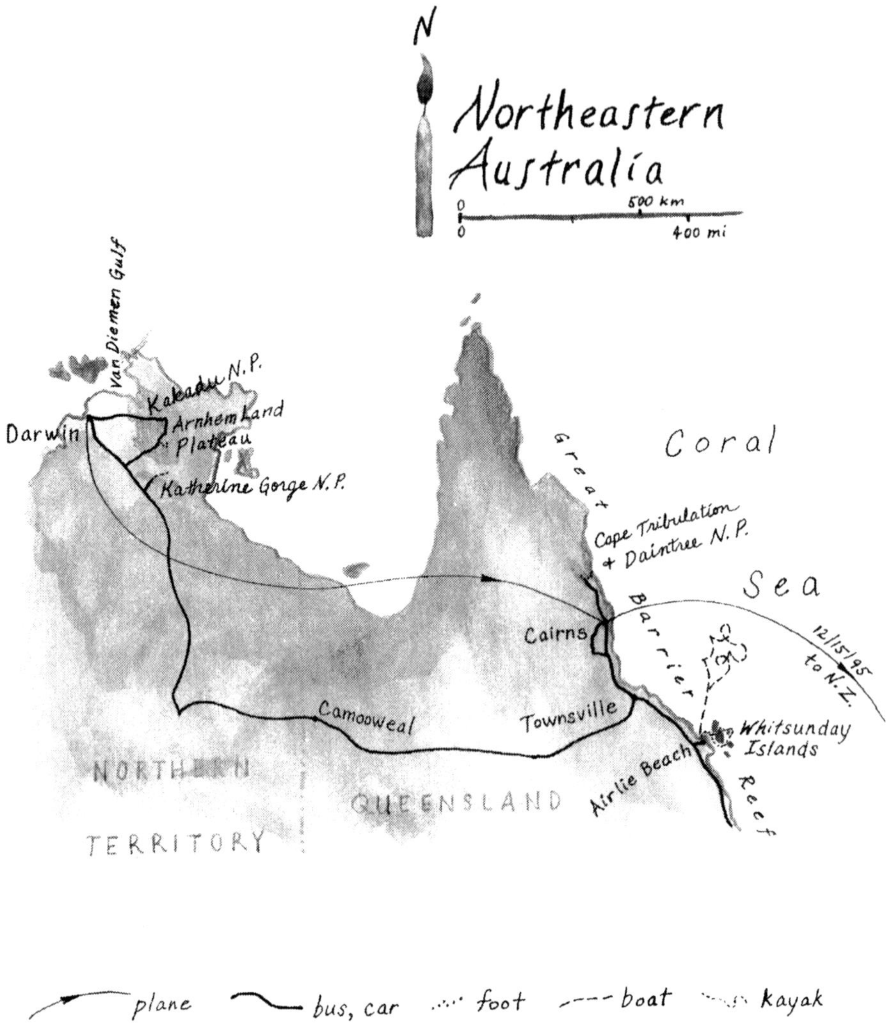
N
Northeastern Australia
0
500 km
0
400 mi
Van Diemen Gulf
Kakadu N.P.
Darwin
Arnhem Land Plateau
Katherine Gorge N.P.
Coral Sea
Great Barrier Reef
Cape Tribulation + Daintree N.P.
Cairns
12/15/95 to N.Z.
Whitsunday Islands
Townsville
Camooweal
Airlie Beach
NORTHERN TERRITORY
QUEENSLAND
plane
bus, car
foot
boat
kayak

3

Into the Outback

All these stories
Tell of earth, animals, Gagudju people.
Our blood, animals' blood and sap of plants.
It all the same, we all the same.
The old people they know this,
That why for thousands and thousands years
This country not change.
This is our culture, our story,
your story . . .
Listen that story.

-Big Bill Neidjie,
as quoted in *Kakadu: Looking After The Country The Gagudju Way*

I confirmed the details in disbelief: "All we have to do is pay you $15/day plus a $500 security deposit and $100 cleaning deposit, both of which will be refunded to us in Darwin?"

"Spot-on, mate," the agent in Cairns replied. "Just make sure you deliver her intact to Darwin in five days. She'll be right."

"She'll be right as long as we remember to stay left," I thought, but didn't say as we rolled out of the Brits Australia lot in our 4-wheel drive Toyota Landcruiser. I pulled over at the first vacant piece of land we saw, so Ann and I could practice driving. Everything about the vehicle seemed backwards: the steering wheel was on the right and I had to shift left-handed; I kept looking to my right for the rearview mirror; and the car may as well not have had turn signals at all. Luckily, the accelerator and clutch pedals weren't reversed, or my only hope would have been to drive the next 1,800 miles to Darwin with my legs tangled; left foot on the clutch, right on the accelerator. By the end of the first day, my wrists were sore from strangling the steering wheel.

The rental agent had warned us to watch out for road trains—three or four trucks hitched together like freight train cars up to 100-feet long. He neglected to mention two other salient facts: road trains travel at the speed of light, and they brake for no living thing. No previous driving in my life prepared me for the unnerving experience of two-way traffic on a single lane road, with road trains periodically approaching at upwards of 80 miles/hour. On numerous occasions we escaped a head-on collision only by pulling off the road onto the baked desert clay the instant we spotted one of these behemoths. Few kangaroos are as fortunate. My romantic notion that we would frequently see kangaroos bounding across the outback was quickly dispelled by the numerous dead roos littering the road. There was a 50-mile stretch of road west of Camooweal, where I counted an average of one pancaked roo per mile.

Traversing the outback we saw many emus, crane-like brolgas, flocks of galah parrots, and solitary raptors, as well as domestic sheep and two-humped cows. The landscape was a palette of crayon colors—burnt sienna clay; crumbling, copper termite mounds; white-barked trees; wispy, cultured-oyster clouds; and endless robin's egg-blue sky that reminded me of the Sonoran Desert in Arizona. Scattered clumps of forest green, weeping foliage were the only variation from the dominant hues of red, white, and blue.

The Bee Gee's, Carole King, Supertramp, and Styx belted out ballads on the radio as we traversed the desolate outback. The only signs of human life were an occasional drab roadhouse, ramshackle cattle station, or dilapidated windmill, all seemingly sucked of vitality by the relentless desert heat.

After three days of hard driving, the warm waters of the Katherine River were a welcome respite. I held my breath and arched my back, floating motionless, as large bats, known locally as flying foxes, circled above me. Everything about the swim felt delightfully tropical: the warm water easing away the tensions of driving; the bats, graceful even in full feeding frenzy; the screw palms lining the river banks; and the warm breeze blowing the last clouds away to unveil the first shimmering stars. Unimpeded by any lights of civilization, the twinkling expanse of sky enveloped us.

Into the Outback

Three different constellations looked to us like the Southern Cross. We chose one and considered that close enough. I let out a long, contented sigh, knowing we had a free day ahead of us with no driving.

The next morning we awoke well before sunrise to munching noises and four sets of glowing eyes. The beam of my headlamp revealed a group of wallabies eating tender grass shoots right outside the door of our tent. Ann and I chuckled as two bouncy young males pushed and punched each other like cartoon boxers.

Unable to go back to sleep, I embarked on a photo-safari, trying unsuccessfully to get pictures of the wallabies, several blue-winged kookaburras, and a frilled lizard. Near dawn, I had better luck photographing the raucous, sulphur-crested cockatoos, and nearby, a brown falcon sitting motionless in the skeleton of a paper bark tree. Brilliant green lorikeets flitted from one eucalyptus tree to another, serenading each other with the high-pitched notes of a trilling flute. With a long lens, and from behind the cover of a thorny bush that kept reaching out to grab my shirt, I photographed a male bower bird meticulously arranging bits of glass, string, and aluminum foil at the entrance to its bower in hopes of attracting a mate. Mornings like this one make me wonder why I don't rise early to greet every new day with a wallaby's bounce in my step and a lorikeet's trill in my throat.

Ann and I rented a canoe for the day and paddled up the Katherine River to the third of 13 gorges. We stroked slowly and listened. The red sandstone cliffs echoed the sounds of our paddles, and whispered legends of the Aborigines, who once called this place home. One such legend tells of spirit people with extra fingers and toes, who live inside the broken rock surfaces on top of these cliffs. If disturbed by excessive or careless changes to the land, these spirits will gulp up people and explode the sandstone cliffs.

Each layer of sandstone was like a growth ring on a tree—a history lesson, a record of climatic events, a timeline. And the aboriginal paintings on the cliff faces magnified the ancient aura of these sandstone gorges. We could make out the outlines of crude human stick figures, handprints, and a spirit figure with extra digits. Weathered paintings of animals still common today, such as kangaroos, turtles, and a brolga with a three-pronged spear through its breast provided a connection to the past. But who left these paintings behind, and what did they mean?

KAWOOSH. We spooked a freshwater crocodile sunning somewhere along the river bank; the violent slap of its tail against the water launched me out of my daydream and nearly out of the canoe. Just an hour earlier, Ann and I had frolicked and splashed in a nearby eddy. And despite a ranger's reassurances that "freshies are harmless," we were reluctant to swim again that day.

As we drifted downstream along the tangled web of screw palm roots lining the base of the painted cliffs, I remembered a partial solar eclipse was happening that afternoon. Ann looked up through her dark sunglasses and there was the sun with a missing crescent, silhouetted behind a cloud. We pulled ashore on a pocket of sand, and traded Ann's sunglasses back and forth, watching the eclipse progress like a time-lapse movie. Just as we had in Baja, where we witnessed a total eclipse on our honeymoon, we watched and listened for any unusual behavioral phenomena. At the peak of this Katherine River eclipse, the cicadas stopped humming, the birds stopped chirping, and I was grateful for the noise of my own breath. Only the occasional fish launching out of the green, still water broke the eerie silence.

Three days later, after safely delivering the Landcruiser to Darwin, we were immersed in the wilderness of Kakadu National Park, and I was cursing the jammed shudder on my new camera. Shudders have failed me on three different brands of cameras, always in spectacular, remote places that I may never return to: sea kayaking in the Sea of Cortez on our honeymoon; traversing the Bailey Range in Washington State's Olympic National Park on our second anniversary; and now entering Kakadu, in the Northern Territory's top end, on the first leg of our world journey.

Ann's suggestion that perhaps some experiences in life are better remembered than photographed was a blessing, though I never would have admitted it at the time. I learned to open my eyes to the world around me rather than always trying to condense life experiences into the aperture of a camera lens. Over the next ten days, I realized just how much the camera influences not only what I see, but how I see.

I first gained an appreciation of Kakadu's grandeur on a bush trail that climbed a steep, rocky valley through pockets of screw palms and up onto the towering sandstone escarpment. Along the way, I watched for signs of the rare and elusive black wallaroo. Known as the *barkk* in the *Gagudju* language, the swift and powerful, kangaroo-like wallaroo favors the fissured Arnhem Land plateau, which dominates the Kakadu landscape. While Ann soaked in a natural pool below, I surveyed the high stone country from the top of Burrunggui, some of the oldest exposed rocks in the world. From this superb vantage point, the layered sandstone pillars and cliffs of the escarpment formed an almost continuous rock wall, 500-to-700-feet tall and 140-miles long. The landscape below was a quilt of open woodlands, wetlands, and parched floodplains. A wave of awe rippled through me, and I remembered well that same sensation the first time I stood on the North Rim of the Grand Canyon. Descending to rejoin Ann, I nearly slipped on a steaming pile of wallaroo dung, and though I never did spot a wallaroo, I liked imagining that one had been watching me as I surveyed his homeland.

Beneath the sandstone escarpment, a variety of woodlands, billabongs, pockets of monsoon rainforest, and coastal mangrove habitats support a remarkable diversity and richness of flora and fauna. The barkk shares his homeland with many other species, including 51 mammals, 280 birds, 77 freshwater fish, and 75 reptiles. Four thousand of the estimated 10,000 insect species in Kakadu have never been described, and more than 100 species of endemic plants of the isolated escarpment are found nowhere else in the world.

Kakadu's mosaic of distinct habitats and species is also intertwined with ancient aboriginal culture. The Aborigines of Kakadu, the *Gagudju*, are heirs to the longest unbroken culture the world has ever known. For more than 50,000 years the Gagudju have lived here in harmony with the environment, as evidenced by carbon-dated paintings on the walls of the escarpment. Fifty <u>thousand</u> years. I can trace my family history back a mere three <u>hundred</u> years.

Kakadu National Park was established in 1979 to preserve not only the aboriginal rock art and culture, but also the critical habitats and species that flourish here. The size of the state of New Jersey, much of the 7,700 square mile area protected in Kakadu is closed to the public in order to protect the traditional lifestyle of the Aborigines, especially their sacred ceremony sites, "dreaming places," and burial grounds. The park is co-managed by the Australian National Parks and Wildlife Service and the Gagudju. Kakadu was designated a World Heritage Reserve in 1981.

This designation places Kakadu in elite company with places that are vital to the world community: Yellowstone National Park, the pyramids of Egypt, the Great Wall of China, and Victoria Falls in Zimbabwe to name a few. Yet, Kakadu is unique among these World Heritage sites because it qualified for listing on the basis of both natural and cultural values of global significance.

Equatorial Crossings

Throughout Australia, whole ecosystems have disappeared: vast tracts of land have been trampled and uprooted by domestic and feral animals; many native mammals and birds were driven to extinction by introduced predators such as cats, dogs, and foxes; and introduced plants continue to make aggressive forays into almost every corner of the continent. Within Kakadu, there's a delicate balance: people and nature exist in relative harmony.

The Gagudju recognize six different seasons in Kakadu. We were there during *Gunumeleng*—the pre-monsoon season from October to December, when the humidity steadily and oppressively rises until the hot, wet air finally turns into monsoon rains. The land was parched and all life forms, including us, were constantly in search of water. On average, we each drank 1-1/2 gallons of water per day, and still felt dehydrated most of the time. Giant cracks opened up in the dried soil of the floodplains, where water used to meander. My nasal membranes dried and cracked too, and I learned to cope with daily nosebleeds. With no perceptible wind, daytime temperatures soared to 40° C (104° F) and I developed a nagging rash commonly known as "prickly heat."

Flies were incessant nuisances, as they probed our ears, noses, and mouths for any signs of moisture. One morning I emerged from the tent to find that my sweaty white socks, which were hanging outside to air-dry, were black with swarming flies. These weren't the insidious biting flies we had experienced in Alaska, but more than once the constant background *whir* of these Australian flies nearly drove me to madness. I recalled the pictures I have seen of caribou herds in the Arctic driven into blind stampedes by mosquitoes, and I could empathize. Our only sources of refuge were the tent—a sweltering sweat lodge in the searing heat and humidity—or smearing DEET all over our faces and wearing irksome head nets. In despair one afternoon, I resorted to tying a bandana completely over my face.

Heat. Humidity. Dehydration. Prickly Heat. Nosebleeds. Flies. The Park visitor's guide might have served as sufficient warning: "Some visitors find the build-up preceding the wet season quite uncomfortable." Now there's some masterful understatement.

Yet, despite our discomfort, we were rewarded with outstanding wildlife viewing, as birds and mammals congregated around billabongs, the only permanent waterholes. Magpie geese were especially abundant, and we watched thousands rototilling the soft mud, as they fed on spike rush roots at the fringes of the billabongs. An estimated 85% of the world's population of these seemingly insatiable geese inhabit Kakadu during the dry season.

On a guided boat cruise on Yellow Waters, one of the largest permanent wetlands in Kakadu, we marveled that thousands of birds could coexist in one place. Among the 280 known species of birds that thrive in Kakadu, my favorite was the lotus bird, also known as the "Jesus bird" or jacana, which is unmistakable because of its brilliant scarlet crest, short beak, and extremely long toes. At sunrise, we watched one jacana literally walk on water as it gleaned insects from around the red lotus lilies enroute to its floating nest.

In addition to the stunning assemblage of birds, we saw barramundi, a large-scaled, bass-like fish prized for its tasty white flesh; archerfish that squirt water up to four feet to knock down their insect targets; and many saltwater crocodiles, undoubtedly one of nature's most efficient predators. A host of other fish, amphibians, and reptiles that we didn't see also flourish in these wetlands, which receive an astonishing 18 feet of rain during the typical wet season.

If Yellow Waters is the vibrant heart of Kakadu, the East and South Alligator rivers are the major arteries. These rivers pulse through the wetlands and floodplains and connect the Arnhem Land Plateau to Van Diemen Gulf. We cruised the East Alligator River with a Gagudju guide, who taught us about traditional foods of his people, medicinal plants, and a few spiritual customs. We practiced throwing spears made of different native woods—ironwood for hunting crocodiles and buffalo, and beach hibiscus for barramundi and other fish.

As the river swept us along a paper bark swamp, we learned of the importance of paperbark trees for making rafts called *guluyami*, as well as torches, bedding, drinking cups, and fire kindling. On many of the trees we could see ocher paint, marking the area where a recently departed Gagudju elder had lived and visited during his lifetime. Within this boundary, he would have known every tree, waterhole, rock shelter, and seasonal sources of food. Knowledge of the land apparently means the difference between life and death, when faced with such climatic extremes.

Our guide idled the motor and grabbed a floating, 3-foot long barramundi. Showing us the half-eaten body, he explained that a shark had probably taken a chunk from the mid-section of the fish while it was still in saltwater beginning its journey upriver to spawn. Later in the cruise, he spotted a freshwater crocodile sunning on the riverbank and tossed the barramundi up on the bank, startling the dozing croc awake. With alarming speed, the croc attacked the fish, flipped it into the air, and munched the bones like a bag of potato chips, leaving the imprint of those CRUNCHES in my skull forever.

On a walk near the Buba (pronounced "Booba") wetland, the air was fragrant with the scent of blossoming paper bark trees. Afternoon clouds hinted at rain, and the whole ecosystem seemed poised in anticipation of the turbulent thunderstorms that would soon break the drought. *Gujeuk*, the time of violent thunderstorms, heavy rain, and flooding, seemed imminent.

Although the heat, humidity, and flies weighed heavily on us, the electric atmosphere kept us charged with excitement. We had front row seats for nature's unfolding drama, the epic story of water and life. Water is central to the aboriginal concept known as Dreamtime. At sacred places called Dreaming Sites, spirit ancestors of the living Gagudju reside in the pools and rocks of Kakadu. *National Geographic* photographers Stanley Breeden and Belinda Wright documented how these people draw on the power and creative energy of the spirit ancestors through painting, song, dance, and other rituals[1]. To maintain the integrity of the life force, the Gagudju must protect and stay in contact with the Dreaming Sites. To these Aborigines, all living things are part of a single life force—a continuing force they call the Dreamtime. Thus, the Dreamtime is the cohesive force that weaves all life and all parts of the environment together into a single fabric.

Perhaps the Gagudju comprise the oldest civilization on earth because they have evolved with the natural world, rather than trying to control it—an evolutionary lesson that most consumer-based western cultures have long forgotten. The wealth of rock paintings in Kakadu is one testament to the evolution of the Gagudju people in harmony with the natural world. These rock paintings, called *gunbiri*, depict the Gagudju's physical, social, and cultural environment. Some of these paintings have been dated to 50,000 years old, the longest historical record of any group of people in the world, and the most prolific body of rock painting anywhere. More than 5000 rock art sites have been identified, and archaeologists estimate twice that many remain undiscovered in the vast sandstone escarpment.

---

[1] S. Breeden and B. Wright. 1989. *Kakadu – Looking After The Country The Gagudju Way.* Simon & Schuster, Australia.

Into the Outback

Laid down in an ancient sea or lake approximately 1.5 billion years ago, the smooth rock faces of Kakadu provided an ideal surface on which to paint important events, animals, and spiritual figures called *mimi*. By dating the rock paintings, archaeologists have discovered a chronology of different styles, corresponding to different climatic periods and reflecting major shifts in animal and plant assemblages. Each of these styles evokes a sense of the painter's personal relationship with the land and the Gagudju spiritual heritage.

Fifty thousand years ago, Gagudju elders made the earliest known rock paintings, simple hand stencils, by sipping natural pigment and forcefully spraying it against the back of their hands and onto the rock. Larger than life-size naturalistic figures of people and animals, including species such as the marsupial tapir and Tasmanian devil that are now extinct on the Australian mainland, appeared around 30,000 years before present (BP).

Among all the rock art styles, my favorite was the X-Ray Style (6,000 to 2,000 years BP), which depicts life-size animals, including their skeletal features and internal organs. At the Nanguluwur Gallery we saw some of the finest examples of x-ray paintings. The anatomical details of barramundi and *al-mangeyi*, the long-necked turtle, were intricately painted in red (ochre), yellow (limonite), or black (manganese oxide) patterns with extremely fine cross-hatchings on top of white (huntite) clay applied in a thin veneer.

At the Ubirr Gallery, we saw rock art that documents the first contact of *Bininj* (Aboriginal people) with *Balanda* (non-Aboriginals) about 150 years BP. Among the many telltale signs of European influence, we saw paintings of guns, knives, axes, white men on horses, and sailboats. To the Gagudju, who share everything and cannot understand the concept of possessions, especially ownership of land, Balanda must have been a profound mystery, both then and now.

Unfortunately, the rock art tradition has diminished since the arrival of the Balanda. Rock painting has been replaced by bark painting, which emphasizes artistry and fine brushwork but is primarily done for the tourist trade. This painting for profit is a dramatic departure from the traditional reasons why the Gagudju painted.

Nayombolmi, a Gagudju elder who hoped to invoke the power of the Dreamtime at Anbangbang Gallery, completed the last known rock paintings in Kakadu in 1964. All the accumulated knowledge of the Gagudju's lore, traditions, and laws now remains only in the minds of a few dozen elders like Nayombolmi. These elders are the libraries, the last repositories, of 50,000 years of Gagudju culture.

For three days we immersed ourselves in rock art, and I knew afterwards that we had only scratched the surface of the traditional knowledge contained in these paintings. The paintings are a visual record of Gagudju history and culture, for which there is no written language. This seems only fitting, though, because no written language could begin to do these paintings justice.

From the rise above the main rock art gallery at Ubirr, we watched the swollen orange sun melt into the horizon. Gazing over the parched landscape, I tried to imagine this place during "the wet." Although the long dry season limits which animals and plants can survive here, the wet defines Kakadu. Protected within Kakadu are some of the largest and most important tropical wetlands in the world.

"There is enough stored water here," according to ranger Anna Pickworth, "to last an estimated 10,000 years; a mere eight to ten inches of rain will raise the water level in the floodplains by 20 feet." That's enough water to crisscross the entire park by canoe.

Wet and Dry ... Wet and Dry ... a cycle older than human life that has etched a landscape and shaped a people unlike any other place on earth.

After five days of cruises, ranger lectures, and rock art galleries, we were ready to venture out on our own and connect with the land. On Anna's advice, we chose to explore Barramundi Gorge, a trail-less expanse in the heart of Kakadu, and one of the few places in the park that has flowing water year-round. We bought some simple provisions and, after carefully packing our backpacks, I called my mom for the first time in three weeks.

She sounded exhausted. I learned that there had been two recent deaths in the family, and that my Great Aunt Gladys was receiving chemotherapy for inoperable colon cancer. The biggest world news was that Israel's Prime Minister, Yitzhak Rabin, had been assassinated. I shuddered as I recalled the triumphant front-page headline from October 6, 1995, the day we boarded our United Airlines flight for Sydney Australia, "Rabin Ratifies West Bank Accord: Vote tight as lawmakers back Palestinian self-rule."

All this news was numbing. I hung up the phone and stood in silence, feeling insignificant. The phone call transported me from the splendors of Kakadu to the reality of life in a complicated world. This was a reminder of how far we were from home, and how separated from the lives of our friends and families, not to mention world events. While we were off celebrating life and making new discoveries daily as we traveled, our friends and families lives were also moving on. At the time, I thought of their lives as static, frozen in time at the instant we left the United States, when, in reality, death, cancer, assassinations, and all life's myriad cycles were proceeding without us. In the wake of this phone call came the inevitable realization that the detachment of being a traveler is both a blessing and a curse. How could we even consider bringing a child into this chaotic world?

The first afternoon in Barramundi Gorge we only hiked a mile before succumbing to the lure of a series of cascades and pools framed by the outlet of a sandstone gorge. As the sun set and the moon rose, we soaked alone in the spring-fed pools. The simple feel of cold water on hot, bare skin was invigorating. Stripped of our sweaty clothes and our worries about heat and bugs, Ann sighed, "I've never seen such an idyllic swimming hole."

I swam upstream from one pool through a slot canyon to another pool, climbed over an exposed boulder, swam through a longer, narrower ravine, and emerged on the upstream end of the 300-foot long gorge. As I drifted back downstream toward Ann, the twilight, the brush of smooth sandstone against sweaty skin, and the rhythm of the flowing water were delightfully sensual.

That night we camped above the gorge, on top of the escarpment, and for once we were able to sit outside and relax in comfort. We listened to the slight breeze and the cascading water, and we talked about the richness of the Gagudju culture. We talked for hours, read aloud from our journals, and kissed with an intimacy both familiar and new. One month into our travels, we could already sense changes in each other and ourselves. We laughed more, talked more, and relished the freedom from deadlines, junk mail, bills, and daily pressures.

The next morning we awoke before 6 am. Ann got up first to cook some oatmeal for breakfast, but was frustrated to discover we had left our fuel bottle in the rental car. I offered to hike the mile back to retrieve it. By the time I returned, Ann realized that the previous day she must have lost her wide-brimmed, canvas hat somewhere between the car and our camp. The hat was her best defense against the relentless sun. She hiked to the car and back, but didn't find it. It was only 8 am, and we were already sweaty and irritable.

We broke camp and hiked in festering heat and silence, along vague animal trails. We plodded on for several hours, stopping periodically for a water break in the scant shade. But the still heat and attacking flies didn't allow for much relief. Our water bottles were nearly empty and there was no stream in sight. Ann, increasingly irritated by all this, as well as the lack of landmarks, collapsed on the ground and resolved, "I'm not going any further."

I was furious. Thinking that she had given up for good, I stomped off to do a reconnaissance of the area. I discovered, after shredding my bare legs on the needle-sharp spinifex grass, that we were only ten minutes from the confluence of two creeks near where we had a permit to camp. I returned, expecting my report to cheer her up: "Guess what, Ann, we're very close to the confluence."

"I don't think so," she countered, her head buried in the map. "We're still at least three miles from Barramundi Falls."

"So, you think I'm lying?" I huffed.

"No," she sniped, "just wrong."

"What?" I erupted, removing the sweat-soaked bandana from my head. My frustration and Ann's condescension got the better of me. I snapped — literally and figuratively — and grazed the back of her neck with the bandana.

Two days later, resting in the shade of a sandstone ledge next to a plunge pool above Barramundi Falls, I directed my flagging energy to writing in my journal. I reflected on why this fight had happened and what it meant for the health of our relationship. At the moment I snapped, I didn't fully appreciate just how fragile Ann's emotional condition was after hours of enduring the inescapable heat and flies. She was dehydrated, physically and psychologically spent from hiking without a trail or a decent map, and feeling absolutely miserable. I was dehydrated too, but invigorated by the physical and mental challenges of bush walking, and feeling like the whole experience was a grand adventure. I unfairly expected Ann to feel the same, and lashed out unexpectedly when she didn't.

The cool soak in the creek, the fiery sex, and the frank discussion that immediately followed the fight had started the healing process, but I couldn't easily dismiss my uncharacteristic rage. I wondered about Ann: was she exploring the same issues in her journal? Are anger and love at opposite poles of some subliminal axis of passion? I childishly wished Aesop were sitting beside me to relate a simple moral to our story.

I scribbled page after repentant page in my journal, the thoughts coming faster than I could write. As I relived the emotional highs and lows of the previous few days, I noticed several thumbnail-size frogs jumping toward me. I put down the journal and watched as these tiny frogs used my body as their dinner table, lunging several feet to snag flies off my sweaty arms and legs. One particularly fearless frog let me hold her in my palm, which she used like a springboard to dive on unsuspecting flies. Four flies in a row she ambushed this way, but after the fourth the frog didn't return to my palm. I noticed a thin, slate-gray snake at the edge of the plunge pool, with the violently twitching, webbed foot of a frog hanging out of its mouth. I gasped.

Ann, who was reading nearby in the shade of a rock shelter she constructed, called out, "What's up?" And I tried to explain the strange juxtaposition of my own fate to comprehend our fight and the frog's fight to change her fate. Life is so full of subtle irony.

I guess maybe the frog and the snake provided me with the simple, Aesop-like message for which I had been searching. Life isn't always predictable and neither is death. Bad days sometimes follow good ones. Fights sometimes follow happy times. Passion sometimes leads to bliss, sometimes anger. But each day the sun still sets and the moon still rises. And the beauty of a healthy marriage is that you don't have to observe the cycle alone.

※

Our time along Barramundi Creek confirmed for me that bush walking is the best way to fully appreciate Kakadu, wandering with all senses focused on the land: fractured and eroded stone country, fragrant eucalyptus woodlands, dank monsoon rainforests, and leg-shredding spinifex grass. The landscape was alive with oddities of nature that I had never seen before. Exquisite butterflies, 20-foot tall termite mounds, a tawny frogmouth owl, sugar bees, and fruit bats were only a few of these. As we followed a water buffalo trail through the monsoon forest and out of the gorge, the images of the ancient rock paintings we had seen at Nanguluwurr, Ubirr, and Anbangbang were still fresh in my mind—*Ngalyod*, the rainbow serpent; x-ray style animals; *Algaihgo*, the fire woman; *Mabuyu*, a fisherman who was robbed of his catch while he slept, and now reminds the Gagudju to tell their children a story that warns against stealing; *Namarrkun*, the lightning man, who carries lightning across his shoulders and strikes thunder off the ground and clouds with stone axes attached to his knees, elbows, and head. But the painting that made the biggest impression on me was of a white man with his hands in his pockets telling the Aborigines what to do.

Kakadu whetted my appetite for foreign travel and opened my eyes to the excitement of discovering other cultures and ecosystems. Trying to understand the superimposed rock paintings was like peeling back layers of time; one painting style overlaid the previous, recording 50,000 years of continuous Gagudju culture. My brief glimpse of this culture filled me with respect for the Gagudju's ancient heritage and traditions, which evolved in concert with a wealth of diverse ecosystems. Perhaps the legacy of the Gagudju may ultimately be this: the key to our survival is creating harmony with the natural world.

I know of few other cultures with such an intimate connection to, and understanding of, nature. And though I cannot claim to fully comprehend the Gagudju's Dreamtime, this compelling concept reminds me to embrace the natural world with reverence—to take my hands out of my pockets and feel the pulse of the land. With the Gagudju as our teacher, we may one day learn that the spirit of the land resides in each of us. We need only to be quiet... and LISTEN.

4

Sea Cadence

> *Patience, patience, patience, is what the sea teaches. Patience and faith. One should lie empty, open, choiceless, as a beach – waiting for a gift from the sea.*
>
> —Anne Morrow Lindbergh, *Gift From the Sea*

Violent gusts of wind lashed our kayak's bow as we crept over the crest and crashed into the trough of wave after wave. "Don't let her turn sideways," Ann cried out, the urgency in her voice alarming me more than the buckling breakers hell-bent on crushing our collapsible double kayak. This chaotic clash of wind and sea shattered our visions of paddling in a sun-cloaked paradise. At that instant, the tropical realm of Australia's Whitsunday Islands, a collection of 70+ drowned volcanoes with peaks rising clear of the sea, seemed a distant mirage. Where were the palm trees, white sand beaches, and leaping tuna that John, the local kayaking guru, had so vividly described?

Forced ashore at Pioneer Point by the relentless wind, we hunkered down among the angular rocks, studied our map, played cribbage, and waited impatiently for a change in the weather. Cockatoo Beach, our intended campsite, was less than four miles across Molle Channel, but incessant north-easterlies and repeated rainsqualls convinced us to stay put. I could see in Ann's eyes the disappointment I, too, felt.

For nearly a month we had lugged, dragged, pushed, and kicked the kayak bags along Australia's eastern coast in anticipation of paddling around the Whitsunday Islands. Now, pinned on this rocky, windswept beach after only two miles of paddling, this rogue storm was a stirring reminder that the sea, the world over, has its own cadence, its own innate rhythm of winds and tides—an interplay of global processes we couldn't even fathom, let alone predict. We were privileged visitors, paddlers with a two-week timetable in a realm where time doesn't matter.

After dark the clouds parted, unveiling a star-studded canvas replete with the Milky Way galaxy, which spanned the sky in one luminous brush stroke stretching from horizon to horizon. I poked my head out the tent door and searched for nearly five minutes before I finally located the Big Dipper, the one constellation I can reliably identify in both hemispheres. Gusty winds periodically rattled the tent walls, and I awoke before dawn feeling like the little drummer boy had spent the night playing *pa-ra-pa-pum-pum* on my eardrums. As the new day began, a growing cloud of sand flies perfectly timed each lull in the wind to alight on the mesh of our tent door. I couldn't rid myself of the image I had of these frenzied creatures—barely half the size of a mosquito—waiting to incise my flesh with their jigsaw-blade, mucus-lubricated mandibles.

A pair of gulls cackled and bobbed on the upside down hull of our kayak, daring us to come outside and face the seething swarm of sand flies. We donned our anti-sand fly garb—rain pants tucked into wool socks, Tevas, fleece jackets zipped to the neck, wide-brim straw hats capping fine-mesh head nets, oily DEET on any exposed skin—and scurried about, cramming gear in the boat and swatting at bugs, both real and imagined. Perpetual motion was our best defense.

We reached North Molle Island after a brisk hour of bug-free paddling, highlighted by two sea eagles soaring overhead in random, widening circles. Lured ashore by a pocket of white sand nestled beneath palm trees, we spent the whole day snorkeling, reading, and practicing our bug survival skills. The newest adversaries were March flies, menacing and relentless pests slightly larger than horse flies, with a shocking bite that left divots in our skin where chunks of flesh had been ripped off. I killed three-dozen in the first hour, and pondered why on earth these vermin are called March flies, if they're so damn abundant in November. Ann still tells the story of one determined March fly that followed her from shore and tattooed the top of her scalp while she was swimming.

The warm, soothing water proved to be the best, and often only, refuge from our growing bugaboo. I immersed myself for hours, sometimes actively swimming, but mostly content to simply hover and marvel at the endless parade of iridescent-colored fish. Parrotfish, damsels, and blue chromis floated, flitted, and flashed around me. Schools of rainbow runners pirouetted in expanding and contracting concentric circles. Mesmerized by the periodic undulations of the brilliant turquoise and green mantle of a kitchen sink-sized Tricana clam with fist-sized siphons, I nearly fainted trying to slow my breathing enough to match its rhythmic inhalations and exhalations.

Near sunset, a pleasant Aussie couple greeted us as they dragged their fully loaded single kayaks ashore. With a familiar collegiality we've found in paddlers all over the world, Lawrence and Judy asked us in near unison, "Where ya' from?" We replied and quickly learned they were avid kayakers from Townsville, who had started a ten-day paddling trip from Shute Harbor earlier that day. Once they had their campsite set up, they invited us to join them for dry-roasted peanuts and Australian Shiraz decanted fresh from the box. Bugs and wind were the recurring themes of our brief, but animated conversation. They assured us that the strong northerlies we were experiencing were atypical and confirmed that the March fly-sand fly-mosquito brigades were not. As we were heading back to our camp, Lawrence promised to update us in the morning with the latest weather report from their marine radio.

The next morning the winds had abated enough that we bid farewell to Lawrence and Judy, then set out in good spirits, full of promise and hot oatmeal. We soon established a comfortable paddling rhythm, and I was pleased at how easily Ann and I fell into synch, both physically and mentally. With ease we dashed across Whitsunday Passage, a 3.5-mile open-water crossing, as much ease as we could muster, that is, in our sluggish nylon and hypalon barge.

Crossing the channel between Cid and Whitsunday Islands, we cruised through three schools of tuna slashing through baitfish, and raucous terns nose-diving to grab the remains. This early in the trip we had not yet gained the strength or confidence necessary to paddle with the leaping tuna. Instead, Ann raised a makeshift sail, fashioned from a rattan beach mat lashed to a kayak paddle, while I ruddered from the stern. And for fifteen exhilarating minutes we glided along, with the tuna and terns a mere 30-60 feet off our port bow.

Moments like this are what I love most about sea kayaking—moments when the mind, heart, and sea are one. Moments when I savor the taste of dried salt on cracked lips and feel the wind sweep its fingers through my hair. Moments when unmistakable smells of the ocean waft not just over me but through me, filling my lungs and head and flinging any thoughts aside like jetsam. I become, fleetingly, a leaping tuna. But this transformation from awed observer to willing participant in the sea's elaborate cadence requires a detached clarity of mind and body that I can rarely sustain for long. At reverent times like this, the sea is neither friend nor foe, but simply is. And I fathom that to be *of* the sea is an infinitely richer, more primal experience than to merely be *on* the sea.

Within seconds of landing at Joe's Beach, our designated campsite, the March flies from hell descended, and I wished we were still in the channel—still in that crystalline mind-heart-sea oneness. Ann whipped up the tent and zipped herself inside. I dashed for the water, pausing only long enough to snag my mask and snorkel from behind my kayak seat. Over our years of paddling together, we've both developed coping strategies for the many challenges we face on a trip of this length. We've also learned and re-learned one of the inherent truths of camping in unfamiliar places: if you think things couldn't get any worse, or couldn't be any more perfect, just wait.

Later in the day, we met Lori and Ann, a gregarious, darkly-tanned, mid-50s couple from Mackay, on holiday in the islands. They had come ashore to search for a fresh coconut, and they invited us on board their luxury cruiser for lunch. Sipping cocktails blended with fresh coconut milk, we explained that we were planning to spend another two weeks paddling and camping in the islands.

"My God," Lori pronounced. "We would never camp this time of year, mate. How ya survivin' the Marchies?"

SMACK. "We're not," I replied through clenched teeth, as the stunned March fly rolled over and flew away.

We went to bed itchy and irritable, and awoke pretty much unchanged. March flies and rain simultaneously inundated us as we were packing up the boat—a daily ritual that involves carefully repacking every item in precisely the right pre-determined space. Wet, itchy, and introspective, we shoved off for Whitehaven Beach, maintaining a slow but comfortable cadence. The monotony of our synchronized paddles carried us forward, though our thoughts were definitely elsewhere.

In aptly named Turtle Bay, we watched three giant sea turtles glide effortlessly across the sandy shallows and then independently surface; their large, rounded heads reminded me of driftwood logs that we call "deadheads" in the Pacific Northwest—logs caught vertically in a tiderip that periodically bob on the surface, submerge, and then unexpectedly reappear. As we left the bay, a favorable flood tide pushed us along, reducing the endless strain that paddling places on the butt, back, shoulders, and abs. From Reef Point to Teague Passage, we shuttled along an erratic, rocky shoreline fringed with towering pines. While appreciative of the free ride, we remained vigilant to avoid the kayak-shredding pinnacles of jagged rock that periodically and unexpectedly gaped from the white foam of breaking waves. Fog pockets hovering low above the water and dark cumulus clouds roiling overhead further added to the uncanny sensation that we were paddling in familiar waters of the North Pacific. Distant views of the occasional palm tree or sea turtle were the only reminders that we were still in the tropical South Pacific. The changing scenery and brooding weather eventually rescued me from my bug-and-wind funk and plunked me back in the present.

At the southern entrance to Teague Passage, we drifted on the tide through a surface boil of baitfish, while I jigged with chunks of rock oysters I had collected earlier in Turtle Bay. I caught and released one vigorous coral trout and one small, lethargic white-lined cod before snagging my line on the jagged rocks and losing the last of my bait. With the oysters gone and Ann's patience wearing thin with my fishing compulsions, we paddled briskly through the passage to discover a white silica beach that stretched north as far as we could see. Bathed in sun from a brief window in the ominous clouds, famed Whitehaven Beach was more stunning than the postcard and poster images plastered on virtually every store window in Airlie Beach.

As we pulled into shore and began our unpacking ritual, the glare off the white sand sent me rummaging through the dry bags for my sunglasses. With the kayak finally offloaded and hauled a safe distance up the beach, we sprawled on our backs in the warm sand and let the tensions of the day ease away. My arms felt heavy and sore as I gently rolled them from side to side, letting the sand flow through my fingers. After six hours of paddling, all we really wanted to do was absorb the sand's warmth and gaze at the melding pink and orange hues of twilight.

Just before dark a torrential downpour soaked most of our gear, still strewn in the same haphazard piles from when we offloaded an hour earlier. Spent, shivering, and suddenly ravenous, we huddled inside the wet tent with a damp sleeping bag draped around our naked torsos. Neither of us even attempted to disperse the gloom, as we inventoried the gear to determine what was dry—"dry" being a relative term, as everything was just varying degrees of wet.

The collective gloom of the first four days hung heavily around us. The reality of bugs, wind, and rain didn't mesh with our expectations of tropical sun, fair winds, and following seas. Scalding tea and boiled noodles elevated our body temperatures and spirits a little. Mostly, though, I was thankful for the bottle of talc powder, a relic that had remained in my pack ever since the prickly heat rashes I developed in Kakadu. A liberal dousing helped take the edge off the wetness, and I drifted into a sound sleep.

We awoke to a day so still that it was difficult to believe we were still in the same sodden place as the previous night. My eyes traced a path across the glistening white sand, across and then into the aquamarine water, and eventually up into a sky as pure blue and cloudless as any I had seen. The fresh scent of wet eucalyptus leaves danced on the occasional puff of breeze. Ann emerged from the tent and gave me a soft peck on the cheek, motioning to a spot down the beach where she wanted to do yoga. Acknowledging her need for time alone, I gently squeezed her hand and wished her a morning filled with light and happiness. As I watched her slowly meander along the water's scalloped edge, I was struck by the simple thought, "I'm a very lucky man."

I spent several hours laying out all our wet stuff, rinsing the sand and accumulated detritus out of the tent and then the kayak, cleaning and oiling my salt-encrusted Swiss Army knife, and attending to nails that needed clipping and cuts and scratches that needed disinfecting and bandages. Occasionally, I would look up to see Ann performing sun salutations, and I could feel the positive energy returning to us both.

As she strolled back to camp, I sensed Ann's smile long before I could see her face. When she walked up and hugged me, I relished the warmth of her body pressed against mine. It was warmth that was deeper than physical; her whole being glowed in a way I both admired and envied. I knew that I, too, needed some time on my own.

Paddling alone often transports me into a stream of consciousness: the haphazard confluence of past adventures, the present moment, and future dreams. My mind first wandered to our maiden kayaking trip together in the icy wildness of Alaska's Glacier Bay, then to our honeymoon in the tropical paradise of Baja's Sea of

Cortez—a three-week paddling trip from Loreto to La Paz. Indelible images of Baja flashed like snapshots through my head: uninhabited desert islands, the riotous colors of the rocky reefs, frigate birds, Ann's tanned body stretched motionless on the surface of languid blue water, lavender mountains at dusk, a torpid six-foot long rattlesnake, and a dazzling solar eclipse. I recalled spending dangerously hot afternoons in carefree siestas, hiking up fragrant arroyos, swimming with sea lions, and savoring succulent fish tacos that we made with fresh tortillas warmed on sun-baked rocks. I couldn't even remember any instances of tension or bad weather, though I knew we had experienced both.

Reflecting on the Sea of Cortez trip, I realized that all of our kayaking trips of a week or longer share certain similarities. Each journey begins with several days of clinging to expectations before letting go and reveling in the present, followed by emotional swings every bit as intense and unpredictable as the weather, and inevitably a sense of post-trip accomplishment manifested by exposing ourselves to physical and mental challenges. My solo paddle helped me to appreciate that this was the first day in a long time that I had really allowed myself to experience the simple pleasure of living in the present, without expectations of Ann or myself.

After several hours, I rejoined Ann at the campsite, where she had carefully repacked all of our sun-dried gear into dry bags. The gear was back in order, and so, miraculously, were our heads. This day, filled with sun, vivid colors, and introspection, reminded us that to live without expectations is to find happiness. The ongoing challenge in our lives is to learn to make such heightened awareness last more than just a few hours, or minutes.

The next morning we paddled out to two private yachts at anchor and replenished our freshwater supply. With 13 liters of water carefully stashed in the shade of eucalyptus trees, we set out to explore Hill Inlet, a drowned river valley that reaches three miles into the mangroves. We swam and splashed and laughed, as the high summer sun caramelized our skin. Manta rays glided away from the shadow of the boat—their dark bodies silhouetted perfectly against the white sand. We snorkeled amidst schools of mangrove jacks and a perturbed barramundi that repeatedly darted in and out of the tangle of mangrove roots lined with oysters. A sunset dinner of fresh crab capped a day of living life to the fullest, a day of rediscovering the joys of harmony.

Equatorial Crossings

After three nights and two blissful days at Whitehaven Beach, we stroked toward Haslewood Island on the fuchsia wavelets of dawn. At the western point of the entrance to Windy Bay, we were drawn into the water by the combination of slack tide, low sun angle, and flamboyant coral heads, known locally as "bommies," less than a paddle's length beneath the boat. We watched in astonishment as a huge tuna torpedoed from blue water to within fifteen feet of us before veering away. For two continuous hours, clown fish, schools of neon blue fusiliers, speckled sweetlips, a few large coral trout, and one enormous bumphead wrasse that was half my body length streamed by, seemingly oblivious to our presence.

During a 6-mile open water crossing to Border Island the next day, Ann asked me in mid-ramble not to talk anymore, confiding that a second straight day of being constipated was making her irritable. In 2-1/2 hours of paddling, the silence was broken only once, by the necessity of working in unison to weave our way through a confusing snarl of five-foot standing waves at the northeastern point of Border Island.

"Paddle hard on the left," I shouted, my first instinct being to muscle our way through the turmoil.

At that instant, tide, wind, and waves converged, simultaneously rebounding off the vertical face of the island directly toward our boat. We both plunged our paddles into a brace, sensing that to capsize here would place us in immediate risk of injury, or worse. Swirling wind and thundering waves heightened my sense of fear, making communication nearly impossible. "Anticipate, don't react," said the inner voice of experience. I forced myself to slow my breathing and to use my head more than my body. By anticipating and pulling hard through the brief lulls and surfing the biggest rebounding waves away from the cliff face, we slowly inched our way out of this frenetic cauldron of sound and energy.

Safely around the point, we slipped into Cataran Bay, laid our paddles down on the deck combing, and trailed our weary hands in the water. We both expressed the relief and inevitable letdown that follows these adrenaline-filled moments when a kayak can seem too small and one's abilities too inadequate to be in such a big ocean — humbling feelings we knew all too well from previous open water crossings.

We pulled alongside the lone sailboat in the bay to ask for a few liters of water, only to discover that *Tethys* was from Port Townsend, a Victorian seaport 40 minutes from our home in Sequim, Washington. The skipper, Nancy, invited us on board, where we met her crew of five women sporting ear-to-ear grins and relishing the last day of their two-week charter. They treated us to a lunch of cheese and crackers, crisp apple slices liberally smeared with peanut butter, and cold beer, while they peppered us with questions. We learned that a mutual acquaintance in Port Townsend built *Tethys*, and that Nancy was presently sailing around the world with women-only crews. We cherished the opportunity to sit amongst this group of newfound friends, fellow adventurers with whom we shared much in common—not only our home state, but a sense of wonder about Australia, the serendipity of our meeting, and the magic of traveling. After several hours of chatting, more food, multiple photos, and their promises that they would send copies to our families "to let them know we were still alive and well," we descended into our kayak with full water bottles and four cans of beer they didn't want. The tension of the crossing only a few hours earlier had dissipated, like morning fog whisked away on a tropical breeze.

Ann and I snorkeled together at a nearby coral reef that the women lavishly described as a "must see." For more than an hour we swam over, through, and around multiple coral arches, and both emerged from the water effusive about the reef's elaborate three-dimensional architecture. Ann captured the splendor of this labyrinthine reef on a waterproof camera, focusing in particular on the giant Tricana clams with their fleshy fringes of blue, green, turquoise, and all hues in between. We were still raving, when we noticed Lawrence and Judy, our friends from Cockatoo Beach, eating a late lunch on the beach next to our kayak. They tried hard to persuade us to stay and camp with them for the night. Short on food and anxious to re-provision, we politely declined, opting instead to head for Hook Island Wilderness Resort.

After more than an hour of bucking the tide and being pushed sideways by lacerating winds, we grew tired of working so hard to gain a mere six inches with each stroke. My arms and hands were tingling, and my right shoulder felt like the muscles were ready to tear any second. Turning around wasn't an option.

I barked at Ann, "Paddle harder."

She retorted, "I'm paddling as hard as I care to, and I'm not going to risk going all out."

In response, I unleashed a barrage of yelling, an ugly froth of commands and criminations. Twice, the mounting swells nearly tossed us sideways onto rocks.

Forty minutes later, in spite of my screaming mouth and muscles, we somehow rounded the northern tip of Whitsunday Island intact, and found protection from the wind and waves in the lee.

Neither of us said a word. Everything in the boat that wasn't inside a dry bag was soaked, and I second-guessed our decision to leave the rudder and spray deck behind. We independently scattered our gear, hoping the half hour of remaining daylight might be enough to dry things a little. I jumped into the water to get away from Ann and the whole situation.

At dinner we both vented, trying but not always succeeding to use a therapist friend's ground rules for conflict resolution, "When you ... I feel ..." I felt Ann had betrayed me by not being there for me when I needed her most. She felt verbally abused and distrusted, because of my yelling and implications that she wasn't willing to paddle any harder at a moment when she was making a conscious choice not to expend all her remaining energy. She emphasized that I could and should have communicated my need for her help sooner and more effectively.

"Do you hate yourself for needing help in these situations?" she asked.

I had no ready answer, only remorse.

We both acknowledged that one part of our relationship we have to continuously work on is our different comfort levels relative to physically challenging situations. I often resent Ann's unwillingness to push herself. Is that fair? Why can't I just accept our differences and not resent her for being cautious and unwilling to risk injury? I feel at times like she is holding me back and that leads to resentment. I get frustrated when her comfort level dictates what we do or don't do. How do we ensure that both our needs are met, when we are both tied to the same double kayak? No wonder some experienced kayakers snidely refer to a double as a "divorce boat."

There are so many inherent challenges associated with being in a double kayak — the need to always paddle in synchrony, communicate constantly, trust each other, and the inability for either of us to just do our own thing. I expressed my pent-up frustration and resentment at feeling unappreciated for all the hard work I do getting us safely from one place to another, and the stress of feeling the majority of the burden for our well-being when we are paddling. I also griped that I have to work much harder than her to keep the kayak tracking in a straight line.

Ann expressed her frustrations with always being in the bow and not being involved as much as she would like in decisions. She, too, felt unappreciated and resentful that I wasn't a better communicator.

"Perhaps," she concluded, "we have evolved in our paddling relationship and abilities to the point that we have outgrown a double and needed to consider two singles for future trips."

We talked at length about expectations we both had for this kayaking trip, and how bugs, wind, and rain had supplanted our romantic visions of tropical honeymoon II. "We seem to go through cycles of good days when we communicate well and both want to do the same things, and bad days when we are totally out of synch," I commented.

"Yeah," Ann replied, "the bad days seem to happen when both of us fail to honestly communicate the state of our physical or mental health."

"Or when we have unrealistic expectations of each other, the weather, or ourselves," I added.

"The best days," Ann surmised, "are those that we allow to unfold without expectations."

Structure, order, and planning are so much a part of an extended kayaking trip. Yet, expectations come with planning, and expectations seem to be the root of many of our difficulties. How do we reduce our expectations and learn to better accept what each day brings? How do I accept that my happiness isn't contingent upon Ann's and vice versa? Why do I let Ann's mood dictate mine? We pledged to search for answers as our world trip progressed, and to work toward finding our individual paths to inner peace.

Eventually, we both mustered apologies. We agreed that the whole conflict could have been avoided if we had stayed at Border Island, but the more significant realization was that we needed to avoid putting ourselves in late-in-the-day, constipated, bad weather, or foul-mood predicaments. The day of paddling had already been long and, at times, intense even before the Border to Whitsunday crossing. We resolved not to undertake any more late afternoon crossings.

After all the venting, discussion, and apologies, Ann again stressed the growing need to be more honest with each other about our feelings and moods. We reminded each other of our marriage vows, and, in the aftermath of the tension, we found consolation in the fact that we were continuing to learn important lessons about communication: lessons that would strengthen our marriage; lessons that we could not have known at the time would serve us well as our world journey progressed and we faced even greater challenges than wind-tossed waves or anger-tossed words.

The following morning we ate toast, cereal, fresh fruit, and yogurt at the Hook Island Wilderness Resort. I gazed in a mirror for the first time in ten days. Initially horrified and then amused by my peeling nose, straggly, grizzled beard, and Rastafarian hair, I readily agreed with Ann's suggestion that showers were the next order of business. The restaurant manager eventually caved in and sold us pasta and rice, as well as fresh veggies and fruit, including an exquisite rock melon. After a short paddle to Saba Bay, we unpacked the kayak, stripped, and washed our grimy, threadbare clothes. In the warmth of the mid-morning sun, we scattered our clean clothes and wet gear on nearby rocks to dry, and snapped a picture of the intertidal yard sale.

At low tide I slowly combed the beach, while ruminating the events of the previous day. I paused often to inspect wave-tumbled stones and the remains of broken nautilus shells, scattered like pottery shards, remnants of another place and time. Near the southern entrance to the bay, I discovered convoluted, multi-colored rocks that coalesced one into another like mudflows. Up close, these variegated rocks looked like concrete with embedded, polished pebbles. I traced my fingers lightly across the spine of one concretion, and then clutched it hard, as if reaching out to reaffirm my connection to Ann after the previous day's turmoil. Not until days later did I realize this was literally a touchstone for me—this clutching of stone symbolic of my desire to find the same sense of solidness in my relationship with Ann.

On the way back to the campsite, I found an intact nautilus shell, perched in a nest of seaweed at the upper edge of the drift line. How did this deep-sea dweller end up here? How could a shell be at once so fragile and so sturdy? Was this my gift from the sea? The words of Anne Morrow Lindberg lapped at the edges of my consciousness: "A good relationship has a pattern like a dance and is built on some of the same rules ... The joy of such a pattern is not only the joy of creation or the joy of participation, it is also the joy of living in the moment."

The joy of living in the moment: wasn't that a big part of what I was searching for on this world adventure of ours? Was it mere chance this day's message came to me in the form of a nautilus shell?

In our double kayak, Ann and I have the opportunity to be true partners, moving to the same precise rhythm—the ebb and flood of the tides, the patterned speech of the wind, the pulse of our separate hearts joined. But the simple joy of such a rhythm, of living solely in the moment, never lasts, and I am inevitably the one to break the spell; the one to desire more speed, or less, to wish I was fishing instead of paddling, to live in my head instead of the moment. I dare not dwell too long in the perfect synchrony of our *reach/dip/pull*—a three-step cadence that reminds me of a slow waltz—for to linger in such a moment makes me fearful the utter harmony will end too soon. Too often I ruin the simple harmony with expectations. I expect Ann to paddle harder, to feel my pain or joy, to intuit my mood and make it hers, rather than letting our separate minds and bodies converge in the purity and rawness of the joint physical exertion.

We've been together long enough now to recognize the pattern, to foresee the signs, and yet, like dancing, paddling demands that both partners be in tune to the same rhythm. To dance well, one must trust his or her partner. To dance beautifully, both partners must let go of expectations. I knew then we hadn't really outgrown the double kayak; we were only just beginning to learn the steps to the dance.

Back at camp, I showed Ann the extraordinary nautilus shell, but couldn't voice the right words to share the revelation it had inspired. The nautilus shell transformed this into a day of lightness for me, following one of lonely darkness and self-loathing. As I would discover again and again over the next year of travels, serendipity has a way of showing her smiling face at the most opportune times.

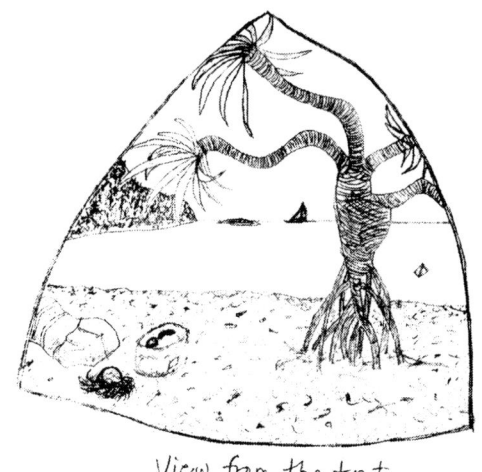

View from the tent
food bag, hat, water jug
Butterfly Bay, Hook Island
(looking NW at Alcyonaria Point)
23-24 Nov.

Equatorial Crossings

For the next three days, we relished the return of sunshine, light winds, and no rain. These were restful, unplanned days filled with lounging, reading, snorkeling, eating when we were hungry, rather than by the clock, and only paddling when we were both in the mood.

One day later, our Thanksgiving dinner on the beach of Butterfly Bay was interrupted by gunshots. We were savoring every morsel of boiled lobster, accompanied by canned corn and ginger snaps dipped in Nutella chocolate-hazelnut spread, when a Park Service boat roared into the mouth of the bay at full throttle.

We remembered reading in Airlie Beach about a goat eradication program, but we had no idea that the Park Service would be shooting goats this close to designated campsites. Captain Cook and other early coastal explorers reportedly left goats behind on many of the Whitsunday Islands to feed victims of frequent shipwrecks on the Great Barrier Reef. The problem is that no hoofed mammals are native to these islands, and now the goats' indiscriminate feeding is wiping out the native vegetation, because no new shipwreck victims arrive to keep the exploding goat populations in check.

The Park rangers eventually pulled their boat into shore and were kind enough to momentarily shut off their fuming engine. They were searching for a wounded goat, which they had shot on the opposite side of the point from where we were camped. After a brief and amusing chat, we convinced them we were not eating their missing goat for dinner. They departed as abruptly as they had appeared, and we resumed reveling in our Thanksgiving feast and the sounds of the sea unspoiled by gunshots or outboards. Our thoughts drifted to friends and families, as we imagined them preparing for traditional turkey and stuffing dinner with all the trimmings. "If only they could see us now," Ann laughed, lobster juices dribbling down her chin as she leaned back contentedly in her Thermarest chair.

Two days later our only remaining food was moldy pita bread, the skim of Nutella left on the inside rim of the jar that was unreachable by spoon or finger, and the last of a mangrove jack I had speared and pan-fried in olive oil and dried herbs the night before. We had exhausted our three favorite recipes for Nutella: on finger, on ginger snap, and on finger dipped first in peanut butter. As we savored the glow of our beach fire, we watched the gibbous orange sun sink below a layer of pink clouds and slowly slip into the sea. Trading the Nutella lid back and forth for the final licks, we knew it was time to head back.

The next morning we sailed downwind across Whitsunday Passage and paddled the mounting surf into Airlie Beach, landing a few feet from where we had departed 14 days earlier. We dragged the kayak up the beach and gazed back toward the islands. This had been a journey of physical and emotional discovery, suffused with bugs, wind, rain and only occasional sunshine; a journey sustained by our deepening love and ultimately endowed with a renewed commitment to our marriage. As we traced our path with strained eyes and wordless gestures, blasts of wind frothed the previously placid Whitsunday Passage into a meringue of stiff white peaks.

5

Coral Sea Odyssey

The land may vary more;
But wherever the truth may be —
The water comes ashore,
And the people look at the sea.

-Robert Frost, *Neither Out Far Nor In Deep*

As I sat on the bow deck with the wind ruffling my scruffy curls, I could not avert my eyes from the turquoise water streaming beneath me. Schools of neon fish shimmered like liquid jewels, and then disappeared in the blink of an eye. Coral fingers stretched skyward, reaching for the sun. I dangled my hand in the water, as if doing so would somehow connect me to the marine life below. I wanted to reach down and touch the outstretched fingers of the corals. I wanted total immersion.

My anticipation of exploring this hidden realm peaked as our 62-foot catamaran, *Pacific Star*, approached Flinders reef, a virgin reef system in the middle of the Coral Sea. Nestled between the coasts of Australia and Papua New Guinea, the Coral Sea is a world-renowned, but infrequently visited, destination for divers. Because of its distance from land, the Coral Sea is only accessible to divers on live-aboard boats. Divers are drawn here by the consistently clear water, often in excess of 150 feet, and the world's largest variety of corals. At Flinders Reef, we were 125 miles from the nearest land, 250 miles from our departure point in Airlie Beach, and 85 miles beyond the outer wall of the Great Barrier Reef. For ten days, this expanse of crystalline water and coral reefs was our home.

Nine other divers, including Richard, our longtime friend from Seattle, joined Ann and me and a crew of four Aussies. Shortly before we left on our journey, Richard had moved from Seattle to Nova Scotia, and this was the first we had seen him in six months. During that time, Ann and I had been together 24 hours a day and communicated mostly with each other. Richard added a lot of diversity and humor to our usual interchanges. I appreciated his upbeat spirit and quick wit, and grimaced at his bad puns. He and I quickly fell into our habitual pattern of teasing and joking; a pattern extending back to graduate school when he was earning his Master's degree in oceanography ("the superior discipline") at the same time I was working on mine in fisheries ("oceanographer wannabes").

Ann, as usual the more perceptive of the two of us, picked up on Richard's more subtle traits: his mastery of the art of listening, commitment to the lost art of conversation, and uncanny ability to express his disagreement and convey his respect in the same sentence. Richard is also good at sensing other people's discomfort, and is quick to provide hugs and words of encouragement; a trait I sometimes lack and therefore deeply admire.

The crusty skipper of our vessel, Gary, was 95% cantankerous and 5% unpredictably giddy. His skills were unquestioned by the crew, and his word was final on *Pacific Star*. Most often I would see him sitting at the helm, cigarette butt dangling from pursed lips, with a distant, glazed look in his eyes. He chain-smoked and kept mostly to himself, and I sensed he would rather be somewhere, perhaps anywhere, else. But when I asked, he replied, "The Coral Sea's my home, there's no place I'd rather be."

Equally at home shooting the breeze with the crew or coddling the divers, Dave, the dive instructor and lead comedian, kept the crew and clients happy. His flat-top haircut, broad shoulders, and dark sunglasses gave him the appearance of the brutish icon on the *No Fear* bumper stickers—the rage among teenage male drivers when we left the States. But underneath this facade was a warm, funny man who loved his job and kept us laughing between the daily cycle of eating, diving, diving, eating, diving, snacking, napping, diving, eating, night diving, and sleeping.

With his chiseled good looks and 6'3" frame compressed into a tiny Speedo swimsuit, Scotty looked like he had just arrived from the set of *Baywatch*. He was the apprentice divemaster, an assignment he engaged with boundless enthusiasm. His puppyish qualities were endearing, and he kept the mood on the boat light and fun. "I'll be dammed if everyone doesn't have a brilliant time out here" was Scotty's mission statement.

Perky Sue was our hostess, cook, housekeeper, and backup divemaster. Although she was more than a foot shorter than Scotty, Sue's big heart exceeded her diminutive size. Her bright smile and cheery attitude made every meal worth anticipating; of course my post-diving appetite was so voracious that she could have served Spam and Velveeta melted on toast slathered with Vegemite and I would have praised her culinary artistry. Instead, she served fresh tuna and mackerel we caught trolling between dive sites, prawns and steaks grilled on the aft-deck *barbie*, lasagna, fresh salads, ice cream, fruit, muffins, and afternoon snacks of cookies, brownies, and popcorn. Sue performed magic with two microwaves and no stove. My stomach certainly didn't suffer, and it was a liberating change not to have to shop, cook, or wash dishes for ten whole days.

Dave was the glue that kept this cast of headstrong Aussies functioning as a team. Everyone liked Dave, even the skipper, which was important for the divers because Dave ran interference between moody Gary, the crew, and the divers. I enjoyed his sense of humor and his ability to keep the diving operations safe and smooth.

"Unbelievable fish and corals" was divemaster Dave's refrain, as we donned our wetsuits for our first dive at Flinders reef. We dived at a site Dave dubbed Cod Wall and my dive log is full of exclamation points:

11/30/95 Cod Wall

Dive buddies:	*Ann and Richard*
50 min dive	*75' max. depth*
Visibility 150'	*Water temp. 82-83° F*

Highlights: A wall dive with hundreds of fish and amazing colors! viz. was outrageous! Saw a school of 25 white-margin unicornfish, 1 chevron barracuda, 1 remora, 1000s of colorful damsels and blue-green chromis, Moorish idols, lots of fairy basslets, and several refrigerator-sized potato cod! Loved the canyons and swim-throughs between the coral bommies. Spectacular green, yellow, and purple feather stars and sea fans larger than a diver! A dazzling array of color and life, almost overwhelming!

Equatorial Crossings

For the next nine days, the exclamation points proliferated. At a dive site called Berlin Wall we saw our first shark, a skittish, four-foot, white-tipped reef shark that showed no interest in us. The next day, on a shallow dive adjacent to an exposed sand cay, I saw my first zebra lionfish with its array of wildly ornamented and highly venomous fins. At Dart Reef, a clown triggerfish that was digging a nest in the sand and alertly defending its territory, charged Richard and me, gnashing its coral crushing teeth.

Richard and Ann compared drifting over the three-dimensional reef structure at Wannastubbie Reef to hiking along a mountain ridge and gazing dreamily into the valleys below. We watched a 100-lb dogfin tuna slice through a school of rainbow runners, which darted and flashed right in front of us like a flock of startled shorebirds. Cleaner wrasses groomed the gills and teeth of huge potato cod. Sue and I admired the graceful glides of a female hawksbill turtle, and the seemingly choreographed pinwheels of a large school of neon fusiliers. A school of barracuda, all exactly the same size, flowed by like a river.

We saw sharks daily: mostly the smaller and more abundant white-tipped and black-tipped reef sharks that circle endlessly, but occasionally a six-foot leopard shark, or a lethargic tawny shark resting on the white, coralline sand. The largest sharks we saw were gray whalers, up to eight-feet long, with huge heads and mouths turned slightly upward at the corners in a menacing smirk resembling that of a great white shark. After a few days, the diver's signal for a shark, a hand formed into the shape of a dorsal fin and placed vertically against the forehead (just above the bulging eyeballs), no longer elicited much response from other divers.

At Midnite Reef, I saw my first cuttlefish, hovering over a coral head. As I approached, it changed from dull brown with white spots to crimson red, then mottled green and black. I spun around to get Ann's attention, noticing in my peripheral vision that the cuttlefish was starting to move. With an uncanny burst of speed and change in color, it disappeared, and I was left excitedly panting into my regulator.

We observed territorial displays, mating, grooming, and foraging behavior of an array of different species. By far the most bizarre behavior we observed, though, was the bubble-eating fish of Cuckoo's Nest. Richard, Ann, and I were diving as a buddy team, when we came to a swim-through, a gap in the reef not much larger than a diver's body. I went through first and spied a small, blue-spotted boxfish that I wanted to see closer. Little did I know that Ann and Richard were beside themselves with laughter, because a large midnight sea perch was 20 feet above me swallowing my air bubbles. Richard eventually got my attention and pointed toward the surface. I looked up, but couldn't tell what he wanted me to see. Richard descended and Ann motioned for me to ascend to her. I watched as the bubble-eater reappeared to gulp Richard's bubbles, swallowing them frenetically, one after another, as if they were its favorite food. We laughed hysterically, nearly choking on our regulators, as we each took turns "feeding" our bubbles to the perch.

The fish life of Flinders Reef was so prolific and colorful that I soon became jaded. Multicolored puffer fish, black-saddled tobies, and harlequin tusk fish no longer excited me. Even the large fish like sharks, tuna, and schools of bludger trevally, and the bizarre fish like lionfish, barred rabbit fish, and bird-nose wrasses seemed too common. I wanted to see something new, more colorful, better. My diving urge was insatiable. I dived four or five times a day.

A fish biologist by training, I was surprised, though, that my attention shifted so readily to invertebrates and algae. Rather than hovering among or above the astounding number of fish, I focused more closely on the minutiae of the reef. I began to notice and appreciate the profusion of shapes, sizes, and colors of the corals, magnificent alliances of animal polyps and symbiotic algae housed together in a calcareous skeleton. I swam through forests of staghorn corals with branching golden limbs reaching seven or eight feet in height. I laid face up on the coralline sand, studying the wavy ridges, valleys, and grooves on the underside of green sheet corals twice my body length. I hovered with my mask inches away from tiny, scarlet cup corals, mesmerized by their intricate fluted edges that reminded me of etched glass. This elaborate, multi-hued coral network was the foundation that supported the biological wealth that surrounded us and provided the Coral Sea with its name.

I watched fuchsia, indigo, crimson, and purple sea slugs slither across the reef top. I found hermit crabs inside giant whelk shells, and spied seldom seen eyed cowries hidden in coral crevices. Giant clams the size of an oven captivated me for one entire dive, as they clamped tightly shut in response to my shadow, and then slowly reopened, unveiling their shimmering, variegated red, blue, and green membranes and softball-sized siphons. At several dive sites, I noticed strange, jawbreaker-sized, translucent marbles, which I later identified to be an unusual alga called "sailor's eyeball." There was just so much to see and explore that five days into our trip I became overwhelmed.

Equatorial Crossings

But our good mate, Richard, helped me to keep things in perspective. Each evening at sunset, he would make us gin and tonics and we would lean against the mast, recapping the highlights of the day. I would ramble on about x species of fish, and y type of behavior, and the ecological implications of z. Ann would describe how the diving reminded her of swimming in an aquarium designed by Walt Disney animators—*Fantasia*-like splashes of color, bizarre creatures of every shape and size, and perpetual movement. And Richard would pose questions like, "What do you suppose that bubble-eating fish did when I farted?"

While Gary shuttled us from one dive site to the next at a speed of 10-12 knots, the divers relaxed in the saloon or on the sundeck, chatted, or napped in their cabins. Between dives, Dave and Scotty washed our dive gear, filled our tanks, and prepared a drawing of the next dive site on the aft deck whiteboard. In the saloon we had access to a CD music collection, videos (mostly dubious diving adventure movies), and a surprisingly complete library of books on diving and coral reef ecosystems. Despite the teasing of my companions about my "nerdy tendencies," I spent an inordinate amount of time in the saloon identifying critters I had seen, revising my dive logs, and reading more about coral reef ecology.

Staghorn Heights was the site of the first of our many night dives, but none was more memorable. Scotty, Rosemary, and I were the only divers, and it seemed we had the vast ocean to ourselves. We had seldom seen lobsters during the day, but at night they were abundant, foraging along the reef crest—their beady green eyes unmistakable once we turned off our lights. We saw many crimson squirrelfish, ideally suited to their nocturnal lifestyle with their large, bulbous eyes, and several flashlight fish, which generate a remarkable greenish light in luminescent semicircular sacs under their eyes. Clouds of shrimp and tiny crabs danced in our light beams. Christmas tree worms vigorously combed the rich water with their feathery, feeding filaments. Translucent jellyfish and comb jellies that are nearly impossible to see during the day, glistened under the beam of my light, highlighted like slides projected in a darkened room. A 5-foot long moray eel, swimming in open water above the staghorn coral, shot us an annoyed look, then slithered into a crevice.

Near the end of the dive, we all turned off our lights again and slowly ascended the anchor line. Scotty led the way, waving his arms and rapidly kicking his fins to show us the bioluminescence: pulses of brilliant green light emitted by microscopic plankton. Thirty feet below me I could see the occasional beam of the flashlight fish and the beady lobster eyes, glowing like a strand of all-green Christmas tree lights tangled in the coral. The night water was alive, twinkling like a night sky filled with fireflies, or like underwater fireworks, but better.

Scotty and Rosemary surfaced and climbed the ladder onto the stern deck. As I was about to surface, I took one last glimpse down. Twelve gray whalers—top predators of the night sea—circled below me, silhouetted by the light of the moon. Like seeing my first wolf in Glacier Bay National Park, my interlude with these sharks was a precious reminder that places untamed by humans still exist.

Buoyed by my sense of good fortune, I hovered motionless and alone above the circling sharks. I realized most people would never see or experience this thrill of the underwater realm, even though water occupies more than two-thirds of "the blue planet." My reverie continued when I finally emerged from the water and Dave exclaimed, "Did you see those sharks below you?" After hundreds of dives in the Coral Sea, Dave is more thrilled by large sharks than any other marine organism, and I knew by the look on his face that he, too, had experienced this same sense of wonder.

On our sixth day at sea, a mandatory no-diving day to allow our bodies to decompress after so many dives, we took the inflatable dinghy ashore on a small sand cay. We were greeted by hundreds of brown and masked boobies, a mixed nesting colony full of recently hatched chicks and nervous parents. The raucous birds had settled on and around an abandoned weather station, and were busy preening each other and incubating their young. I photographed the boobies from a distance and then set out toward the opposite end of the long, narrow cay, beyond some dunes.

At first, I was mystified by broad tracks leading across the four-foot tall sand dunes. I pondered how and why a bulldozer was brought to this remote cay. Later, Scotty explained that these were turtle tracks; the smooth center track was from the underside of the shell, and the adjacent, bilateral divots were left behind by a turtle pushing and pulling her massive bulk up the beach and onto the dunes to lay eggs.

When I met up with Ann and Richard, I discovered that Ann, like me, had been beachcombing. We arranged our collection of shells, feathers, and coral pieces on the sand for a photo and then dispersed them. After several hours in the intense, midday sun, Scotty began ferrying people back to the air-conditioned catamaran. Ann and I opted to stay on the cay longer and snorkel back to the boat. We were the last to leave, and as the setting sun painted the sky orange, we snorkeled hand-in-hand above, and briefly alongside, a loggerhead turtle effortlessly gliding through the water on its five-foot wingspan.

That night a small group of us returned to the sand cay with hopes of watching turtles lay their eggs. We saw ten different turtles, both green and loggerhead, in various stages of digging nests, laying eggs, and struggling to or from the dunes. One mama, who had finished covering her nest, inched slowly back toward the water. She would move half a body length, then slump in the sand gasping. I wanted to run over and help her, but she eventually made it back to the water, completing the innate cycle—a cycle older, perhaps, than the coralline sand grains hiding her eggs.

Then next day we resumed diving, and by the end of our trip I had tallied 36 dives in nine days, with one rest day of no diving. Every day was a new diving high, where the variety of marine life was matched only by the variety of diving opportunities. We dived on sheer, seemingly bottomless walls and among shallow, coral bommies surrounded by turquoise water. We did mellow swims through coral gardens and exhilarating drift dives with enormous schools of pelagic fish. Dave and Scotty led us on several exploratory dives on reefs they suspected had never been visited by divers. With the Coral Sea as my frame of reference, diving will never again be the same.

I think Ann probably best captured the simple joys of this dive trip: "No cooking, cleaning, or decisions other than to dive or not to dive. No bugs. Good sun. Outrageous diving." For a guy who grew up as a large land mammal stranded in the ocean-less geographic middle of the United States, the Coral Sea was ecstasy, shared with my good mate Richard and my soul mate Ann.

The remoteness of the Coral Sea may help protect these reefs. I hope so, because in Cancun, Cozumel, Belize, Indonesia, the Florida Keys, and the Bahamas, I have witnessed first-hand the negative effects humans can have on reefs: ocean dumping, fishing with dynamite, over harvesting, and the deepening human poverty that results from the destruction of the very resources that provide these communities sustenance. The statistics are alarming. Ten percent of the world's coral reefs are damaged beyond repair. Another fifty percent will be in the next 50 years. Within that time, some researchers estimate that one of every five fish species living on coral reefs will be lost. I shudder to think what could happen to the reefs of the Coral Sea.

As we surfaced from our last dive, an Omnimax-movie-like drift drive along a vertical wall, the beauty of the Coral Sea overcame me. I paused on the ladder to reflect on what I had seen and learned. I pondered whether just by coming here I had already contributed in small, intangible ways to the decline of these reefs. I worry now that by writing about the Coral Sea and unveiling some of its mystery and splendor, I will encourage others to go there. I took a few photos, and left no footprints. But what did I really leave behind? And what did I really take away?

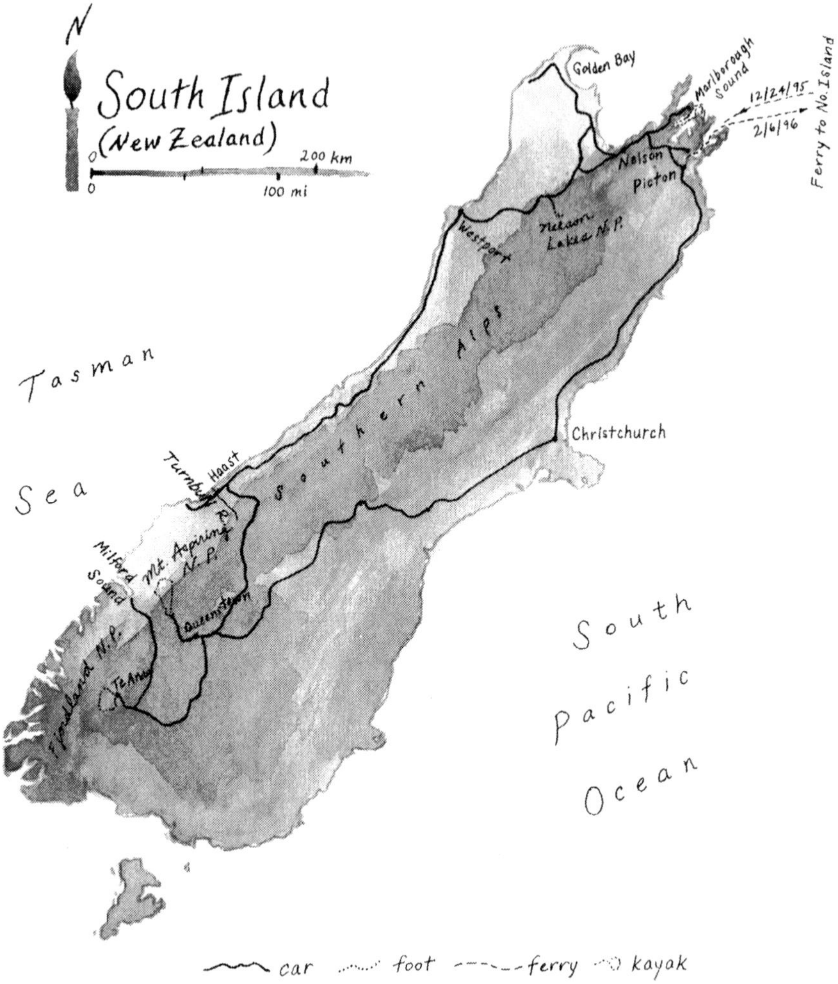
N
South Island
(New Zealand)
0
200 km
0
100 mi
Golden Bay
Marlborough Sound
12/24/95
2/6/96
Ferry to No. Island
Nelson
Picton
Westport
Nelson Lakes N.P.
Southern Alps
Tasman
Sea
Christchurch
Haast
Turnbull R.
Mt. Aspiring N.P.
Milford Sound
Queenstown
Fjordland N.P.
Te Anau
South
Pacific
Ocean
car
foot
ferry
kayak

Tale of the Turnbull

Time is but the stream I go a-fishing in.

-Henry David Thoreau

Like a majestic river, my Grandpa meandered through my life, nurturing and inspiring me. Part of his legacy is the art of fly-fishing, which he cast upon me with patience and plenty of good barbs. Growing up, my brother, Doug, and I spent countless hours exploring the lakes and rivers of Michigan, Missouri, and Illinois with Grandpa.

He wasn't a particularly talkative man, but I admired his quiet strength and integrity. I remember his large, brown hands, tan year-round, and the way they dwarfed the butt of a fly rod; the childish grin that spread like river-born fog across his weathered face whenever we were fishing; and the crescendo of his laugh as it pried free of his ample belly, reverberated along the canyon of his throat, and cascaded off the sill of his fissured lips. And I know now that these excursions were about much more than fishing. Fly-fishing was Grandpa's way of teaching me about life—about patience, pursuing one's passions, and living for the moment.

For three weeks, I stalked the famed trout of New Zealand's South Island with a second-hand fly rod I purchased at a thrift shop in Nelson overrun by spiders and dust bunnies. The west coast of the South Island reminded me of the west coast of my Olympic Peninsula home: a convergence of mountains, glaciers, rainforests, and beaches, linked by wild rivers. But the differences were as dramatic as the similarities. The watersheds of the South Island were intact: no dams, no clear-cut forests, no listings of threatened and endangered species, and a sparse human population. Short, steep, tumultuous rivers connected the Southern Alps to the Tasman Sea. These rivers were clean and pure. Dream palettes. Trout waters.

Brown trout are not native to these waters, but have adapted magnificently since the government began stocking these dark-spotted beauties in the 1880s. Nourished by the nutrient-rich, unpolluted habitat of the South Island's streams and rivers, trout have flourished. Brown trout, although introduced, became for me as much a totem of the wildness of this place, as my beloved native salmon are a totem of the Pacific Northwest.

After many consecutive days of steady rain, broken clouds, and little sunshine—oh yeah, and no trout landed—I welcomed the sweat beading on my forehead. As the Kiwis say, it was a "cracker day." My spirits were high as I drove along the south bank of the Turnbull River at the southern extent of the West Coast Highway near Haast. Quivering with excitement as the river came into view, I tried to drive, smear bug dope on my face and hands, and scout for promising trout water all at the same time.

Even the clouds of frenzied sand flies flitting across the inside of my windshield didn't break my concentration. In the distance, I could see the valley where the Turnbull emerged from the beech-covered mountains, before meandering through sheep and cattle pastures. I drove a little faster.

Moko, the '77 Ford Cortina we bought cheap in Auckland from another backpacker, lurched and struggled to respond to my pulses of excitement. She was enveloped in dust; a thin film covered the dashboard and adhered to the bug dope on my face. A glance in the rearview mirror confirmed my suspicion; my Brillo-pad hair and dust-rag face made me look like I belonged in a commercial for extra-strength cleaning products.

The dirt road ended at a sheep station, where there was no obvious public access to the river. I drove back downstream and pulled to the side of the road next to a blackberry thicket. A pocket of slow moving, gin-clear water immediately caught my eye. I left my fly rod in the passenger seat, figuring it was too hot and bright for any trout to be active. My goal was simply to identify likely fishing spots that I could try near dusk.

After thrashing through the blackberry thicket, I could see several pockets of deep water with root wads and submerged tree branches that provided excellent trout cover. I knew intuitively that this river reach held promise, but I couldn't see any fish. I walked downstream along the crest of the bank, stopping periodically to brush away and spit out sand flies, but still I saw no trout.

I kicked a pebble into the river and turned to trudge back toward the car, when fifteen feet below me in two feet of water I saw the biggest brown trout of my life. Had it risen to the pebble I booted in disgust? Suspicious that this fish was a sand fly-induced delusion, I plodded upstream, away from the log-trout. I bent over to extract my bootlace from the tenacious grip of a blackberry vine and there it was again, directly below me. Cruising slowly upstream, the monstrous trout, easily a ten-pound fish, was feeding right next to shore.

For ten minutes, I knelt in the blackberry thicket glorifying this fish, and cursing the sand flies that descended on me like a steaming cow pie. I couldn't stand it any longer, and I bolted for the car, pausing only long enough to mark the trout's location with a dead tree branch at the side of the road. I grabbed my fly rod, snipped off the bead-head nymph, and tied on a larger brown stonefly nymph. I threw on the only sand fly protection I had—nylon rain pants and a Gore-Tex parka—foolishly foregoing another lathering with bug dope. At full run, I returned to my marker branch, nearly tripping on the bottoms of my rain pants, which had fallen below my heels because the elastic waistband was no longer elastic.

I crawled up the berm and crouched to look over the top of the blackberry thicket. The big brown trout had vanished. For an hour and a half I stalked the bank, hoping somehow to cast a fly near the dream trout. My desire to catch this fish became an obsession. After another half hour, I came to the brilliant conclusion that I was never going to catch this or any other trout with my line out of the water.

At a bend in the river, where a large tree stump overgrown with tall grass masked my shadow, I descended to the river's edge and thrashed the surface with several awkward casts. With no room to back cast, I was only able to flick the fly out twice the length of the rod and no farther. After a dozen casts or so, I climbed on top of the tree stump to look for the big brownie. Thirty feet downstream I saw the reddish-brown side and unmistakable hooked lower jaw of the huge trout.

Convinced the trout would see me, and then spook, I flattened my body against the stump and spooled out fifteen feet of line. I carefully dropped the stonefly nymph into the current, using the tip of the fly rod to feed out the line spooled in my hand. Nothing. I began a slow retrieve. Still nothing.

I leaned out a little farther and flipped the nymph into the current again. This time an 8-inch rainbow trout shot out from under a boulder ledge toward my fly. In my excitement, I jerked the fly from the ambushing rainbow, launching it out of the water, over my head, and into the blackberries behind me. When I looked downstream again, both my dream trout and the little rainbow were gone.

I strolled along the top of the riverbank back to the car, keeping an eye out for other cruising trout. Three fourths of the way back, I saw the same big brown trout again, this time cruising downstream, but still right next to the bank. I slithered on my belly fifteen feet upstream of the trout and slid on my butt down the berm and through the blackberries. The fish was still holding in the same spot. Putting all the concentration I could muster into one cast, I flipped the stonefly nymph in a near-perfect arc. It fell to the water five feet upstream of the trout. The trout pivoted and closed the five-foot gap in what seemed like milliseconds. I tensed, bracing for the strike, but the wary trout braked inches from my fly, took one brief look, and shot out of sight into a deep pool.

Again, I marked the spot with a piece of driftwood, which I pounded into the moist ground at the edge of the road. I climbed in the car and drove back to the campground, arriving more than forty-five minutes late for my dinner date with Ann. I was drenched with sweat, bleeding from the blackberry thorns, plastered with sand fly bites, and happy as could be. At dinner, I regaled Ann with tales of my encounters with the big brown trout. She was amused, but mostly thankful that she had spent her afternoon in more relaxed pursuits—swimming, napping, and reading.

At dusk, I zipped off again in pursuit of the dream trout, and I went straight back to the same stretch of river. After two hours I had tried every fly in my collection, and I hadn't seen a single trout. A few fish were rising in the middle of the river, well beyond the limits of my casting ability. At 9:30 pm I quit fishing, when I snagged a tree limb behind me and snapped off my last pheasant-tail nymph.

On the way back to the campground, I decided to scout the north bank of the river, in case I wanted to fish again the next morning. I drove for three or four miles without seeing a single likely fishing hole. Just before dark, I stopped alongside the gate to a sheep pasture and walked across the road to take a closer look at the river. With distinctive smacking sounds that sent ripples across the surface, trout were rising everywhere to feed on a prolific insect hatch.

In what little light remained, I tied on the biggest dry fly I had, a #10 black gnat. Not concerned with being stealthy, I scrambled over the boulders right down to the water's edge. I could no longer see where the trout were rising, but I could hear the repeated *smack, smack*. The silhouette of a half submerged tree branch provided the only clue of the main river flow, as I watched the water curling around it.

I made a short, too hurried cast and my line and fly slapped the water surface. Before casting again, I composed myself and stripped enough line to reach the current curling around the tree branch twenty feet away. This time my cast was spot on, landing just downstream of the branch. Seconds later, I sensed tension in the line and thought, "Oh perfect, I'm snagged on a submerged branch I couldn't see." The branch then started spooling line off my reel. Fish on!

It wasn't until I applied enough pressure to turn the fish out of the current that I realized I had hooked into a beauty. The trout finned once at the surface and then surged into the strongest current. Never had I hooked anything this big before on a fly rod. I started talking to myself out loud, as Grandpa's sage advice echoed through me, "Be patient . . . Let the fish fight the current . . . Keep your tip up . . . Give the fish some line to run, but not too much . . . Relax, enjoy it." My own thoughts were more like, "Your rod is cheap your leader is four-pound test and this fish is way bigger than that so you'll never land this fish don't screw up."

After ten minutes, I had only regained fifteen feet of line. The fish made two more strong runs; the second one jerked me off balance, and I nearly fell in as I was making my way across the boulders in search of a flat spot where I could attempt to land the fish. It was nearly pitch black and my eyes hadn't yet adjusted to the darkness. My feet found a flat, stable rock next to a small pocket of gravel, as the feisty fish went on its last and strongest run, pulling out all the line I had regained, plus more. I let it run, afraid to try and stop it with only four-pound leader.

Fifteen minutes later, the fight was mostly gone from the fish and I slowly reeled it in. I quivered at my first glimpse, thinking, "Wow, it's a salmon." "Please let me land this fish. Oh Please," I whispered to the darkness, or perhaps Grandpa. After one last desperate run, I finally had the fish next to the riverbank. I scooped it with both hands and hoisted it up onto the bank, falling backwards in the process. My hands shook uncontrollably as I examined the massive fish. It was a regal brown trout, a chunky male with a hooked lower jaw and huge spotted body. Was this the same fish I had stalked all afternoon?

My personal code of catch-and-release angling demanded that I relinquish the fish. But the deluge of childhood memories and my irrepressible desire to share this moment with Grandpa convinced me to keep it. In the stillness of the night, I could almost hear again Grandpa's raspy cackle, the triumph of mirth over emphysema-riddled lungs.

The black gnat was deeply embedded in the trout's lower jaw and took several tries to pry loose. As I was rinsing my reel and cleaning the fish scales from my hands, the mighty fish flopped twice and landed inches from the water. I pounced on it, trembling all over once again.

I crawled up the riverbank—fish dangling in one hand, rod in the other. Back at the car, I searched for something big enough to hold the fish. The best I could find was a plastic grocery bag with handles. Half the fish fit inside. I laid the bag on a rubber mat on the floor of the passenger side and started driving.

The evening chill had set in, but I rolled my window down anyway to savor the cool breeze. As I slowly drove back to the campground, I thanked the brown trout, the Turnbull, and my second-hand fly rod for providing me with such exhilaration. I also thanked Grandpa for nurturing my fishing passions, and for instilling in me the courage to explore and the humility to treasure life's infinite possibilities.

Back at the campground, a Kiwi, who had just returned from his own fishing excursion, asked me how big the fish was. "Dunno," I replied. He threaded a rope through the gills and mouth and hung the trout from a spring-loaded scale he pulled from his fishing vest. At 7-1/4 lbs this trout was by far the biggest fish I had ever landed with a fly rod. The Kiwi loaned me a fillet knife and I sliced the trout into twelve thick steaks. I gave him two for his help, put the rest in the campground refrigerator, and collapsed into our tent.

For lunch the next day, Ann and I made a wood fire and grilled several of the trout steaks with fresh lemon juice, chives, and butter. The meat was salmon-pink in color, succulent, and flaky: the richness of a pristine watershed converted into its flesh and now ours. To accompany this grand feast, we had fresh salad greens and grilled, crusty bread with local black currant jam. That morning on a drive out to

Jackson Bay, Ann and I had discovered an organic fruit and vegetable stand by the side of the road. We selected the jam, salad greens, and chives, and left some money in a coffee can marked "donations."

We were careful to save all the bones and skin from our first meal of the brown trout. Then, following the tradition of many Indian Tribes in the Pacific Northwest, I returned the bones and skin to the Turnbull River. As I shook the fish remains from a plastic bag into the smooth current, I offered a blessing:

> *I am grateful for the gift of your flesh and the nourishment and pleasure it provided me. With profound respect, I return your skin and bones to your home stream in the hope that others, too, may benefit. May trout always prosper here.*

Grandpa would have been proud. He cherished a good fish story, and this one's for him.

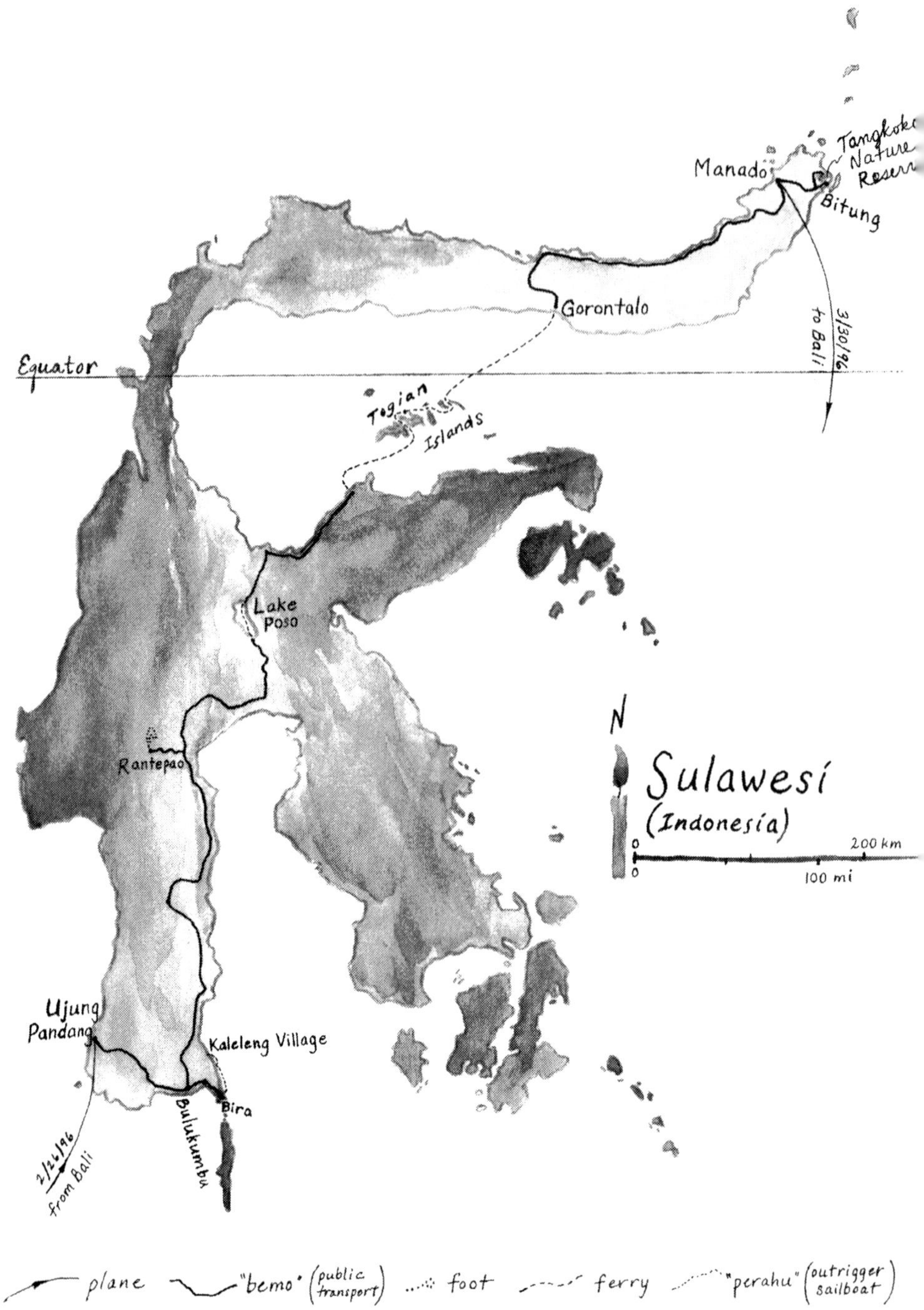
Tangkoko Nature Reserve
Manado
Bitung
Gorontalo
3/30/96
to Bali
Equator
Togian Islands
Lake Poso
N
Sulawesi
(Indonesia)
0
200 km
0
100 mi
Rantepao
Ujung Pandang
Kaleleng Village
Bira
Bulukumbu
2/26/96
from Bali
plane
"bemo" (public transport)
foot
ferry
"perahu" (outrigger sailboat)

7

Sailing to Kaleleng

I find the great thing in this world is not so much where we stand, as in what direction we are moving.

-Oliver Wendell Holmes

Her name was *Puteri Mandar*, "Princess of the Mandar Sea," and we crossed paths fortuitously on the island of Sulawesi, one of more than 17,000 islands in the Indonesian archipelago; the one where the beautiful Princess led us on one of the most extraordinary adventures in our thirteen months of world travels. But to fully appreciate the serendipity of our meeting the Princess, I must begin in Ujung Pandang, the bustling port city of southern Sulawesi.

We arrived in Ujung Pandang by plane, after spending a decadent week on Bali savoring the local color, culture, and cuisine amidst the terraced rice fields of Ubud. At the Ujung Pandang airport, we made a hasty decision to take a small bus, a *pete-pete*, to a nearby hostel—a decision prompted by imminent rainfall. Crammed together in one seat with our backpacks still on, we were the source of great amusement for the driver and other passengers. We leafed through our phrase book, trying out our limited vocabulary of the national language, *Bahasa Indonesian*, which only added to everyone's amusement. In Ubud, we got by fine knowing only English. It was clear within 10 minutes of arriving on Sulawesi that English wouldn't cut it here.

Equatorial Crossings

At stoplights, or whenever the traffic slowed, our driver would shout out to another vehicle something that caused both drivers to erupt in laughter. The only word I could make out was "American," and it was clear we were the butt of his jokes. Seemingly oblivious to other vehicles or the flooded roads, the driver further amused himself by reading our phrase book, while swerving in and out of traffic. As passengers got on the bus, he would say in broken English, "Plees seet down." Occasionally, he would glance back at us, give us a thumbs-up sign, and beat his hands on the dashboard to the rhythm of static-filled rock music blaring from his radio at eardrum-crushing decibels.

We arrived safely, but a bit shaken, at the "central terminal"—merely the intersection of five serpentine streets with no street signs—and were immediately besieged by *becak* riders. Enroute from the airport, we had watched as these tiny men furiously pedaled and weaved their three-wheeled bicycles, passengers first, headlong into traffic. We had seen enough to convince us that walking was the more prudent alternative. Besides, this was our first experience traveling in a country where English is seldom spoken, and we were nervous. Who could we trust? How could we be certain a becak rider wouldn't take us down some back alley, where his friends were waiting to mug us?

Using a crude map in our guidebook, we oriented ourselves and headed towards the waterfront. Along the way, my definition of filth was redefined. Soiled clothes, piles of human feces, and every imaginable form of garbage lined the edges of the streets. The walls of the shoddy buildings seemed to slope inward and close in upon us, as did the smells from the cesspools of standing water left behind by the morning rain. We eventually found a street sign and determined we were only five minutes from our destination, the local hostel.

After a troubled nap in the still, muggy air of the top floor of the hostel, mounting worries about malaria motivated us to look for a mosquito net. The search took us to an enormous, three-level department store called Mata Hari, where we tried in vain to make someone understand we wanted to buy a *kelambu*. First we were taken to housewares, where two young men showed us placemats. These men escorted us to women's accessories, where two helpful women showed us panty hose, before enlisting the help of others. Ultimately, six different people were anxiously trying to help us, without a clue what we were looking for. We even resorted to play-acting, making our fingers and lips into buzzing mosquitoes and slapping our arms. The response was blank stares and muffled snickers. Finally, a woman who spoke a little English explained (we think) that we could find a mosquito net in the morning at one of the vendor stalls on the lower level of the eight-story building next door.

Sailing to Kaleleng

On the way back to the hostel, we stopped at a fruit stand on the street. We were astonished to see the vendor was selling apples, but not just any apples—Red Delicious apples with "grown in Washington" stickers. We bought two each, amused that these apples appeared in our path at the precise instant when our distance from home and the present language barrier seemed insurmountable. When we pointed to the stickers, saying W-A-S-H-I-N-G-T-O-N and drawing pictures in the air of our home state, we nearly brought the vendor, and a growing crowd of spectators, to tears laughing. We joined in, reveling in our serendipity and savoring the familiar explosion of juices and flavors that connected us to home with each crisp bite.

On a whim, we stopped at a textiles shop across from the fruit stand and asked again for a kelambu. After saying the word for the third time, slightly slower and louder, the clerk's face lit up and he motioned for us to follow him to the back of the store. There, in a neat stack, we found pink, blue, and white mosquito nets. We even had three sizes to choose from. We paid his asking price without even trying to barter, happy just to have succeeded. But the self-congratulation was short-lived. Our one afternoon of wandering was enough to convince us that Ujung Pandang was an ugly, filthy, unplanned sprawl. We had just arrived and we were already anxious to leave.

The next morning, I met a man named Riswan in the lobby of the Legends Hostel. He owned several bungalows in Bira, a seaside village near the southern tip of Sulawesi, which is known for its white sand beaches, fishing, boatbuilding, and weaving. Riswan persuaded us, with little difficulty, to come stay with him. Little did we know that the journey would involve two pete-petes, and three different underpowered, overloaded Nissan mini-vans called *bemos*.

The resulting transportation scenario became a familiar one: fumble to make our destination understood; sit around for hours and wait until every possible space was filled with either bodies or cargo; wear our packs or worry about someone stealing them once out of our sight; and then endure foul air and rutted, body-jostling, mind-jarring roads for hours on end. On the last bemo from Bulukumba to Bira, we sat for two hours while the driver stuffed 22 people, luggage, bags of rice, boxes of noodles, and cases of beer inside. He then lashed sheets of plywood and two large, door-sized mirrors onto the roof. When I thought we were as packed as we could possibly get, he handed me a crate of eggs to hold in my lap. I laughed so hard I thought my spasms might scramble the eggs.

Equatorial Crossings

For the next two hours, I was smooshed against bags of rice and the back door of the mini-van with six women pressed against me, a little boy vomiting on my sandaled feet, and the acrid stench of cigarette smoke filling my lungs. And, as if simply breathing wasn't enough of a worry, I was convinced that if I broke even one of the eggs, some horrible tribal ritual awaited me.

Amidst the confusion of women's breasts, thighs, and buttocks protruding in my face, I couldn't even see Ann, though I could hear her reassuring voice a few feet away—"Ah, paradise found." I smiled as I recalled the freedom and, in my present circumstances, seeming luxury of driving our own vehicle in New Zealand just a few weeks earlier. The man behind Ann sang softly throughout the journey, and later she wrote, "These people accept and survive hardship with more grace and humor than I imagined possible. I could take a few lessons!"

We arrived at Riswan's bungalows just after sunset. The 70-mile journey that we guessed would take five hours had taken eleven. We set up our new mosquito net, ate a quick dinner, and collapsed in bed, exhausted from our first day and a half on Sulawesi.

We awoke at sunrise to the universal *cock-a-doodle-doo* of roosters and were promptly served fried bananas and crispy, sugar-coated doughnuts. We ventured out with the intention of visiting the boat building center in Marumasa, but never made it there. At the ferry pier, the handmade wooden boats, the see-through water, and the shimmering morning light enchanted us. A young man named Asnewil introduced himself to Ann. He was studying to be a ship captain and was quite anxious to practice his English, which was fortunate for us because we clearly needed to learn a little Bahasa Indonesian. After a pleasant conversation, we said goodbye and walked to the end of the pier. Ten minutes later Asnewil returned with a gift of rice crackers, a humble expression of his appreciation that we had stopped to talk with him.

The highlight of the morning was seeing a local spear-fisherman at the end of the pier. He was a tiny man, with weathered skin and sunken eyes, sitting cross-legged in a narrow dugout canoe the exact width of his hips. The canoe and the man were one. He was wearing only threadbare shorts and a frayed balaclava-style hood. Resting on his head were hand-carved, wooden goggles with thick, glass lenses that looked like they were probably made from the bottoms of Coke bottles. He demonstrated with great pride and precision how he dives down to the reef with his wooden spear gun and shoots a fish with a flanged metal spear. He then resurfaces at the boat, which is tethered to his ankle with a long, braided hemp rope. In the bow of the dugout were a large cuttlefish and two small reef fish—his morning's catch. When I motioned that I wanted to take his picture, he flashed me a grin that revealed chipped, broken, and missing teeth. The lines of his face and his gnarled hands told a story of a grueling life at sea, but I was tormented by my inability to talk with him. I knew a lifetime of stories remained locked behind his weary eyes. He was likely the last of many generations of traditional spear-fishers.

Next to the ferry pier, we watched a father and son team, in translucent water up to their chests, pulling a net in consecutively smaller and smaller circles. After half an hour, they had caught only two fish, both less than six-inches long. We moved on, strolling the white sand beach and taking photos of the many massive wooden sailing vessels at anchor in the still, turquoise water.

"Are you wishing we hadn't shipped the kayak home?" Ann asked, reading my mind.

"Yes and no," I replied. "It's fun to imagine kayaking these tranquil waters, but I sure don't miss the hassle of schlepping all that gear around."

As we neared the end of the line of boats, a voice emerged from the trees up the beach from us, "Come here you guys."

We turned, startled first by the English words and then by the image of this stranger coaxing us to him. His hair was bleached white from the intense equatorial sun. The skin on his face was drawn tight and cracked like peeling drywall, and his lips were badly blistered. He was wearing a lovely silk sarong beneath a ratty T-shirt, which exposed his pasty arms. We approached with caution, unsure what this suspicious character might want with us. Only one thought entered my mind: he either wants to sell us drugs or fleece us.

"What's up?" I asked warily.

"Come here, I want to show you something," he replied, with a European accent that I couldn't place, pointing toward one of the ramshackle houses on stilts. We looked to where he was pointing. Then, without introducing himself, he came toward us and simply stated, "I want you to see the sarongs the local women are making."

Three hours later, we were sitting with our new friend, Horst, inside the house on stilts, discussing plans to go sailing with him. Horst was working on a PhD in anthropology with the Coastal Societies Research and Development Project at Hasanuddin University in Ujung Pandang. He was from Cologne, Germany originally, but had lived in southern Sulawesi since 1987. At the time, he was living with different families in Panrang Luhuk, one month with each, before moving on. The focus of his research was the sailing and fishing communities of southern Sulawesi, and how traditional knowledge is passed on from one generation to the next. He spoke fluent Bahasa Indonesian, including the local dialect called *Konjo*, in addition to English, German, and a bit of Dutch. Eager to interact with westerners, he shared with us his wealth of knowledge about the local people, their boats, and their subsistence culture.

As the afternoon wore on, Horst's host family served us sugary tea and tasty boiled cakes, called *umba-umba*, made of rice flour, coconut, and red sugar, while the women gave us a show of their exquisite silk sarongs. These were far nicer than the cotton sarongs we had bartered so hard for on Bali. Horst explained that the social fabric of the local culture is based on the women weaving and caring for children, while the village men are away fishing. The conversation kept returning to sailing and fishing, and we eventually learned that Horst had his own *perahu*, a traditional wooden sailboat. He offered to take us sailing in exchange for a contribution to a scholarship fund he had established to help send local students to the University in Ujung Pandang.

Ever since Australia, Ann had been hoping to go sailing, and now the perfect opportunity had been dropped in our laps. Horst took us down to the beach to see his sailboat. At first glance, the hull seemed to be a simple dugout canoe with bamboo outriggers. But as I studied the perahu's lines, I marveled at the high degree of artistry and craftsmanship. "Hard to believe this was all done with hand tools," I gushed.

The 24-foot long hull was made of *tepulu*, a soft, light wood that is resistant to borers and lasts 100 years or more. The mast, boom, and outriggers were *patong*—bamboo roughly ten inches in diameter. The rudder, hull decking and ribs, and outrigger spars were teak. Rattan was used to bind the spars to the outriggers and hull, as well as the boom to the mast.

Horst described how every inch of her hull had been carefully shaped with a *bingkung*, a square-bladed adze, and hand axes; how every joint was pegged with hand-carved dowels; and how the whole boat building ritual progressed according to strict traditional rules of construction. The boat was built for Horst in 1988 by a Mandarese *panrita lopi*, a master boat builder whom Horst had met during his research.

The Mandarese people, Horst explained, traditionally used perahus for fishing. They sailed across open water as far as Australia, 1,000 miles away. But wooden boat building is a craft on the brink of change. According to Horst, the 1970s saw the advent of motorized vessels, and a subsequent decline in sailing and seamanship. Voyages once set by knowledge of stars, landmarks, waves, and clouds, are today fixed by compass and chart. Traditional wooden boats that were operated under sail lasted up to 60 years. In contrast, many of the motorized wooden vessels built today rattle apart under the strain of diesel engines within five to eight years. In fishing communities all along the southern coast of Sulawesi, wooden boat building is being transformed from a traditional undertaking to a modern industry involving advertising, marketing, and power tools. According to Horst, the generation of panrita lopi still building boats by hand today will be the last guard of Sulawesi's centuries-old boat building tradition.

My eyes danced along the glossy white hull of Horst's perahu, then up, and up the bamboo mast, which supported a gigantic triangular sail called a *sombalaq*, 650 square feet of heavy, canvas-like cloth. Horst had made only a few concessions to modern materials; all the lines were polypropylene and he had a solar panel to run his tape deck and laptop computer.

"What's her name?" I asked.

A proud grin gave needed warmth to his creased face, "*Puteri Mandar* — Princess of the Mandar Sea — she's won many races." I could already imagine the wind blowing through my hair, and the crystalline water lapping at her hull.

"Where do you want to sail?" Horst asked.

"Wherever you and the Princess wish to take us," I blurted, still bouncing along the waves of my daydream.

Ann expressed her desire to learn how to sail Puteri Mandar, snorkel, and maybe visit a local fishing village. I heartily concurred. We made plans to meet Horst at 7 am the next morning, and left in excitement on a mission to buy gifts for fishermen and villagers that we might meet on our journey. Horst had recommended hair accessories for women and flashlights for men. He volunteered to buy cigarettes and food to give away as gifts also.

Leap day, February 29, 1996, was still and hot — as Ann noted, "perfect for lounging on a white sand beach, but not for sailing." While Horst and Daeng, a village fisherman who would be our deckhand, carried supplies to the boat and checked all the rigging, Ann and I played frisbee with several children. They quickly mastered throwing and catching the flying disc. Abdullah, the youngest child of Horst's host family, was especially coordinated. He could throw the disc forehand, backhand, and upside down, and he stretched his long legs and arms with the grace of a gazelle and the radiant smile of an Olympic gymnast. Daeng's daughter, the oldest of six kids, also joined in. Horst told us that Nani, this shy but striking eleven year old, was responsible for taking care of Daeng's house and her five siblings, since her mom died a year earlier.

Equatorial Crossings

We shoved off from Panrang Luhuk around 8:30 am. Our first task was to paddle the sailboat into water deep enough for Ann and me to lower the solid, six-foot rudder, while Horst lashed it into place. Daeng taught us how to raise the *bong* with the *manteleq* and hoist the *sombalaq*, while Horst translated. We caught a fresh northwest breeze and glided for a while at a comfortable 8 to 10 knots. Ann and I inundated Horst with questions about the boat, sailing, the Konjo language, the spear-fisherman we had met, and the local cultures. Within an hour, the wind picked up and Horst explained that Daeng and I would have to stand on one of the bamboo outriggers to keep the boat from heeling over too far. Daeng scampered out effortlessly. I gripped the spar with my arms and legs and inched out on my butt.

Out on the pontoon, Daeng made a sling for me out of a sarong and attached it to a line coming from the top of the mast. We were cruising at 20 knots, and as my confidence grew, I was able to grip the pontoon with my toes and lean back at a 45-degree angle to the water, letting the sling support my weight. Flying fish leaped out of the bow wake, and twice I had to duck to avoid a mid-air collision. Occasionally, I glanced over my shoulder to see the limestone bluffs and shoreline zipping by.

I later learned that many Konjo fishermen believe the ocean is a kingdom ruled by spirits, who control man's fate at sea. These guardian spirits control the winds, currents, waves, and weather. The flying fish is traditionally regarded as a divine spirit endowed with the power to observe everything that happens, both below and above water. Seeing a flying fish is a good omen. I didn't ask whether getting smacked in the face by one is also.

Offshore from a small village called Ara, we dropped the sail and anchored in the sand on the inside of a coral reef. Ann and I snorkeled, while Daeng and Horst fixed lunch. The diversity of fish far exceeded my expectations for such a small patch reef. The water was crystal clear with visibility in excess of 75 feet. Ann saw a reef shark and a small turtle, and together we watched a spotted eagle ray with a missing tail glide along the reef crest. My favorite fish were the iridescent blue and turquoise damsels. We were thrilled to see so many of our favorite fish from the Coral Sea again: lionfish, triggerfish, fusiliers, and Moorish idols. I could have been content to spend the next two days anchored right there.

We emerged to find a meal of tea, biscuits, *indomie* (noodles), *ikan* (fresh fish), and *nasi goreng* (fried rice) waiting for us. Daeng had prepared the meal on an ingenious clay stove the size of a small Dutch oven. The stove was circular, with an open top exactly the size of Daeng's rice pot and a small slot to feed kindling underneath the pot. He grilled the fish, skin-on, right on the glowing coals. It was hard to keep from drooling, as the fish juices dripped and spattered on the coals.

Ann teasingly pinched me to make sure that I wasn't dreaming. A half day of sailing had already been a feast for the senses: tropical breezes on our skin, rhythmic rocking of the sailboat to massage our bemo-bruised muscles, jazz from the solar-powered tape deck for our ears, the sweet smell of a wood fire for our noses, and a palette of equatorial blues and greens for our eyes.

After our meal, Horst, Ann, and I swam to shore to look for a freshwater cave that Horst knew about but had never visited. Two young men, who were riding a motorcycle on the beach, took us to the cave. A shaft of light shone through the entrance and illuminated the water, which was so flat and clear that we thought we were looking down at a pond many feet below us, when in fact we were looking through the water inches from our feet. The candle flame quivering below us was actually the reflection of a candle hidden in a ceiling nook, outside our view. It was one of those moments when my brain couldn't register what my eyes were seeing. We took a refreshing swim in the spring water, rinsing off the crusted salt before returning to the sailboat.

Daeng had readied the boat for sailing, and we hoisted the sail and resumed our journey north up the coast toward Tahanaberu, a fishing village where Horst had many friends. Moments later there was an explosion, which I thought was thunder. Ann remarked that something must haven fallen overboard and slammed against the hull. Horst suggested that the sailboat must have hit something floating. But Daeng explained that it was a bomb, set off by Bugi fishermen who were collecting fish by dynamiting the coral reef.

Horst was livid. The local people of Panrang Luhuk and Ara despise bombing as a fishing technique. However, the Bugis are nomads, who move often, never settle, and take no responsibility for maintaining the reef fisheries.

"Pillage and move on," I sighed in disgust. "It's apparently the same default choice the world over."

Within an hour, the sky blackened and powerful gusts of wind heeled the boat over to starboard, thrusting the windward pontoon ten feet out of the water. Daeng and I tied lines to our waists and scrambled out on the port pontoon. Too giddy to be frightened, I waved to Ann, who was nestled in the cockpit next to Horst, with the deck hatch pulled under her chin. Horst shouted, "We're doing 25 knots." He seemed confident that we could sail north fast enough to outrun the storm from the west. No such luck. Rainsqualls soaked us and the wind continued to build. As the winds mounted, Horst was forced to point closer and closer into the wind. We were rapidly closing on the shoreline and its fringing reef, when Horst felt a warm blast and hollered, "It's getting stronger. Get back on board, NOW!" With Ann's help, Daeng and I yanked down the sail seconds before the Princess was lambasted by violent winds and driving rain.

For the next 15 minutes, the boat was in utter pandemonium. The reef and shoreline that we previously admired were now enemies. Decisions had to be swift and correct. Horst braced his feet and pushed with all his strength against the rudder, struggling to avoid the reef while still keeping us pointed into the wind. Daeng, Ann, and I fought with the billowing sail, trying desperately to lash it to the boom. Loose lines were whipping. The end of the mainsail halyard went overboard. Ann's palm leaf hat, handmade for her by an Aborigine woman in Australia, took flight in the tempest. "I'm sorry," Horst hollered, acknowledging to Ann without saying so, that there was no way we could retrieve her hat. Ann's eyes traced its path, as we gathered in the sail. And amidst the fray, Horst looked entirely in his element: dark sunglasses shielded his eyes from the pelting rain, which trickled in rivulets down his cracked cheeks and off his stubbly chin; the sarong wrapped around his head bled maroon dye down his face and neck; and the smoldering butt of a cigarette hung precariously from his lips.

Using a long bamboo pole, Daeng hooked the halyard and the three of us secured the sail to the boom. No longer in danger of crashing into the reef, we could now drift and wait out the storm. Without the deafening chatter of the sail, we could also converse again. Ann expressed her concern to Horst about Daeng, who was shivering uncontrollably. Horst appreciated Ann's concern, but assured us that Konjo fishermen like Daeng are "incredibly hearty and self-sufficient." He added, "All he needs is a cigarette." Sure enough, Daeng crouched in the cockpit to smoke a cigarette and afterwards seemed less chilled. Ann and I huddled together under a plastic tarp. I was buzzing from the adrenaline rush, too caught up in the moment to notice that Ann was trembling. It is this exact experience of being out of control that Ann has always disliked and feared about sailing. The apparent urgency, yelling, and frenetic action had frayed her nerves. Horst stood and stretched his arms toward the sky; the bulging veins in his neck slowly receded.

The force of the storm lessened after 45 minutes, and the sun reappeared. Horst and Daeng conversed awhile in Konjo, deciding that we should set sail again before the wind and waves pushed us onto shore. I went out on the pontoon alone for my most exhilarating ride yet. I played around with shifting my weight and hanging my head all the way over backwards so the shoreline was zooming by upside down. In a short amount of time, we traveled a significant distance, well past Tahanaberu, which was too exposed to the wind and waves to risk anchoring. Horst had sailed this stretch of coast many times, but he had never anchored overnight. He decided to take us into a sheltered cove near a village he had seen on his previous voyages, but never visited. It was late afternoon when we dropped the sail just outside the reef at the entrance to the cove. Ann and I paddled, while Horst and Daeng poled us through the narrow gap in the reef.

As we entered the cove, I could see several kids running excitedly along a pocket of beach next to the dense, intertwined mangroves, then some more kids, and then adults. Horst and Daeng secured the Princess with the bow anchor and a stern line to a mangrove. Horst smiled at us and said, "Well, here's your chance to visit a fishing village. They'll have more fun with you if I don't go ashore."

The *National Geographic* theme song was playing in my head, as I surveyed the growing group of villagers, the wooden boats lining the shore, and the houses on stilts. Fishing nets hung from rows of pilings, parallel to each other and perpendicular to the shoreline. Coconut trees and mangroves appeared to be the dominant vegetation landward of the muddy shoreline and mangroves. Four perahus, smaller versions of Puteri Mandar, were lined up at the water's edge, as if ready to be launched in a hurry. Plywood houses with rusted metal roofs and windows without glass were perched on stilts in a line facing the water, less than fifty feet horizontally from the high water mark, but ten to fifteen vertical feet above the mud.

Still drenched and chilled, we slogged through the silty mud and mangroves to greet the awaiting crowd. We approached cautiously, so as not to trip on the mangrove roots — worried that tripping might make us look even more pathetic than we already did. Having only been in Indonesia ten days, we couldn't say much more than, "*Saya nama* David, *Saya nama* Ann," and "good afternoon, *selamat sore*." We were greeted with total silence. Women, girls, and children were standing in small clumps holding one another. The men were behind, arms crossed against their chests. There was a little shuffling, but no one spoke. Regretting that we left our phrase book on the boat, we attempted a few clumsy words of Bahasa Indonesian, like *perahu* and *sarong*, pointing to the items as we said the words. Some people smiled, others laughed, but the kids encouraged us to say more. "America," one boy said. "Yes, we are from America," Ann replied enthusiastically. For ten awkward minutes that crept by like ten excruciating hours, we tried to communicate. No one was quite sure what to do or how to act.

Ann went to the sailboat to get our phrase book, some dry clothes, and a point-and-shoot camera. Her camera finally broke the ice. The little kids became especially excited, as they clung to one another and giggled. We took pictures of them, and they took pictures of us, gathering around us like we were royalty. Two chairs appeared and we were invited to sit. The villagers surrounded us, and the kids pulled my arm hairs and touched my beard, as if they had never seen a man with body hair before. Everyone laughed nervously whenever we attempted to speak.

One young man asked, "You speek English?"

"Yes, English, not Bahasa Indonesian," I replied.

Darna's limited English was better than our limited Bahasa Indonesian, and by pointing to words and passing the phrase book back and forth we managed to converse. We started with easy stuff like numbers, and eyes, ears, nose. Then, we progressed to family relationships—a short-lived topic because they all seemed to be related. We explained that we were Americans, married, and in our thirties, and that we had sailed to their village from Panrang Luhuk. Where were our children Darna wanted to know? He looked very worried when we answered *tidak punya*, "no children." Several of the women gasped.

Horst came ashore eventually, but went straight inside one of the stilt houses with several of the village elders. After an hour or so more of stumbling discourse, Darna and his buddy paddled us in a dugout back to the sailboat. We had hoped to return to the boat for a respite from all the attention, but there were already five men on board smoking cigarettes with Daeng, and Darna and his buddy also got out.

Horst eventually returned and filled us in on his meeting with the village elders. The name of this village was Kaleleng and westerners had never before visited. We were stunned. "But why are many of the kids wearing American T-shirts, and where have they seen a camera before, and how come Darna speaks a little English?" I demanded.

"Easy, Dave, be patient," said Horst. "I will explain everything."

Horst prepared a sack of rice and noodles, gave us some cigarettes, and told us to gather up the gifts we brought. He then escorted us to the *Kepala Desa*, the home of the village headman. The village elders had invited Ann and me to spend the night as their honored guests. Enroute, Ann pulled Horst aside, nervous about spending the night with people we couldn't even ask a simple question like, "Where's the toilet?" He reassured her everything would work out.

Sailing to Kaleleng

Once inside the Kepala Desa, we were introduced to the headman's family, but only the males. Our host encouraged us to sit on chairs in the main living area and we were offered hot tea. Horst explained that because this was a Muslim village, females must stay in the kitchen or back room unless the headman invites them into the main room. Ann quickly escaped into the kitchen to deliver our food sack and to be with the women and girls. I sat quietly, uncomfortably, for a long time, while Horst and the headman talked in Konjo and chain smoked. Periodically, Horst would convey what he was learning.

These people were suffering greatly because their corn crop had failed due to lack of rain. The conditions weren't right in this area for growing rice, and thus their diet was mostly protein—fish, goats, and chickens—plus some seaweed, coconuts, and bananas. The closest road was ten miles away, and most everything they needed was brought to the village by boat. The community was devout Muslim and they had their own mosque and school. Most of the adults in the village had traveled to Bira or other villages in southern Sulawesi, but few of the children had ever left Kaleleng, other than to go fishing. No one in the village owned a camera, but they had seen cameras before in Bira and other larger villages. Horst speculated the T-shirts had arrived in Ujung Pandang from an American aid organization. It was unclear exactly how the shirts made it to Kaleleng, but not too surprising to him, given the active trading and bartering that occurs throughout Sulawesi.

Horst kept the headman well supplied with cigarettes, and the stories kept flowing. Of the six men in the room, I was the only one not smoking. Unwilling to smoke, and unable to converse, I felt increasingly out of place. When Ann came back into the room to tell me about her interactions with the women, they all followed her. The headman repeatedly thanked us for traveling "all the way across the ocean" to visit his village. "We are honored to stay in your home," we assured him. Horst interpreted, while we passed around postcards from the Olympic Peninsula, and photos of our families. The looks on their faces ranged from delight to disbelief. The headman's brother insisted it was impossible for trees to get as big as the ones on the postcard of the Hoh rainforest. The women squealed at the postcards of Dungeness crabs and killer whales. Surprisingly, the photo everyone liked best was a picture of Ann and me sitting between my mom and brother on a couch at my Aunt Dorothy's house. Several people asked to keep that particular photo, but we explained that these family photos were our cherished connections to home.

Ann gave the hair bands, barrettes, and a pair of her earrings to the headman's wife, who distributed them to her daughters, keeping nothing for herself. I presented a small metal flashlight to the headman. We both passed out hologram fish stickers to the younger kids. The headman's wife kept the postcard of the breaching killer whales. The headman's brother wanted to keep the Hoh rainforest postcard, which we gladly gave him, with our address and several wildlife stamps on the back—a symbolic bridge between our distant cultures.

The day was exhilarating from start to finish. And exhausting. Late that night, Horst got up to leave and the headman's wife announced that dinner was ready. We were served rice and noodles, the food we had brought as gifts, with two tiny fried fish added. Taking half a fish, the equivalent of one bite, Horst commented with surprise, "They are much worse off than I thought."

After the meal, the headman's wife gave us each a clean, neatly folded sarong to sleep in, and we were shown to our room. This must have been the master bedroom, because we had a comfortable double bed with elaborately quilted pillows and a wardrobe with a full-length mirror. We stripped and looked in the mirror. For the first time in five hours, we had our own private space: no questions, no stares, less naked in our nakedness than hours earlier in our wet, clinging clothes, surrounded by strangers.

As we donned our sleeping sarongs, Ann filled me in on her interactions with the women and girls in the kitchen. The headman's wife had greeted Ann with a welcome smile and offered her a chair. Ann sat and was soon flanked by women and girls on all sides. She was served tea and peanut butter cookies called *planta*, while they all played *apa ini* (what is) this and *apa ini* that. One young woman was particularly taken with Ann. She took Ann's hand and gently held it for a long time, staring into her eyes. Ann dearly wanted to know whether she was a teacher, or somehow better educated than the others. Why did this woman seem so urgent to make a connection?

We curled up in bed, and Ann let out a heavy sigh. She expressed a little discomfort with the foreignness of this place, mixed with excitement about the extraordinary events of the day. She told me she was embarrassed to admit that she was tense. I was asleep before she could elaborate. I woke up only once, in the middle of the night, feeling as though I had emerged from some bizarre dreams, but remembering nothing about them. Ann remembers waking up and feeling cozy and secure. The sounds of roosters, crying children, and wood chopping brought me to consciousness the next morning. I lay in bed for awhile, but couldn't go back to sleep. At dawn, Muslim prayers and singing were broadcast from a loudspeaker on the roof of the mosque. We laughed that, even in this village with no electricity, they have a loudspeaker.

I snuck outside and managed to take a dozen photos, before several kids noticed me and begged me to take their picture. The morning light was soft and peaceful, and I was thankful for the brief opportunity to explore the awaking village. The tide was completely out and the Princess was grounded, except for the offshore end of her pontoons. Mudskippers skittered across the mudflat, dodging the brown coconut husks. I examined the fishing nets hanging from the pilings, curious why they hung in such disrepair. I walked past rows and rows of dead corn stalks, at the edge of what seemed to be a graveyard. The kids followed me, monitoring my mood and expressions, chirping words I couldn't understand.

When I returned to the Kepala Desa, Ann was cornered on the couch, flipping through the phrase book and trying to answer questions. I could see the relief in her face that I was back and could help her out. Together, we organized several family portraits out in front of the Kepala Desa, some with Ann in them, others with me. The previous night the headman had told us about a sacred *gua*, a cave near the entrance to the cove, and he was now anxious to take us there.

The limestone cave was hidden on a small peninsula at the southern entrance to the cove. The headman motioned for us to go inside. We followed the coral shingle, hunching progressively more as the walls and ceiling narrowed. The cave extended back for about 30 feet, where we discovered a small ledge covered with wilted flowers, blue-striped sticks, coins, cigarettes, and neat piles of rice on banana leaves. The walls and ceiling were adorned with colorful shells, driftwood, and other beach combings tied to pieces of string and suspended from sticks wedged into crevices. At the entrance to the cave was a saltwater pool, a perfect circle eroded in the limestone.

We were sifting through our phrase book for words that would allow us to understand the significance of the cave, when Horst showed up, and translated as the headman told the story of the cave. The people of Kaleleng believe this cave is the place where all peoples originated. According to Horst, this origin story is a common oral history among all Konjo villages. The headman wanted us to understand that his people take part in a special ritual here, which consists of eating a carefully prepared rice dish from a banana leaf, bathing in the saltwater pool at the cave entrance, giving an offering at the back of the cave to the Guardian Spirits, and finally, making a wish and hanging a talisman—a string of shells or wood. Their belief is that if the wish comes true, then the individual must return to the cave, remove the talisman, and cast it into the sea. The headman urged us to hang our own talismans. Both Ann and I did, and someday we hope to return to cast ours into the sea.

After the cave visit, we went back to the Kepala Desa and sat again for an uncomfortably long time. As we made motions that we needed to leave, a grand meal appeared. We were served rice, lentils, steamed seaweed, green beans, noodles, three small fried fish, and octopus in spicy oil. Horst said that some of the village men had gone out in the middle of the night to catch the octopus, a revered delicacy among these people. The octopus was exquisite, but we were careful to refrain from eating as much as we would have liked. The fact that we were the only ones eating was an awkward reminder that we were different and special in their eyes. We felt honored and humbled by their generosity.

The meal concluded with an obligatory final cigarette for Horst and the headman, followed by emotional farewells and promises that we would send more photos. We shook hands all around and said a heartfelt *terima kasih* (thank you very much) to our host and hostess, and *selamat tinggal* (farewell) to all the villagers as we waved goodbye.

When we arrived back at the boat, Daeng was busy preparing us rice, eggs, and tea. While he worked, we lay down on the deck. It was an unexpected opportunity to relax and let go completely. We sailed in good wind and good spirits for an hour or so to the south. Horst wanted to deliver some photos to friends in Tahanaberu and also buy several liters of "the best coconut oil in the world." Ann and I tagged along, wading ashore with our cameras held at arm's length above our heads. The village kids recognized Horst's boat and were anxiously waiting for him on shore. Horst handed us some money and asked one of the girls to help us buy some cigarettes for him and traditional cakes for us. The kids followed us around like we were pied pipers, yelling out random words of English: "Hello Meester;" "Wan, Two, Tree, Four;" "Watt's your name?" and "Tank you very much!" Amidst the giggles, Horst trotted off to find his coconut oil.

We were shocked at the differences between Tahanaberu and Kaleleng. In Tahanaberu, the houses were all in good condition; some had glass windows, and several even had satellite dishes. Apparently this village had converted from traditional fishing boats and methods to modern boats and diesel engines. According to Horst, the village was settled in the 1950s and had quickly become a prosperous base for fishing. Yet, we still couldn't fathom the disparity in wealth between the two villages, given their relatively close proximity to each other.

When we all met up back at the boat, Daeng was cooking again. Ann and I decided to snorkel, while the water was boiling for tea. The small patch of reef had been bashed by storms, and broken coral was heaped in a long ridge parallel to shore. Nevertheless, we saw fair numbers of fish, including another lionfish, several anemonefish, a brilliant blue triggerfish, and five sweetlips each greater than 1-foot long. Having just learned that this is a vigorous fishing community, I was surprised to see any harvestable-size fish.

For several hours, we remained anchored here, while Daeng struggled to keep the fire hot enough to fry potatoes and prawn crackers in Horst's fresh coconut oil. Still licking the hot coconut oil from our lips, we pulled up the anchor as the sun was setting. Pinks and reds flickered in the wispy clouds. Ann and I looked at each other, thinking of the adventure ahead — sailing at night on the tropical sea. The wind was strong and consistent and we rounded the first cape in no time. But shortly after dark, the wind died and we crept along with the sail luffing. Horst put on some classic rock to "heat up the wind." I dozed off.

When I awoke, a land breeze to starboard was shuttling us down the coast. I rode the rest of the way to Panrang Luhuk sitting on the outrigger spar. Horst wouldn't let me use the sarong sling for fear I would fall asleep and slide overboard. What he didn't know was that my mind was way too active processing the events of the previous days for me to drift off again. The shoreline was clearly visible beneath the three quarter moon and Orion twinkled straight overhead. A trail of bioluminescence fanned out behind the rudder. We slid silently across the water, except for Horst or Daeng's occasional calls for wind in the Konjo sailor's tradition. Two days of sailing had evolved into two days of bliss, and I slipped in and out of reverie as the waves lapped at the hull and the moonbeams danced across the deck.

Abdullah, the young boy from Horst's host family, galloped down to us as we beached the Princess. He gleefully chattered to himself, while he assisted with unloading and tying up the boat. Abdullah welcomed us into his family's house with such enthusiasm we knew he would be a grateful and proud new owner of our Frisbee. It seemed such a small token of appreciation for the gift of his smile, and I wished that I could adopt him on the spot. All kids should be so happy.

Despite our weariness and readiness for bed, Abdullah's father, Ahad Ballo, insisted on hearing all about our adventures. Ahad, a former head of his village, was once a gifted sailor and fisherman until debilitating bronchitis landed him ashore permanently. He listened intently to our stories, as Horst once again translated. Ahad interrupted frequently to clarify details, but he seemed especially curious about our strong emotional responses to our experiences in Kaleleng. As we swapped sea stories, his girls served us another feast — our fourth that day.

Once again, sleep found us with full stomachs. The last thing I remember before drifting off was Ann reflecting that, "these must be the two days of my life most filled with living." Seldom do I remember dreams, but that night my dreams were a vivid collage of sailing and snorkeling, and Ann giving birth to a lovely Indonesian girl that she named Nani. I awoke to the *cock-a-doodle-do* of roosters, wondering in what new direction we were moving.

8

The Flight of the Kinglet

Out of the welter of life, a few people are selected for us by the accident of temporary confinement in the same circle.

-Anne Morrow Lindbergh, *Gift From The Sea*

New Year's Day, 1997, marked the final blows of one of the worst winter storms in decades. We had been back from our world travels just three months, and for more than a week, we were lambasted with snow, followed by freezing rain, followed by not-quite-freezing rain, flooding, and massive mudslides. Winds up to 60 miles/hour hailed in the new year. New Year's morning, I was gazing out our bedroom window to see if my favorite Western hemlock had survived the blast, when I heard a thud against the kitchen window.

Out on our deck I found a stunned golden-crowned kinglet, gasping for air. I gently cupped the kinglet in my palm and brought it inside to the warm kitchen, where I used an eye dropper to feed it sugar water. Our neighbor Jimmy, a wildlife biologist, had once explained to me how he sometimes revives injured birds in this way. The helpless kinglet, one of our tiniest resident winter birds, involuntarily gulped the sugar water, and its glazed eyes slowly rolled back under membranous lids. I carried the motionless kinglet back outside and hid it underneath a hemlock bow, which I placed over the top of a cedar flower box fastened to our deck railing. I didn't have much hope it would live. I shuddered, both from the brisk morning breeze and the still-vivid memory of my own brush with death nine months earlier.

※

After weeks of anticipation, we were enroute to the Tangkoko Nature Reserve in northern Sulawesi, and we could barely contain our excitement. What drew us to Tangkoko is the same charismatic macrofauna that so deeply puzzled the famous British naturalist, Alfred Russell Wallace, in 1859: six-inch tall spectral tarsier monkeys, a teddy bear-faced tree dweller called a bear cuscus, flying lizards, dog-sized buffalo called anoas, red-knobbed hornbills with the wingspan of a condor, and most of all the crested black macaques. Lesser known are the seemingly infinite diversity of insects and plants in this lush tropical rainforest. Tangkoko Reserve is one of a few increasingly rare places left on earth where new species continue to be discovered each year. It is also, sadly, a place at risk from humans.

Thoughts of disappearing wild animals were foremost in my mind, as we waited in the relentless sun for the next bemo. The air was rank with the smells of rotting produce—smells that were equally repulsive to the stench of overcrowded humans that is my lingering memory of our ferry journey from the Togian Islands to Gorontalo. I recalled the subsequent 14-hour bus ride from Gorontalo to Manado that tested the limits of my bladder. When the driver refused to stop the bus, I finally had to pee into a narrow-mouthed water bottle, while Ann shielded me as best she could with her body. The short, breezy bus ride from Manado to Bitung early the following morning seemed insignificant in comparison to our travel marathon over the previous 72 hours.

But in Bitung, the nearest village to the reserve, we were both overcome by violent nausea within 10 minutes of each other. Two days earlier we had devoured a scrumptious concoction of shaved ice, beans, various fresh fruits, and peanuts at a night vendor's stall in Gorontalo, following the nearly sleepless 40-hour ferry journey from the Togian Islands. For two days we had gone without a place to lie down and no food, other than some stale powdered-sugar doughnuts we begged from two German backpackers. Having endured so much, we were hardly anxious to abort our trip to the wildlife reserve, but the idea of traveling another three or four hours over muddy, rutted roads to reach the remote reserve convinced us otherwise. We checked into a local hotel. That choice probably saved our lives.

The Flight of the Kinglet

By late afternoon when Ann and I checked into the dingy hotel, there was no point in wearing clothes anymore. Our vomiting and diarrhea were uncontrollable. We were paying the price for eating bad ice.

For the next five hours, we played musical chairs with two of us and only one toilet. Too weak to stand, we took turns crawling, neither of us able to retain any fluids. We tried water, Gatorade, and the oral re-hydration solution from our well-stocked first aid kit. Nothing helped. So extensive was my fluid loss that I began having severe cramps in my hands, feet, and calves. By 10:30 pm that night, I looked like I had aged 50 years. My muscles lost all definition and my skin was loose and withered, especially on my hands, which I no longer recognized as my own.

Ann tried several times to massage my cramps, but after each attempt she collapsed in exhaustion. Our situation was growing increasingly desperate, and we both realized the urgency of getting medical attention.

Ann somehow summoned the energy to get out of bed, wrap up in a sarong, and crawl down the stairs to find help. I lay in bed writhing. The pain from the cramps was excruciating, worse than anything I had ever experienced: worse than losing control while telemark skiing through Cascade cement snow and testing the laws of gravity with my face and the trunk of a subalpine fir tree; worse than the time a spunky girl I was teasing at recess in fifth grade slammed the door to our classroom, shattering the ring finger on my right hand; worse than nearly splitting my left thumb in half with an axe on a Boy Scout campout; and even worse than falling on my skull from more than 20 feet, when the rope I was climbing in high school P.E. class pulled out of its ceiling mount. The cramping pain was worse. Much worse. The pain was also magnified by my fear. We were 10,000 miles from home and I didn't have a clue how or where we were going to find help.

The first person Ann found happened to be an off-duty policeman, chatting in the tiny lobby with the hotel manager. Tindatu spoke only a few words of English, but he understood right away that we were in serious trouble and needed to get to a hospital immediately. He and the hotel manager helped me out of bed, draped a sarong around me, and carried me down the stairs to the curb. I vomited in the street before getting into Tindatu's van, and excreted several times inside, at first dismayed by my complete loss of bodily control and increasingly frightened by my mounting loss of mental control.

Equatorial Crossings

At the *rumah sakit* (literally "house of pain"), I laid down on a wooden bench in the lobby for less than one minute before I had to hobble outside and void myself in the street. I was too weak to move and rolled over onto the curb. I was nearly unconscious when the hospital staff came and lifted me onto a stretcher.

The cramps were occurring with greater frequency, and in the examination room, I pleaded with Ann, "You gotta help me."

"Please, can't someone help us?" she cried. "Can't you see his pain is unbearable?"

But no one spoke English and the best Ann could do was search our phrase book for anything related to pain, re-hydration, medicine, or IV. She, too, was battling rapid dehydration and struggling to stay coherent enough to figure out a plan—phone for emergency evacuation, call our physicians in the U.S., hire an interpreter? When the admitting doctor asked to see our passports, Ann handed hers over and I realized I didn't have mine. My passport, money, camera, and all our possessions were in our unlocked hotel room. This realization nearly pushed me over the edge.

I was consumed by fear. I screamed from the pain. I screamed from the fear. I screamed in despair. Over and over again, I screamed.

My fear was contagious and Ann joined in, "*Sakit! Sakit!* Pain! Pain!" "Get an IV!" "Please do SOMETHING!"

But our screams went unanswered. How could these doctors and nurses show such a monumental lack of compassion? They obviously couldn't understand English, but surely they could understand the universal language of pain? The doctor did nothing other than point to my right calf, knotted up the size of a softball, as he scribbled something on his notepad. Someone laughed. At me? Was I becoming delusional?

For what seemed like several hours, the admitting doctor, one consulting doctor, and four nurses milled around in apparent confusion and debated what to do with us. Tindatu, the off-duty policeman who drove us to the hospital, made the only effort to alleviate my suffering. He calmly massaged my calves and feet, and I sensed he understood my pain; I could see the compassion in his eyes. Did he also understand my fear? He went back to the hotel to find my passport and bring our backpacks to the hospital. When the episodic cramping subsided and I could focus on something other than the pain, the fear took over again.

Finally, a new nurse appeared with an IV bag and a packaged, sterile needle. She presented them to us with a questioning look on her face.

The Flight of the Kinglet

"Yes! Yes! DO IT!" Ann jumped up and cried, incredulous that it took the doctors so long to determine the obvious.

Nurse five started my IV and wheeled me away on the stretcher. Ten minutes later, Ann arrived in a wheelchair with her own IV dangling from her right arm, which looked like a limp spaghetti noodle. On top of everything else, it scared the hell out of me to see my robust partner looking so frail.

Glancing around, I realized the admitting staff had moved us to our own private room with two beds. I imagined my last meal being intravenous fluids and the six unidentifiable pills the nurses forced me to take every few hours.

After hours of surprising mental stamina, given her deteriorating physical condition, Ann, staring at the possible phone numbers we might call, realized with despair, "Our insurance coverage for emergency airlift evacuation is useless. No one at this damned hospital speaks English and the closest phone I know of is a half mile away."

Delirious, I wondered what my mother would think about my showing up at the hospital in a soiled sarong and no underwear, after teaching me as a child to "always wear clean underwear when you're going to see the doctor." I pondered how I would explain to my friends that I was shitting all over my fleece jacket, a towel, and whatever clothes the nurses could find in my backpack, because Ann and I had saturated all the available sheets and the hospital had no more. The absurdity of such contemplations magnified my fear. I began imagining my imminent death, absolutely certain I had cholera, or worse.

During a brief respite from my cramps, I recall sobbing in desperation to Ann, "I don't think I can make it through the night."

"Dave, Please don't say that—I know you're in horrible pain and scared, but DON'T GIVE UP!" she pleaded, suddenly realizing it would be up to her to sustain hope. Ann summoned her strength and calmly proclaimed, "I love you . . . I need you."

But at the same time, Ann had grave, unvoiced concerns that our IVs weren't helping, that the exact same fluid going into us was coming straight back out. "How are we ever going to recover?" she asked herself, enveloped by a shadow of gloom. Adding to the misery was the relentless buzzing of mosquitoes. Staring up at the holey mosquito netting draped over her bed, Ann silently feared malaria.

Equatorial Crossings

We both lay awake, each pondering our demise. The physical separation was too much to bear. Ann reached out several times to try and touch my outstretched hand, but couldn't. In the middle of the night, Ann sensed my panic and insisted to the nurses, "We must talk to a doctor . . . D-O-C-T-O-R!" The doctor who eventually came was the same uncaring sloth who had admitted us. Clearly angry that the nurses had summoned him, the doctor glanced at our charts, glared at us, and lumbered off, shoving the clipboards at the nearest nurse with venomous words we couldn't translate. Instructions? Reproach?

I had known physical and emotional pain in my life, but this overwhelming fear was an emotion with which I had no previous experience. In my youth, I had experienced the fear of pinning the nose of a canoe under a submerged log as the vortex of a class-III rapid sucked me underwater; hanging by my sweaty fingertips from a rocky spire after free-climbing hundreds of feet off the ground; and gaping at the splintered wooden deck that could have been, and nearly was, my head, after a wire cable on a research vessel's 500-lb metal dredge snapped with me standing underneath it. But dying in this hospital, so far removed from friends and family was a paralyzing notion, because I was powerless to do anything about it.

I didn't want to die feeling as though my life had no meaning. My fear was intertwined with the burden of guilt that comes from being born into a society where self-verification is all-important. If I were to die here in the rumah sakit, would I leave the world a better place? By what accomplishments would people judge me? Would my life be considered a success?

It was unthinkable that I might never hike, fish, ski, or even smell fresh air again. How could I die without the opportunity to see or talk to friends and family one last time? But, most of all, I couldn't bear the thought of leaving Ann. Our life together was just beginning, and we were filled with such boundless hope. We were kindred spirits, lovers, and life partners enmeshed in the thrill of discovery. Dying in a foreign hospital wasn't part of our master plan.

That night was the darkest of my life. Lying in pain in my own shit, I anguished over admitting my fear of death aloud. Intellectually, I knew I wasn't ready to die, with so much left to live for, but my body was quitting on me. I struggled to deal with my guilt, on top of the pain and fear. As I drifted in and out of consciousness, I wallowed in self-pity, unmindful of Ann's suffering. Where was my compassion? How could I ignore Ann's condition?

I vomited again and again, without either the strength or resolve to aim for the bedside bucket. Every half hour the nurses would come to change my drenched bed. I curled into a fetal position and simply prayed that I would see the morning light. Sleep was impossible. Too much emotional baggage and no way to check it.

The next thing I remember is screaming in pain from a torturous cramp in my left calf. The muscles were knotted so tight I was certain my calf was going to explode right before my eyes. I sobbed from relief when a smiling nurse appeared with a hypodermic needle, and gave me the first of several injections of an unknown painkiller. I passed out. What seemed like days later, I rolled over, and light sprinkled through the curtains. Morning light!

That afternoon a young doctor from the hospital in Manado, a tourist destination three hours away, showed up on his weekly rounds. He was everything the admitting doctor was not—competent, compassionate, and genuinely interested in answering our questions and allaying our fears. He also spoke nearly flawless English. He patiently explained why we were taking each of the medications, and his assessment that we had a severe case of gastroenteritis, not cholera. He assured us that fluid replacement and rest were the keys to our recovery. As he was leaving, Ann flashed me a big smile—the one medicine I needed most.

Later in the day, our new friend, Tindatu, stopped by to see us. I made no attempt to hide my tears, knowing he had probably saved my life. That evening my cramps finally stopped, after nearly 30 straight hours. The hospital priest didn't come to say prayers for us, and I took this to be a good omen; such a good omen, in fact, that I said a silent prayer of my own, grateful beyond words that Ann was with me. To this day, I shudder to think what might have happened had she not been.

Our friends have often joked that Ann and I lead "charmed lives," but never had I believed it with the resolve I did at that moment. I will forever marvel that we just happened to be in one of the few villages in Sulawesi with a hospital; that Tindatu just happened to be visiting his friend at our hotel that night and was able to get us safely to a hospital; that the kind doctor from Manado just happened to have rounds at the Bitung hospital the day after we were admitted; and that the nurses took such exceptional care of us, when other patients were surely worse off.

Tindatu came to visit us every day, always with the same reassuring smile and look of peace. I felt blessed to be the recipient of his selfless generosity and compassion. On the third day, he brought along his wife, son, and daughter to see us after church. I was touched beyond my limited ability to tell him. I sensed how awkward this was for his family, especially the two kids, who were clearly repulsed by the way we looked and smelled. But he didn't bring them for their benefit; he brought them for ours.

He made Ann and me promise that we would let him drive us to Tangkoko Nature Reserve, once we were feeling up to it. His very first assignment as a police officer was at the village of Batuputih, on the outskirts of the Reserve, and he was both excited and proud to have the opportunity to show us his former home.

By the afternoon of the third day, Ann was feeling almost normal. Her diarrhea and vomiting had passed and her appetite returned. She even felt well enough to sketch our dreary, concrete hospital room, to this day a poignant reminder of our brush with death. That evening, I, too, was feeling much better; my vomiting and diarrhea finally ceased, and I could sit up in bed without help. The fourth day, our IVs were removed, and Ann and I whittled away the long hours watching Indonesian TV, playing cards, and practicing our Bahasa Indonesian with the friendly nurses. They allowed me to go for a walk through the hospital, during which I realized that we had been given the only private room in the entire house of pain. Some rooms had as many as six adult patients. I knew, then, we were getting special treatment, and returned to our private room feeling ashamed and guilty: ashamed that I had been so loud and demanding; guilty for the way I had negatively judged the very people working to save my life. But above all I was profoundly grateful.

In the waning light of dusk, a lithe, young man from a nearby room came to visit us. He explained in broken English that his wife was in labor with their first baby, and he relieved his nervous energy by flitting around our room with a device that looked like an electrified tennis racket, swatting mosquitoes and zapping them in mid-air. The surreal sight of this stick-armed caricature lunging and leaping around the room made me laugh, until the laughter turned to tears. We were going to live.

Before we went to sleep that night, the nurses used body language and Bahasa Indonesian to explain that we could leave in the morning. For the first time since entering the hospital, I whispered, "I love you Ann," overwhelmed that I had lived to say those words—words, thereafter, I would strive to say daily.

The Flight of the Kinglet

The morning of the fifth day, we took bucket showers and put on our own clean clothes, freshly washed and neatly folded by our new nurse friends. Three times I lathered every surface of my body, frantically trying to scrub away the feelings of filth. I rationed the water in the small bucket to savor every tickle of its warmth trickling down my emaciated torso. I counted my protruding ribs. With my toes, I probed the brown soap scum that slowly circled above the clogged drain. Clumps of hair and skin—my hair, my skin—bobbed in the foamy froth. The flotsam and jetsam of my former existence lay at my feet. Like a recently molted crab, I emerged soft and vulnerable.

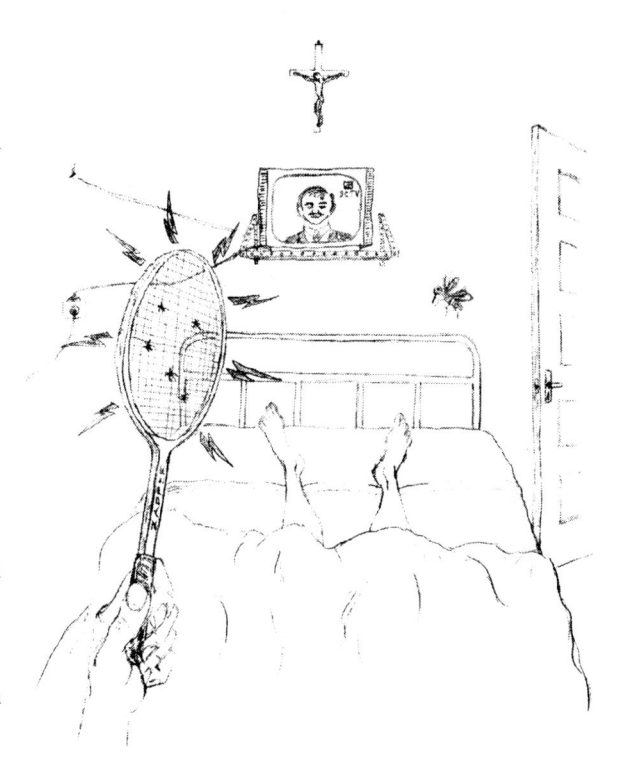

After a huge breakfast, which we ate sitting in chairs like normal human beings, we caught a bemo into town and went to four different banks before we finally found one that could give us a cash advance on our credit card. We returned to pay our bill, the equivalent of $400 US for the two of us, and discovered that the nurses had prepared a six-dish, farewell feast for us. Astonished and immeasurably touched by this gesture, we were speechless. For several days, the nurses had been trying to get us to eat more. In a mere four days, I had lost more than fifteen pounds. One slender nurse teased me about being too skinny. I can still picture the hilarious way she sucked in her breath and nearly encircled her waist with her hands, pantomiming me as a skinny man. We returned later in the day with a large arrangement of silk flowers and a cash contribution to the nurses to show our appreciation for their wonderful care. It seemed so little to give in comparison to all they had given us.

⋙•⋘

The morning after the New Year's windstorm, I spent an hour picking up debris. Chilled and anxious to get back inside by the woodstove, I noticed the injured kinglet. I watched as the frail but determined bird emerged from the flower box and flew past me to a nearby hemlock. Its tiny wings beat in a labored rhythm, and so, too, did my heart. As the kinglet flitted past, I sensed it's incredible will to survive. In that instant, I realized how unpredictable life can be and how truly lucky I was to be alive. I looked up at the bird in wonder — filled with awe at the innate will to survive I had discovered hidden beneath the fold of my fears. And here was the power of hope embodied in the flight of the kinglet.

Above: *Leaving the U.S. with fully-loaded backpacks and a two-person collapsible kayak (photo by Hildy Pehrson).*

Below: *The "essential" gear from our backpacks (not including the dogs) spread out on the porch of new friends in Merrickville, Australia; our kayak, lifejackets, paddles, and other paddling accessories are not shown.*

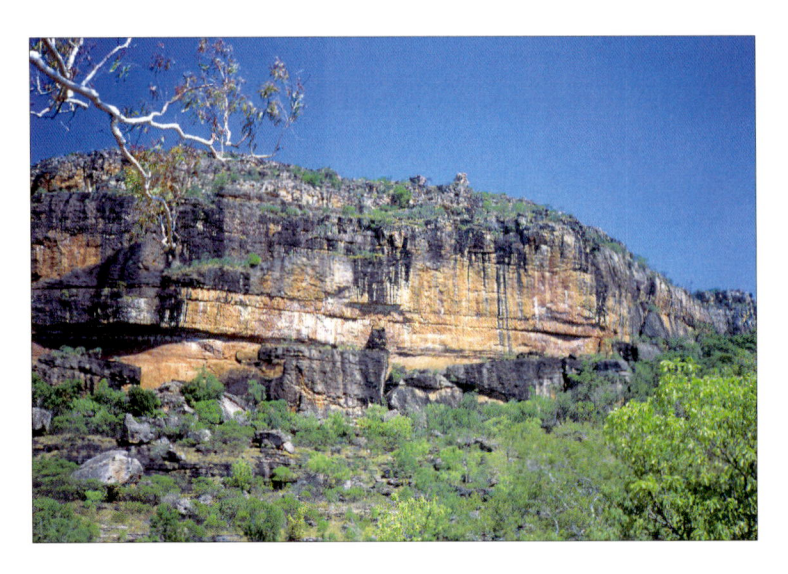

Images of Kakadu National Park, Northern Territory, Australia

Above: The ancient sandstone escarpment of Kakadu's "stone country."

Left: Aboriginal rock painting of the fisherman Mabuyu, the subject of an oral history lesson that teaches children not to steal.

Below: Ann hiking through the trail-less, eucalyptus-dominated monsoon forests of Barramundi Gorge.

Images of Australian Wildlife

Above: *Rainbow lorikeets* (Trichoglossus haemotodus), *Airlie Beach, Australia.*

Right: *Boyd's forest dragon* (Gonocephalus boydii), *Cape Tribulation World Heritage Area, Queensland, Australia.*

Below: *Sulphur-crested cockatoo* (Cacatua galerita), *Katherine Gorge National Park, Northern Territory, Australia.*

Above: Sailing our kayak among Australia's Whitsunday Islands, using an improvised sail made of a rattan beach mat and a kayak paddle.

Below: Diving with Richard on one of many relatively unexplored reefs of the Coral Sea, 85 miles beyond the outer wall of the Great Barrier Reef.

*Along the west coast of New Zealand's South Island, we explored remote beaches **(Top left)**, temperate rainforests **(Top right)**, glaciated mountains **(Left)**, and crystalline rivers like the Turnbull River near Haast **(Below)**.*

Left: *The Muslim village of Kaleleng, a Sulawesi fishing community inaccessible by road.*

Below: *Sailing Puteri Mandar, a traditional wooden perahu, along the coast of Sulawesi near Bira.*

Right: Ann and Dave with the people of Kaleleng, most of whom had never seen westerners (photo by villager).

Above: Ann and Dave looking down from 20 feet up the hollow inside of a network of strangler figs, which "strangled" a tree that has since rotted away, Tangkoko Nature Reserve, Sulawesi.

Below: A crested black macaque (Macaca nigra), Tangkoko Nature Reserve.

Above: Boys collecting crayfish in a creek that forms the boundary of the Tangkoko Reserve and the village of Batuputih.

▸ *Overleaf:* Tharu villagers make a daily commute across the Rapti River on the border of Royal Chitwan National Park, Nepal.

Below: Kids from Batuputih playing in a rainstorm with boats improvised from string, a sandal, Styrofoam, and plant leaves.

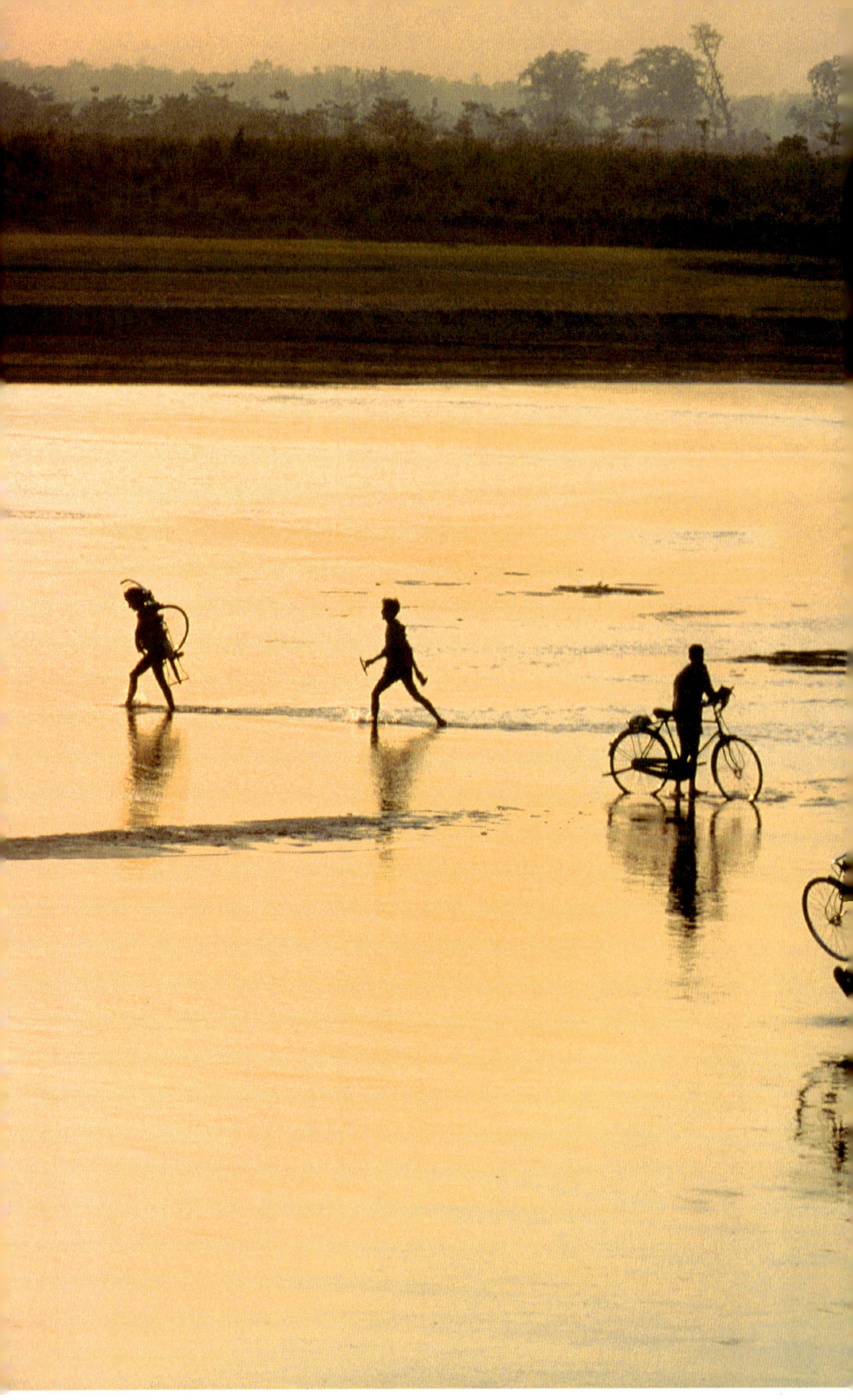

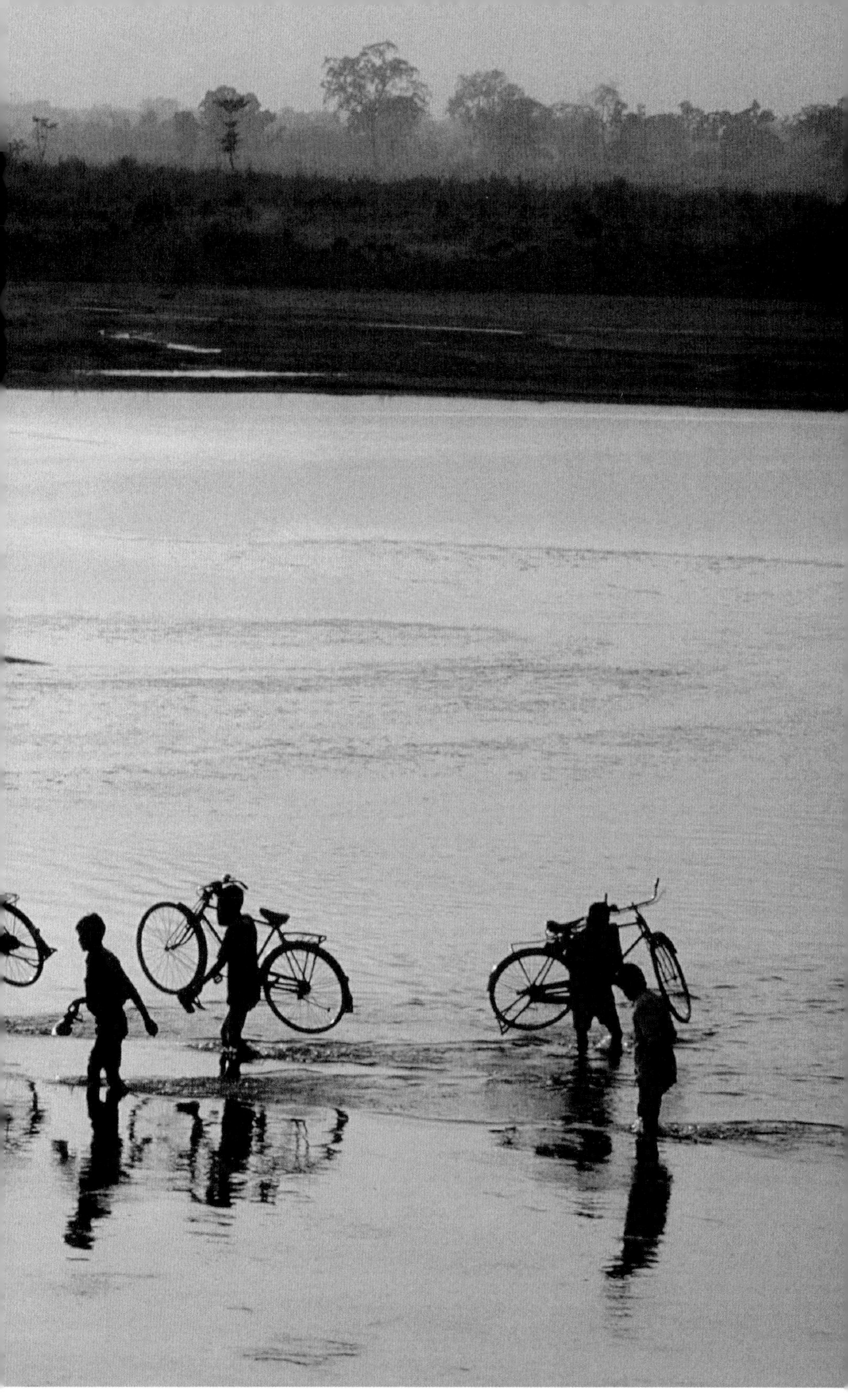

Above: *Trekking with Hildy, Dorothy, Mike, and 19 porters, cooks, and guides on the Annapurna Circuit, near Landrung, Nepal.*

Left: *One of our porters, Pemba, begins the Annapurna Circuit carrying Ann's backpack, Mike's duffel, Dorothy's duffel and cooking supplies — a load of more than 100 pounds.*

Above: Ann receives affection from a family in Marpha, Nepal; we often saw children as young as three carrying and caring for younger brothers or sisters.

Below: Hildy delights Nepalese kids in Landrung with a portrait she drew of them.

Above: *Dave, Ann, and Dorothy dance the night away in Tatopani to Nepalese folk songs played by our beloved guides and porters (photo by Hildy Pehrson).*

Left: *Dorothy and Hildy are all smiles after 12 days, 75 miles, more than 8,500 feet in elevation gain, and a lifetime of memories on Nepal's Annapurna Circuit between Dhampus Phedi and Kagbeni (photo by Ann Soule).*

Above: *Ann and Mike with good-luck tikas freshly painted by a sadhu at Muktinath Temple, a Buddhist and Hindu sanctuary, in Muktinath, Nepal.*

Below: *Dave, Mike, and Ann at the summit of Thorung La (17,755 feet), the high point of the Annapurna Circuit (photo by Nima Tenzing Sherpa).*

Above: Braga Monastery clings to the cliffs near Manang, Nepal.

Below: Sherpa women who have just completed a pilgrimage to the Braga Monastery to celebrate Buddha's birthday.

Above: *A young Sherpa girl hauling water near Ghyaru, Nepal; Annapurna II (26,040 feet) looms in the background.*

Below: *Terraced fields enroute to Besisahar, Nepal, near the end of our Annapurna trek.*

Images of the Solu Khumbu Region of Nepal

Above: *Panoramic view of Everest (29,035 ft), Nuptse (25,790 ft), Lhotse (27,890 ft), and Makalu (27,765 ft), from the summit of Gokyo Ri (17,519 ft).*

Left: *Moonrise over Kyajo Ri, from Maccherma.*

Below: *Ama Dablam (22,494 ft) under full moon, from Chukkung.*

Top: *The precipitous village of Thame, where we trekked to observe the lama dance festival, Mani Rimdu, a 19-day sequence of secret ceremonies and empowerment, culminating in a 3-day public dance festival.*

Center: *Thame Monastery lamas begin the dance festival with cymbals, horns, and drums.*

Bottom: *The resplendent Thame Monastery altar just prior to the beginning of the dance festival.*

Above: *Dave receives a prayer scarf and blessing from the rinpoche of Thame Monastery (photo by Ann Soule).*

Below: *Lamas dance to ward off evil spirits; this and other sacred dances convey Buddhist teachings for those that do not have the opportunity to study and meditate extensively (photo by Ann Soule).*

Above: Sunset on the Tibetan Plateau, near Old Tingri.

Below: Colorful prayer flags adorn a high pass on the Tibetan Plateau; the flag colors are symbolic of sky (blue), clouds (white), fire (red), water (green), and earth (yellow).

Above: Tashi Lhunpo Monastery (1447 AD) in Xigatse, Tibet was the home of the Panchen Lama, Tibet's second most revered spiritual leader, before he was kidnapped and taken to China in 1995.

Below: A turquoise swastika — the world's most ancient good luck symbol — embedded in the floor of the Tashi Lhunpo Monastery.

Above: Soaring more than 350 feet, Lhasa's impressive Potala was completed in the mid-1600s. Formerly the home of the 14th Dalai Lama and thousands of monks prior to 1959 when China invaded Tibet, the Potala now sits mostly empty.

Below: Monks debating Buddhist philosophy at the Drepung Monastery in Lhasa, Tibet; established in 1416 AD, Drepung was once the largest monastic institution in the world, housing an estimated 15,000 Buddhist monks.

Top: *A young monk holding butter sculptures (thorma) in front of Lhasa's Jokhang Temple, built in 647 AD. This temple and the surrounding Barkhor are the centers of Tibetan culture in Lhasa; pilgrims (in the background) come from all over Tibet to worship here and to seek a peaceful liberation from China.*

Bottom: *A grandfather and grandson selling juniper incense outside the Jokhang Temple. The incense is placed in giant mud ovens (in the upper right of the photo) that billow fragrant plumes of juniper day and night, purging the sacred square of negative thoughts and deeds.*

Above: The rocky, treeless expanse of yak pastures near Damxung, Tibet.

Right: We spent hours jumping creeks, hurling yak patties, and searching for wishing stones with kids from a yak-herders village outside of Damxung.

Below: Ann with some of our newfound Tibetan friends.

Above: *Ann's adopted Tibetan family outside of their home. Saathi is second from the right. Ani is second from the left, wearing Ann's backpack (the sky has been digitally altered).*

Left: *Ann's Ama braids her hair in the traditional Tibetan manner with long strands of interwoven turquoise and brown yarn.*

Below: *Dave's Tibetan family: Ama Chookoe, Tseten Dhondup, and Nima Pinza (photo by Ann Soule).*

Above: *A Tibetan man's prayer wheel appears frozen in time as he completes his daily circumambulation of the Jokhang Temple in Lhasa, Tibet.*

Below: *Jampa Phuntsok and Ann at the Namgyal Monastery, directly across from the Dalai Lama's residence in exile in Mcleod Ganj, India. Above Jampa's head is an API photo of him crying "Free Tibet!" at a 1988 demonstration in front of the Jokhang Temple.*

Above: Sunrise over Lake Baringo, in Kenya's Rift Valley.

Center: A golden-backed weaver (Ploceus jacksonii) weaves an upside down nest on the end of a flimsy branch to thwart potential predators.

Below: A Pokot tribesman leads us on a guided hike near Marich Pass, Kenya to observe birds and medicinal plants.

Above: *Zebras* (Equus burchelli) *and wildebeest* (Connochaetes taurinus) *are among the many grazers that find an abundant food supply on the floor of the Ngorongoro Crater, Tanzania.*

Below: *A herd of African elephants* (Loxodonta africana) *follow the matriarch upstream at Tarangire National Reserve, Tanzania.*

Above: Female lions and cubs (Panthera leo) *devour a freshly-killed cape buffalo, Masai Mara Nature Reserve, Kenya.*

Center: Sometimes called the "upside down" tree, the majestic African baobab (Adansonia digitata) *can grow to 80 feet and live for over 1,000 years.*

Below: Because of their size, sharp horns, and unpredictable temperament, Cape buffalo (Syncerus caffer) *are among the most dangerous animals (to humans) that inhabit Masai Mara.*

Above: The dhow is the traditional sailing vessel of the Kenyan coast.

Below: Off the southern tip of Kenya's Wasini Island, overfishing poses a serious threat to the coral reef community.

Above: The Kangai Family (Nancy, Kudzi, Phebion, and Munya) made our long and perilous journey from Kenya to Harare, Zimbabwe well worth the effort (photo by Ann Soule).

Below: A full moon over the mountains of Chimanimani National Park, Zimbabwe graced our last night of camping before leaving Africa, causing us to tearfully reflect on more than a year of adventures.

9

A Prayer for the Living

The secret of life is enjoying the passage of time...

-James Taylor

The sinewy fingers of dawn had not yet penetrated the dense rainforest canopy as we scurried to the base of the sleeping tree. Two hundred feet above us we could barely discern through binoculars the fuzzy silhouettes of awaking crested black macaques. Sakar, the local naturalist we had hired, assured us that once ample light tickled the forest floor these coal black, baboon-like primates would descend and begin their daily search for food.

As he promised, Tindatu had driven us to the Tangkoko Nature Reserve two days after we left the hospital. That night, we had our first taste of this jungle wonderland, when Sakar guided us to a mating pair of spectral tarsier monkeys, the smallest and among the most primitive of all primates. At first, we caught only glimpses of one six-inch tarsier darting in and out of the beam of our headlamps. As it sprung through the tangled hollow of a strangler fig, the monkey periodically froze in a deer-in-the-headlight stare. With its enormous eyes, oversized ears, delicate padded digits, long tail, and owl-like ability to rotate its head 180 degrees, this tarsier was magnificently equipped for its nocturnal lifestyle. Eventually both tarsiers crept out in the open to stalk moths, grasshoppers, and cicadas. Capable of bounding up to six feet, twelve times their body length, these tarsiers treated us to a gymnastics display that would have left even the most accomplished Olympic athlete bewildered. But the thrill of our first tarsier encounter was only the beginning of our wildlife odyssey.

At precisely 6:30 am, the crested macaques jumped, slid, and swung through the sleeping tree like Balinese shadow puppets flitting in and out of filtered light to the tune of the dominant male's vibrato chirps. The monkeys filed down the trunk and casually strolled around us while picking through the forest litter for insects and figs. I stood motionless, mouthing to Ann, "Can you believe this?" We had heard from other travelers that one could see macaques up close at Tangkoko, but we never imagined that "up close" would mean within a few feet, or even *at* our feet.

At first, we were reluctant to even move, for fear of startling or annoying the macaques. Sakar, perceiving our dilemma, assured us it was ok to walk around. He suggested we tread slowly and not stare directly at the adult males, some of whom have been known to interpret a stare as a territorial challenge. With Sakar as their guide, British researchers had intensively studied this particular group of 45 macaques for three years, and thus the "Rambo II" group was remarkably habituated to humans, and to Sakar in particular. I was so completely moved by the beauty and proximity of these animals that I temporarily forgot about the camera dangling around my neck.

For the next several hours, we watched as the monkeys foraged, groomed, and played, making their way nonchalantly toward the black sand beach that fringed this luxuriant rainforest. As they walked, their pointed triangular crests of black hair reminded me of party hats at a children's birthday celebration. With a quietness approaching reverence, we slowly followed, until a chilling alarm cry jolted us from our hushed adoration. The hairs on the back of my neck stood on end, as the eerie, incessant squeals reverberated through the forest.

Without a word, Sakar sprinted off toward the source of the cacophony. Ann and I followed at a near run, unsure whether this was prudent, but quite sure we didn't want to remain behind. We crashed blindly through plants with elephant-ear-sized leaves. Over downed logs and around giant trees, we crashed through the understory with gasps and heaves.

When we finally caught up to Sakar, he stood rigid, pointing at a 12-foot long reticulated python, stretched horizontally along the edge of a rotting log. The assembled macaques sat in a semicircle, quietly sizing up the python, one of their few natural predators. Apparently pythons only need to eat once every ten days to two weeks, and Sakar speculated that this one must have eaten recently. Yet, he had a hard time convincing us this enormous snake was a "small one" and "no danger." He told us how he and the British researchers had once watched the Rambo II group attack and kill a 30-foot long python. One subset of the group poked and pulled at the tail of the gargantuan snake, while another bashed the snake's head in with sticks.

According to Sakar, if these macaques had sensed any threat from the 12-foot python in front of us, they would have thrown rocks and sticks, at minimum, and possibly tried to kill it. I took a few photos of the python with a 200-mm lens, and from behind the seeming safety of the lens, I noticed the exceptional beauty of this snake. Solid muscle and the size of an inflated fire hose, the python had repeating oval patterns of caramel, copper, and chocolate, rimmed with black and an occasional tinge of blue when the filtered light struck the scales at just the right angle.

One young macaque approached us and sat an arm's reach from my feet, looking directly and inquisitively into my eyes. I didn't know what to do. Talk? Reach out? Attempt to make monkey noises? I cocked my head slightly toward my right shoulder and smiled. The monkey blinked twice, scratched the bridge of its nose, and ambled back over to the group. After a half hour or so, the monkeys lost interest in the python and resumed their daily progression to the beach, led by one large, silver-chinned male. From behind, we could easily distinguish the females in heat because of their crimson red, swollen bottoms. We also noticed two females with tiny, hamster-sized babies clutched to their chests. I would have been elated to keep watching these macaques, but Sakar insisted that he had many other exciting things he wanted to show us.

So, we set off in search of red-knobbed hornbills, listening for their characteristic dog-like bark. Along the way, Sakar showed us fresh scat from a sloth-like bear cuscus, fruit bats hanging upside down in a partially hollow fig tree, and many bizarre native plants with leaves larger than my arm span. He also identified the calls of every bird, and knew the natural history of virtually every animal or plant we inquired about.

After several more hours of hiking, Sakar was ready to give up on finding any hornbills, when he heard a distant bark and took off running. We were off again on a chase, through ravines and up and over ridges. Drained and drenched by the oppressive humidity, we finally caught up with Sakar. He was beaming. Six red-knobbed hornbills were perched several hundred feet above us, plucking ripe figs from the sagging branches. He pointed out the differences between the larger males with red crests and anvil-shaped beaks and the smaller females with yellow crests. Far larger than I ever imagined from the pictures I had seen, these "flying dogs" had up to a 9-foot wingspan.

During the mating season, Tangkoko supports the world's highest density of red-knobbed hornbills—30 birds per square mile when figs are ripe. Sakar explained that mating takes place between August and October and that hornbills mate for life, often returning to the same nesting tree year after year. When the female is ready to lay eggs, she uses her fig-laden fecal paste to cement herself into a hollow slit in a fig tree. The male is then responsible for bringing the female and any fledglings the choicest ripe figs, the single most important part of their diet.

On the trail back to our guesthouse, we found the Rambo II group again and I asked Sakar, "Can I please stay and watch the macaques longer.?"

"So sorry," he replied. "No tourists in Reserve without guide."

"Please," I begged, strategically playing my "I'm a scientist" card.

"OK," he relented, "but no getting close, and don't tell any persons."

Sakar and Ann returned to the guesthouse, and for the next 2-1/2 hours I became immersed in the most extraordinary wildlife experience of my life. I smiled as young males played, chased, and practiced mating, under the watchful eye of a large adult male, who was sprawled supine in the notch of a tree, arms and head dangling into a window of sunlight. Most of the monkeys were no longer on the ground, preferring instead to eat or groom in the lower branches of small trees. I watched one in particular, as she meticulously devoured a ripe coconut half, savoring each thin white strand. After an hour or so, the monkeys descended again and started actively feeding, mostly on a fruit that looked like a miniature pineapple and smelled like rotting fish. I followed them for a while, until I realized they were resuming their stroll to the beach. Running back to the spot in the trail where I had stashed my rain parka and camera bag, I decided to race to the beach ahead of the monkeys, and wait.

One lone female emerged from the rainforest and sat on a drift log next to me at arm's length, while she ate a rotting-fish fruit. In full sun, I was even more profoundly moved by the humanness of her face and her expressions. Another female allowed me to photograph her as she cuddled and breastfed her hand-sized baby. The tiny newborn looked so fragile and helpless clinging to its mother's chest as she walked, jumped, and climbed through the vegetation fringing the black sand. Two young macaques frolicked like kids at the water's edge and jumped nervously back whenever the surf broke. The silver-chinned male sat at the tide line, hands on knees, taking everything in. And the memory of this regal black monkey crouching on black sand and gazing out to sea gives me pause to this day.

Because of these encounters, it is impossible for me not to ascribe human qualities to these macaques. I now appreciate more fully why Jane Goodall, Diane Fossey, and other selfless researchers dedicated their lives to understanding primate behavior, and why protected places like Tangkoko Reserve are so vital to the earth's well being—and even, perhaps, our own.

According to Sakar, the population of macaques in Tangkoko was estimated at 20,000 individuals when he was a teen in the late 1970's. The British research team he worked with estimated in 1995 that only 1,000 to 1,500 remained. The researchers attributed this shocking decline mostly to wanton poaching. Low salaries and a lack of funds burden Reserve rangers as they attempt to halt the poaching, but macaque meat continues to be sold openly in Manado's public markets.

The hopeful sidebar in this otherwise grim saga is that farsighted, local management of Tangkoko appears to be working. The Reserve has initiated a successful program to educate locals about the importance of protecting the natural wealth that surrounds them. No tourist is allowed in the Reserve without a trained, English-speaking guide, and all guides are hired from within the local community of Batuputih. Two of the three guesthouses in Batuputih are owned and operated for and by the Reserve. At a small, thatched-roof visitor's center, locals sell *Save Tangkoko* stickers, T-shirts, and glossy color enlargements of the Reserve's unusual flora and fauna.

We were especially impressed with Sakar's resolve to protect this treasure. His love for the Reserve so clearly came from his heart and his thirst for knowledge, rather than a love or thirst for tourists' money. He was tangible proof of the success of managing the Reserve with locals, for locals. The steady influx of eco-tourist dollars fuels this social experiment, but long-term success will depend on whether protecting macaques (and the Reserve's many other spectacular animals) provides locals with the means to acquire better food than eating macaques.

On our final day in the Reserve, we awoke to a symphony of warblers, cicadas, and crested macaques. Their discordant whistles, chirps, and cat-like meows welcomed the dawning of a new day in the jungle, punctuated by the unmistakable staccato *arf arf* of a distant red-knobbed hornbill and the territorial squeaks of a tarsier duet. As we sat on the porch of our bungalow, mosquito coils smoldering beneath our chairs, we reveled in the primal sensory experience of being enveloped in the verdant, dripping wealth of the Tangkoko understory.

We relished this opportunity to reflect on the many things we had to be grateful for, not the least of which was simply being alive. For nearly seven months, we had been on the move. Each day brought new insights and fostered an enduring closeness between us that we didn't even perceive until others, like Sakar, pointed out our "much good love." We were so often overwhelmed by the richness of our experiences that we failed to realize just how much we had grown emotionally and spiritually. The fights we had early on—the Barramundi Gorge brawl, the Whitsunday welter—seemed like ancient history. And the relationship lessons we had learned since then seemed so elementary with the benefit of hindsight: communicate more and expect less; slow down and enjoy whatever each day may bring; embrace serendipity, and each other.

In the aftermath of our near-deaths in the Bitung hospital, our time in the jungle of Tangkoko felt like a miraculous gift—a gift that revitalized my spiritual connection with nature and filled me with a sense of indescribable wonder. Our two days in the Reserve were a celebration of life in all its infinite variety. And in rare moments, when I am able to silence both heart and mind, I can still hear the chorus of the Tangkoko rainforest at dawn, a prayer for the living.

Central Nepal

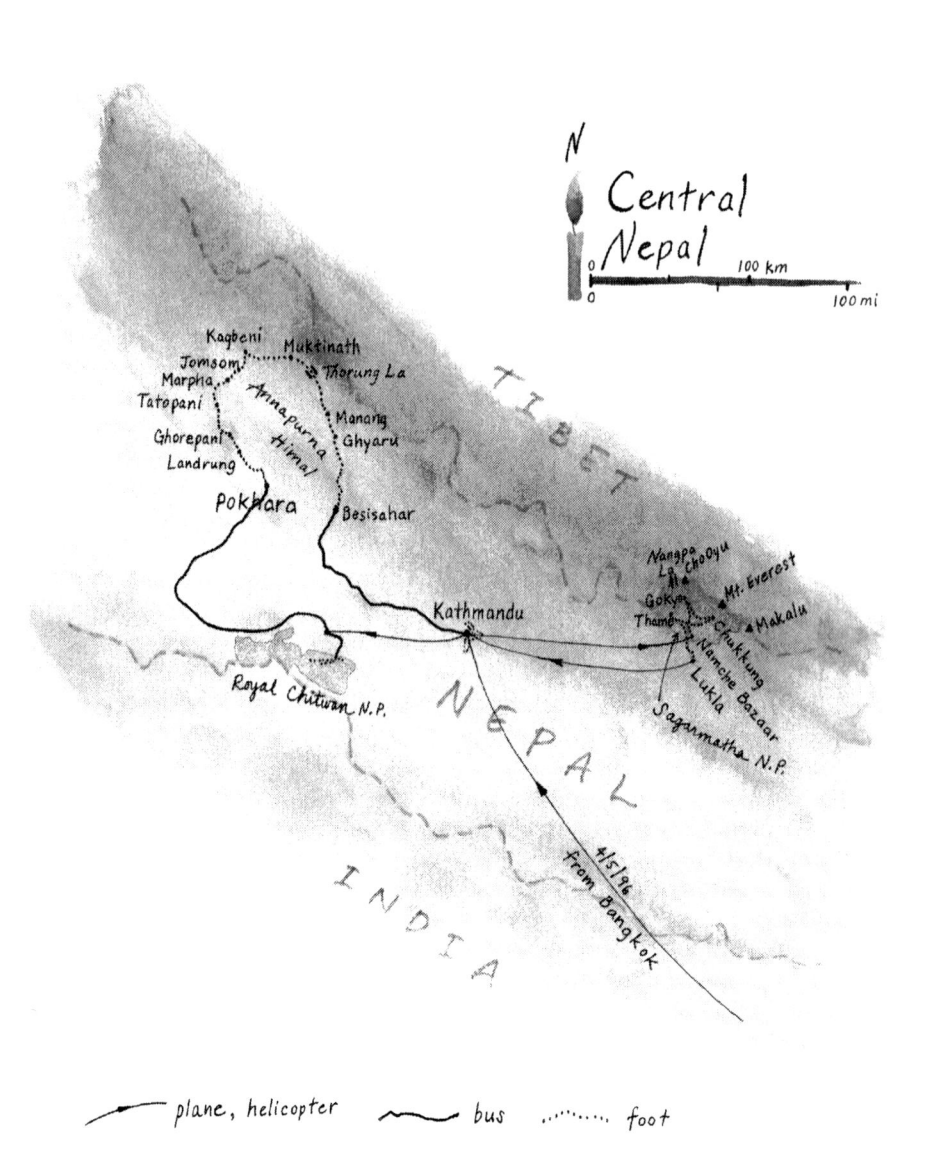

N

0 ——— 100 km
0 ——— 100 mi

TIBET

Kagbeni Muktinath
Jomsom Thorung La
Marpha
Tatopani   Annapurna
Ghorepani   Himal   Manang
Landrung   Ghyaru

Pokhara   Besisahar

                                Nangpa   ChoOyu
                                La   Mt. Everest
                                Gokyo   Chukkung
                                Thamo   Makalu
                        Kathmandu   Namche Bazaar
                                      Lukla
Royal Chitwan N.P.   Sagarmatha N.P.

NEPAL

4/5/96
from Bangkok

INDIA

⟶ plane, helicopter   ⁓ bus   ········ foot

10

Role Reversal

Love has no other desire but to fulfill itself. To melt and be like a running brook that sings its melody to the night. To wake at dawn with a winged heart and give thanks for another day of loving.

-Kahlil Gibran, *The Prophet*

Just before dark, the clouds furled, revealing the broad ridge of Annapurna South and the forked pinnacle of Machhapucharre, the sacred fishtail mountain. Their snowy summits glowed in the setting sun, distant reminders of the journey that lay ahead. Filled with wonder, we clutched each other in hugs, savoring this moment and the long awaited start of our trekking adventure in the Himalayan Mountains of Nepal.

Two weeks earlier, my mom, Dorothy, and Ann's mom, Hildy, (affectionately dubbed "the moms"), met us in Bangkok, and our friend Mike from Olympia, Washington met us in Kathmandu. All together, at last, we spent five days exploring the Kathmandu Valley and then three more days stalking one-horned rhinos on foot, paddling a dugout canoe, and riding elephants in search of Bengal tigers in the hot, muggy lowlands of Royal Chitwan National Park.

After more than a year of planning and anticipation, the five of us had just completed our first day of trekking along the Annapurna Circuit. For Mom, our Annapurna trek marked the first time in her life, at age 60, that she would wear hiking boots, sleep in a tent, or carry a pack. For Hildy, at 62, this journey would be a dramatic new challenge in comparison to hiking in her familiar Sierra Mountains. For Mike, Ann, and me, this trek would fulfill a long-held dream of exploring the high Himalayas. For all of us, the trip was an opportunity to revitalize old friendships and rejoice in new ones.

Snuggled in my toasty, down sleeping bag that first night of the trek, I chuckled as I replayed the day's events: the hair-raising, body-thrashing bus ride from Pokhara; the short but steep climb up worn, stone steps from Dhampus Phedi, through a mature oak forest; the hot, tangy juice waiting for us when we arrived at our camp on a flat, grassy knoll; the indulgence of stretching and lounging in the warm, mid-afternoon sun, while our porters sang Nepalese folk songs to the erratic rhythm of drum and guitar; the simple pleasure of playing cards and eating garlic soup as wispy clouds danced above us; and the sacred feeling I had seeing the unclimbed 22,966-foot summit of Machhapucharre disappear into the golden clouds of sunset. But the lingering image, as I rolled over to kiss Ann goodnight, was the spectacle of 19 porters, cooks, and guides with loaded head baskets bounding up the trail just to support the five of us.

Two porters carried our personal duffels; the other 17 carried food, tents, stoves, fuel, lanterns, a guitar, and a drum. Who were these men? Did we really need such a big team? How could they possibly carry such heavy loads in bare feet or flimsy flip-flops? I drifted off to sleep, cloaked in the day's memories and the thrill of being together with Mike and the moms in such a majestic place.

The next morning became the unfortunate template for others to follow. Ann was nauseous. Dorothy had hacked all night long and suffered through a bought of diarrhea. Mike raced out of his tent several times to vomit and had not slept at all. Hildy and I were feeling fine, but couldn't help but wonder when their same fate would overcome us. In this state of collective indecision about the wisdom of continuing, we began our longest day of trekking.

Clear views of the mountains and the steep, terraced fields kept us inspired and moving until late morning when the clouds rolled in, adding to the growing sense of gloom. Mike, Ann, and Mom were all too nauseous to eat any lunch. Hildy and I were ravenous. After lunch, we resumed climbing, and climbing, and climbing. Several times I thought Mom might collapse from exhaustion, but never once did she complain. Her body language spoke her pain. Hildy roused the only laughter of the day, when she called Dorothy "the little engine that could."

After ten hours of hiking, Mom and I finally arrived at the campsite in Landrung. When she saw Ann, Mom began crying—a mixture of relief and total physical and

Role Reversal

mental exhaustion. The mood at dinner was subdued. Mom was too weak to eat, but Hildy and I coaxed her to drink hot tea and nibble on some crackers. Ann was still suffering from intense stomach cramps, and simply pushed the food around her plate. Mike's nausea had passed; he ate lightly and then decided to get a room in a guesthouse to catch up on badly needed sleep. Hildy and I were, as usual, disproportionately hungry relative to the energy we had exerted. That night, I lay awake for a long time ruminating the enormous accomplishment it was for the moms just to get here, pushing themselves beyond any physical limits they had previously experienced or even imagined. I wondered whether they felt the effort was worth it.

Three days into the trip we began slowly settling into a rhythm. Morning tea in bed at 6 am, followed by eggs, porridge, toast, and more tea. On the trail by 8 am. Hot lunch at noon. A snack of popcorn or cookies with hot drinks at 4 pm. Soup, followed by a huge dinner, sometime between 5 and 8 pm, depending on when we arrived in camp. Singing and dancing until we were too tired to move, followed by deep, fitful, sometimes rejuvenating, but predictably unpredictable sleep.

There was a certain comfort in having a set schedule, and there was ample opportunity in between for exploring villages, lounging, and practicing the national language, *Nepali*. Appetites came and went, as did periodic diarrhea, cramps, giardia, and nausea. Meal conversations often revolved around bodily functions, and Hildy and Ann developed a humorous rating system for the vile outhouses. The constants were the natural beauty of our surroundings and our Nepalese crew, and the growing bond between the five of us.

Makar, the head cook, created traditional Nepalese meals such as *dahl baht* (rice and lentils), vegetable *momos* (dumplings), and curried potato soup, as well as special treats like fruit cake with meringue topping, pizza, and even apple pie, when he sensed we needed a familiar boost. The assistant cooks, Suki Ram and Sanu, served all our meals with good humor, and after a few days we began to understand their playful antics. Goman, the number three Sherpa and most graceful dancer, willingly took on the role of helping my mom. He was a bundle of raw, youthful energy; he sprang, jumped, and ran like an excited puppy, but he also had a quiet, compassionate side, and he seemed intuitively to know when Mom needed his help. For most of the next nine days, Mom and Goman walked hand in hand.

Because of their shared love of music, Hildy was drawn to Basu, the guitar maestro of the group and number two Sherpa. Mike often hiked with Makar, and I admired their closeness, the way they hiked holding hands—two cultures united. Nima, the *sirdar* or head Sherpa, lead singer, and spirited leader of the group, kept both the crew and the clients smiling with his humor, songs, and practical jokes.

As we began to learn a few words of Nepali, we also bonded with the porters. At first these men with unfamiliar names like Pasang, Ram Prasad, Dewakar, Giribah Raj, Chandra, Surya, Krishna, Pemba, and Dawa seemed like hired servants, but after a week together, we became friends. We eventually accepted that their role was to carry all our gear, set up camp, and serve us meals. Each morning Suki Ram or Sanu brought us tea in bed and hot water for washing. There was nothing we were going to do or say to change the system. They showed extraordinary pride in caring for us, and we ultimately learned to enjoy their pampering.

Ann wrote in her journal:

> *Where does our little assemblage of Americans fit into the overall fabric of this place? We are like a needle, pulling another thread through it as we trek along. So many thousands of threads, each unique, have added to the fabric that is mostly woven by the Nepalese people. What do the moms think of this wild experience? How are they feeling inside? . . . What seem like luxuries to us allow the moms to persevere against many challenges. Our new friends have become our support system. We laugh, sing, and grunt our way up the trails with them. Our appreciation grows each day as we become more and more entranced with Nepal, and the magical experiences they patiently make possible for us.*

Song, dance, laughter—these were our common language, our unifying refrain, our sustenance. I still hum those Nepalese folk songs, and I can still visualize the fluid, elegant dances that Krishna and Goman taught us, and the energetic, free-form dancing of Suki Ram and Dawa. And I am thankful for the universal gifts of music and laughter, and the positive energy they spread.

One of the highlights of our trek was strolling through a forest of blooming rhododendrons between Banthanti and Ghorepani. The massive rhododendron trees stretched up to 60 feet skyward, and their flaky, reddish bark reminded me of madrona trees back home. They seemed almost human, like something in a Disney animated movie, and it wasn't hard to imagine these trees having distinct personalities and the voices of Robin Williams or Eddie Murphy.

Mom was feeling reasonably healthy for the first time in four days, and I was heartened to see her become immersed in her surroundings. Mike and Ann adorned themselves with fallen, crimson, rhody blossoms and broke out in a spontaneous dance accompanied by the rhythm of our laughter. Basu climbed a tree and plucked fresh blossoms for Mom and Hildy to wear on their hats. I shot three rolls of film, trying unsuccessfully to capture the magic of this rhododendron forest, and in the process realized all over again that Ann is right: some experiences are better left to memory.

In the fifteen years Mike and I have been friends, we have shared life's sorrows and joys in a way few men do. Before meeting Ann, it was Mike who was my avid travel companion. Canada. Mexico. Belize. Europe. Skiing. Diving. Sailing. Hiking. We are fellow adventurers, and having Mike along on the journey was like traveling with two soul mates. But it wasn't until sunrise from Poon Hill—a 10,000-foot bump with unobstructed views of 20,000-foot Himalyan peaks—that I realized just how much he meant to me. The realization came as I was taking his picture. He was sitting on a stone wall with Dhaulagiri-I towering over his right shoulder. The soft glow of first light made his cheeks look radiant and made me feel radiant. It was a simple, quiet moment that left me with a sense of peace and a renewed appreciation for the power of friendship.

The low point of the trek for me was on day five, when Mom sat down on a rock next to the trail and broke down in tears. I sat next to her and put my arm around her shoulder. "What's wrong?" I asked softly.

"I'm just exhausted; the upward trek has taken its toll on my legs," she sobbed . . . "and I'm frustrated—and angry—that my legs feel too short and my boots too heavy."

I joked that we could trade, "boots, that is, not legs."

She smiled, but poorly-timed humor was definitely not the boost she needed. She was at a physical and emotional low. The cumulative effect of many nights of poor sleep, diarrhea, sore knees, and lower back spasms had zapped her strength. I sensed, too, that she was still grieving Dad's death eighteen months before, and that anytime she felt sad she cried. I didn't know what to say or do and hated feeling helpless.

"I wish I knew how to help you," I said.

"I thought that a few months with a personal trainer would prepare me for this," she confessed, still trembling, "but obviously it didn't." She took a drink of water and blew her nose.

I re-wrapped the Ace bandage on her tender left knee, struggling not to cry as I realized I had become her umbilical cord. Goman was her physical support system, but I was her life-blood.

Mom wiped the tears from her glasses and stood to test the knee. Goman held her by the arm, ready to assist, however she needed him. Ann and I encouraged her to go on, slowly, one step at a time.

"Come on, Dorothy, you can do it," Nima reassured her. "Tomorrow is a planned rest day."

Each morning thereafter, I would ask Mom how she was feeling, and whether she wanted to continue. I didn't want her to quit, but I wanted even less for her to suffer day after day. We delved into topics that were difficult for both of us to discuss: bowel habits, sore knees and back, and self-doubt. Her biggest concern, though, was that she was ruining the trip for the rest of us, that she was slowing us down and depending too much on others. Not once did she think of herself or what was best for her.

I was on unfamiliar ground. Parenting a parent was not something I'd done before, or even contemplated. I knew Mom was reluctant to ask for my help. I also knew she needed all the encouragement I could give her.

At first, I wasn't comfortable with the burden of carrying this emotional load for both of us. Yet, as the days passed, I could feel my legs and lungs growing stronger. And with my newfound physical strength, I gained emotional confidence. I gradually became more comfortable with my nurturer role. My hugs were from the heart instead of the head. And my respect for Mom's courage grew daily, as she refused to quit, in spite of huge challenges.

One afternoon, in one of the rare instances in eight days that I hadn't been at Mom's side, I hiked alone with Ann for several hours. Uplifted by the sun and the glistening snow on a mountain called Tukuche, we each rummaged for the right words to verbalize the powerful emotions evoked by trekking with our moms. Our conversation gradually drifted to the pros and cons of having children, and was precipitated by Hildy's earlier comment, "*When* I have grandkids ..." The certainty of her statement made us realize we needed to tell the moms and Mike that we had not decided for sure to have children, and that we wouldn't even consider the possibility until after our travels.

That night I explored my thoughts on parenthood in my journal:

> *My uncertainty about parenthood stems primarily from not wanting to lose my freedom — the ability to hike, kayak, ski, travel, or pursue whatever passions whenever. I wrestle constantly with whether I am being selfish, but inevitably return to the realization that loss of freedom is a common change I've witnessed in the lives of friends who have become fathers.*
>
> *I love our marriage just the way it is — solid, yet pliable. Wouldn't becoming parents change everything? What if our child(ren) were cursed with my ugly feet, my flaws and foibles? What happens if we decide to get pregnant and can't? Would we consider adopting?*
>
> *Fatherhood seems so daunting, so grown up. It's not like playing baseball, distance running, mountain biking, casual dating, or other pursuits I briefly and passionately embraced, then cast aside. Fatherhood is permanent.*

> *I also dwell on the responsibilities of bringing new life into an already overpopulated world. Here I am, in the midst of our travels, trying to simplify my life, while faced with escalating, complex, moral and evolutionary decisions. Why on earth did we ever call our pre-trip newsletter "A Prelude to Parenthood?"*

So often in our married lives, Ann and I seem to be in synchrony. Thus, it came as no surprise when Ann revealed that she, too, had been pondering the pros and cons of parenthood in her own journal:

> *Another special thing about the walk down here to Tatopani was that D. and I hiked together much of the way alone! And we could talk because the down slope wasn't hard on the lungs. I told him about my discomfort with casual or joking talk about our future children, since we haven't decided whether we want children or not. We expressed our concerns to each other, and agreed that it would be best to explain to Mom^2 (and Mike) that it's not a forgone conclusion we will have children.*

For me the crux of the parenthood decision was my concern about loss of freedom; for Ann a big hesitation was the potential for passing her own anxieties on to another generation. She felt she wanted to grow more as an individual before she would truly feel ready to be a parent—and, for the same reason, she wanted our marriage to experience more growth, too.

Just having these conversations seemed to, in fact, precipitate some of the growth Ann was hoping for:

> *Dave reminded me that in our relationship's history we have taken care of situations we didn't like somehow, and we would undoubtedly be even more careful to find resolution if we had children. We would talk to friends, read, get counseling, etc. to help us. His simple confidence made me feel more confident in our ability to maintain a healthy relationship. And he reminded me that since we never do ANYTHING without hours and days of research and thorough discussion, having and raising children would be the same.*
>
> *I can't let myself be afraid of failing — especially when I don't believe "failure" to be definable with regard to parenting. There's no such thing*

as perfection. Another reminder to myself to trust my – and our – creativity.

Ann wanted me to understand that she had never had an instinctive desire to be pregnant, though her mothering instincts were alive and well. She definitely wanted children in her life, but she could probably be satisfied with those from an extended family, or perhaps she could achieve more exposure to children through a deliberate change in career. Adoption was also perfectly viable from Ann's perspective, and she felt we needed to define "having a child" broadly, partly because getting pregnant was not a given. If we waited to start a family and conception seemed at all doubtful, then we could always adopt a baby. Indeed, our desire to expose an adopted child to new and diverse cultures might galvanize our commitment to travel throughout our lives, especially if we adopted a foreign baby.

In Tatopani, the next rest day, Ann and I shared our parenthood dilemmas with Mike and the moms. No one was too shocked, but they all insisted we would be "really great" parents.

Hildy added emphatically, "No experience in life can replace parenthood."

Mike chimed in, "I'm looking forward to being an uncle for a little scruffy or baby Ann."

I suppose Mom captured their general sentiments when she said, "We all respect your decision, whatever it ends up being, but I think you have so much to offer children . . . I would regret for you not to have the experience of raising your own."

I squirmed, glanced at Ann, and sensed in her distant gaze that perhaps she was already imagining life as a mom. Was parenthood destined to be a new chapter in our evolving relationship?

As rain pelted the tin roof, the conversation glided into an honest appraisal of our trek and whether everyone's expectations were being met.

"I expected the trekking to be hard, but not this hard," Hildy said.

"Or this steep!" Dorothy echoed, with a characteristic laugh.

"I could do without the recurring stomach cramps and diarrhea," Mike added.

"And yet, look at us," Ann smiled. "Collectively this is the healthiest we've been in a week, and we're still making progress."

"Thanks to our Nepalese friends," I replied. "It's hard to imagine where we would be now without them."

"Isn't that the truth," Hildy answered. "I'm very moved by the way our porters and guides are so uninhibited about touching, grooming, and holding hands."

Ann said, "Yeah, it makes me wish I knew more Nepali, so I could talk with them and with the local people along the way."

Mike, who had picked up bits of the language the fastest, suggested, "I think they really do appreciate any efforts we make to communicate, however feeble."

We all nodded our agreement. The rest day, the hot tea with honey, and the conversation had elevated everyone's spirits. Hildy joked about taking advantage of the local supermarket and pharmacy: "We are, after all, spending two nights here in *civilization*." "Don't forget about the beauty shop and dry cleaners," Dorothy added, with another laugh belying her pain.

The rain finally stopped and we went outside for a treasure hunt that Ann and I had secretly been planning. Earlier in the trek, Ann had bought plastic replicas of Tibetan *dzi* beads, and she made five matching necklaces for each of us. Together, she and I created a list of clues written in Nepali that Mike and the moms had to translate in order to find the hidden necklaces. Several of our crew were fascinated by the game, and became excited enough to help translate the clues. By the tenth of twelve clues, most of our guides and cooks, and several of our porters, were participating in the hunt, anxious to see the treasure.

From that day on, the five of us wore our matching necklaces, as a common symbol of our camaraderie. We found out later that Hildy didn't remove hers until Ann and I had safely returned home from our world travels. Mike often still wears his necklace when he goes hiking or climbing. Since the Annapurna trek, he has worn his dzi necklace to the summits of three of Washington's highest volcanoes. My necklace now hangs on our bathroom mirror, where I see it each morning as I start my day; its reflection inspiring my own reflections of this distant place but not so distant memories.

At dinner the night of the treasure hunt, Makar beamed when he saw five clean plates. He was both thrilled and relieved that everyone was finally feeling healthy enough to polish off one of his lovingly-prepared meals. After a relaxing soak in the natural hot springs (*tatopani*), we danced with fervor. Mike even convinced Dorothy to dance for the first time, and the porters, picking up on our high energy, all danced too. We reveled in the moment and fueled the fervor with homemade fudge that Mike delivered—a gift from our friends Bill and Lynda that came wrapped in wax paper and new, ironed underwear for Ann and me. The ensuing celebration marked one of those rare times in life when everything seemed perfect.

As we ascended the Kaligandaki River valley, the deepest in the world, the vegetation became more sparse and the landscape more arid. Most of the way, we were flanked by the Annapurna Himal and Nilgiri to the east and the Dhaulagiri Himal to the west. For four straight days, we experienced luminous blue skies, stunning mountain views, and strong winds. Enroute to Marpha, a small village nestled among terraced apple orchards, clouds of fine river silt blasted us. We hiked for most of one day with hats, sunglasses, and bandanas covering our ears, eyes, and mouths, but grit still made its way into many uncomfortable places grit doesn't belong. One gust knocked Dawa with his fully loaded basket right off his feet, and then sandblasted his torso, while he lay there laughing. Each new day of hiking up the valley drew us a little closer to Kagbeni, and our inevitable separation from Dorothy and Hildy.

Kagbeni was an oasis, an island of green, irrigated wheat fields, set amidst a dry, desolate landscape. This was the last village on the ancient Tibetan trade route, and the furthest point north we could travel without a special permit to enter the Tibetan region of Nepal, known as Mustang. For the moms this was the highest elevation they would reach (9,200 feet), before returning back to Jomsom for their helicopter flight to Kathmandu.

I knew our moms had been deeply moved by this journey; I just didn't know how deeply until Hildy's farewell salute to the crew. During our final night of singing and dancing together, she eloquently expressed the joy she felt.

"I am so grateful to each of you," she began.

"Thank you for showing me your beautiful country. Thank you for sharing your music and dancing. Thank you for helping me to reach Kagbeni."

"Most of all," she said through quivering lips, "Thank you for your warmth and kindness . . . I didn't expect us to become friends."

"*Namaste,*" she trembled, bowing to them.

Nima translated for the crew as teardrops glistened on the faces of some of the porters and guides. As I gazed toward them, I was suddenly warmed by a realization that should have been apparent much sooner. Nepal is a land of many faces: the sculpted faces of the world's highest mountains; the diverse faces of the multiple ethnic groups that inhabit the Himalayas; and the mirrored reflection of my own face in the smiles of our newfound friends. I went to Nepal expecting to see stunning natural beauty; the revelation was discovering the hidden beauty within each of us.

Twelve days, 75 miles, more than 8,500 feet in elevation gain. A lifetime of memories. On our last morning together in Kagbeni, Mom and I went on a walk alone, as did Ann and Hildy. Mom and I walked slowly and took photos of the verdant wheat fields and the gleaming glaciers of Nilgiri.

"Mom," I said, "I want you to know how proud I am of you for making it this far, and for not quitting when that choice would have been so much easier than continuing."

She stopped walking, gazed out at the mountains, then replied, "I know that once I return home, the good memories will overwhelm the bad. I will always cherish the memories of the singing and dancing, the spirit of the Nepalese people, the beauty of these mountains." She paused, the tears now streaming down her cheeks, "and the love I feel for you, Ann, Hildy, and Mike because of this incredible bonding experience."

I hugged her and whispered, "It's been so hard for me to see you in such pain and discomfort, but now your accomplishments seem even greater."

We returned for group photos, more tears, trembling hugs, and goodbyes. Nima and Dawa escorted Hildy and Dorothy back to Jomsom, as Mike, Ann, and I began our slow ascent toward Muktinath. Later that morning, Ann and I shared with each other our parting conversations with our moms. Ann summarized the feelings she had expressed in her journal:

> All in all, trekking with the moms was pure inspiration to me. I got high just being with them, seeing them rise to the challenges and experience the thrill of astounding beauty, the people's deep warmth, and their own physical achievements.

We were surprised to learn that both our moms had expressed their profound admiration for us, and their hopes that we would continue our travels as long as possible. What did they see in us that we couldn't see in ourselves? How had we changed as individuals? As partners?

We were so wrapped up in their accomplishments that we hadn't taken the time to realize our own, not only in terms of this Annapurna trek, but also our previous seven months of traveling together. Ann reflects in her journal that:

The Moms both seem to have noticed something in Dave and me that pleases them enormously, and has made them appreciate the effect our traveling has had on our relationship. Mom is hoping we will be able to complete our year's journey, and is strongly encouraging us to face the financial challenges to make it work. I think she is anxious that we get the full benefit of these relationship lessons by being gone as long as possible!

Perhaps Hildy and Dorothy sensed our delight in pursuing our dreams. Perhaps they witnessed our vigor and growing self-reliance — the confidence that comes with embracing new cultures. Perhaps they sensed the growing strength of our marriage; we had condensed so many life experiences into such a short time period — fear, pain, anger, joy, laughter, wonder, and nearly death. Perhaps our moms had seen for themselves how enriching foreign travel can be; how one cannot visit a place like Nepal and leave unchanged. Or, upon their departure, perhaps they simply wanted to re-reverse the nurturer roles, and let us know they will always be our moms.

11

From West to East

> *We never become truly spiritual by sitting down and wishing to become so. You must first undertake something so great that you cannot accomplish it unaided.*
>
> -Phillip Brooks

After twelve grueling days of trekking, our moms were clearly ready to return to the comforts of home. But for Mike, Ann, and me the eastern side of the Annapurna Himal still beckoned. Sixteen more days of trekking lay ahead, and our biggest physical challenge—crossing Thorung La (17,755 feet)—was yet to come. Tears welled in my eyes, as we ascended the steep, arid slope out of Kagbeni.

I was still thinking of how long and hard we had hugged with our moms, clinging to each other's fleece jackets as if doing so might prevent the precious memories from slipping through our fingers. Mom's final words reverberated through me. I reached out for Ann's hand and held it, saying nothing. At the top of the slope, I shared with Ann my mom's parting words: "I had hoped to honor your father, by asking you to leave a dried rose from his funeral at Thorung La." The forgotten rose lay on her kitchen table in St. Louis.

Ann and I clutched and cried, both touched by the depth of Mom's love for Dad. I admired Mom as never before, realizing that the real challenge of the Himalayas for her was not the many physical obstacles she had surmounted—diarrhea, nausea, cramps, headaches, low back pain, weak knees, and the curse of too short legs and too steep steps—but the emotional obstacles to letting go of Dad.

Equatorial Crossings

As I gazed out at the breathtaking views of the Dhaulagiri Himal and Annapurna South, and traced the desolate, upper Kaligandaki River valley from Kagbeni to where it originates in the Mustang region on the Tibetan border, I knew I would somehow fulfill Mom's wish to honor Dad and my own to find meaning in his premature death.

In Muktinath, a picturesque village perched in the mountains high above the Kaligandaki River valley at 12,460 feet, we pitched our tent on the windswept roof of a guesthouse. I spent hours recording where we had been and imagining where we were going. I lay awake, having silent, long overdue conversations with Dad:

> *Here I am, Dad, having the time of my life, and I can't get you out of my head. Why did you give up on life when you had so much living left to do? And I had so much left to tell you? I don't pretend to understand your hellish battle with alcoholism, and I try not to judge you too harshly now. I only know that I feel empty at times, cheated of your companionship – your patient mentoring – at too young an age. I wanted you to spend time getting to know Ann. I wanted you to see the house we finished building on Lost Mountain. I wanted to understand your passion for your career, to mimic your wry sense of humor, to unlock the lifetime of emotions you kept so tightly locked inside. I wanted to know you better, Dad, because I am after all half you.*

Nilgiri, the Dhaulagiri Himal, and Mustang Peak dominated the skyline to the west. Thorung La, the high pass and traditional trade route between the eastern and western flanks of the Annapurna Himal, loomed to the east. I slept fitfully—too hot, too cold, got up to pee three times. Thin air. Heavy expectations.

We spent two full days in Muktinath, resting and letting our bodies adjust to the altitude. Our porters took us to a protected area, a religious and environmental sanctuary, nestled in a grove of trees above the village. Interpretive signs in English asked trekkers to donate money for the "adopt a tree" program, a last ditch effort at forest preservation in a region where most trees end up as firewood.

The sacredness of the sanctuary was palpable: long strands of colored prayer flags danced in the wind; silk prayer scarves dangled in the trees; saffron-robed Hindu *sadhus* sat in deep meditation; piles of stones known as *chortens* dotted the ridge; *mani stones*, flat stone tablets carved with scriptures by Buddhist lamas, were heaped several feet deep at the base of each chorten; a hunched, nearly blind Tibetan man on a horse was guided to the sanctuary by his smiling son; and Buddhists and Hindus freely intermingled and bathed together in the holy water called *jaul*. Muktinath is a natural sanctuary where all are welcome and free to worship, regardless of one's nationality, race, sect, or religious beliefs. I was heartened to learn that such havens still exist in our troubled world of ever-growing intolerance.

Hindu and Buddhist pilgrims come here from as far away as India to pray and bathe in the holy water. Many of our porters collected a bottle of the jaul to take home to their family members, who will drink it and sprinkle it on their heads. We were blessed by a Hindu holy man, who painted red *tikas* on our foreheads and scattered dyed-red rice on the top of our heads to bring us good luck for our Thorung La crossing.

At a nearby Buddhist temple, our guide Nima convinced us to pull back the curtains underneath a Buddha statue. Three cobalt-blue natural gas flames shot out of fissured rock, and Nima explained that Buddhists believe these "eternal flames" have been burning since the earth was formed. Ann and I each lit a candle in honor of our departed dads. This day, April 29th 1996, would have been my dad's 63rd birthday.

The next morning, we left Muktinath, and climbed another 1,000 feet to a small, ramshackle hut at Chubarbu. This hut was to be our last acclimatization stop before crossing Thorung La. Mike, Ann, and I spent the afternoon playing cribbage and roaming. Near the hut, in a steep gorge filled with sculpted boulders and a trickle of water, I found a saligram, a fossilized marine organism that resembles a nautilus. Both Hindus and Buddhists believe these fossils are holy, and good fortune comes to the finder. At that instant, I knew exactly what I would do to honor Dad.

We ate a huge meal at sunset and I went to bed soon afterward, feeling warm, healthy, and fit, but anxious. Our room in the hut was like a cave with sooty walls, a dirt floor, and a low wood ceiling. A raised dirt platform with pine boughs on top served as our bed, but the anticipation of climbing higher than I ever had, and my preoccupation with honoring Dad at the pass prevented me from sleeping.

At 1 am Makar delivered hot juice to us in bed. Like a dazed bear emerging from interrupted hibernation, I plodded from our cave to find a brilliant, nearly full moon illuminating the path to the pass. After a quick meal of hot porridge and eggs, we packed and began our ascent by the light of the moon.

We made slow but steady progress, climbing as a group for the first hour. After a water break, the terrain became steeper, the air noticeably thinner, and the gaps between us widened. My breathing became more labored, as my lungs adjusted to the colder, drier air. In the pre-dawn light, I paused often to survey the rugged terrain and remind myself of the magnitude of this undertaking. Once, I glanced over my shoulder just in time to see the radiant moon drift behind the Dhaulagiri range, and I remember feeling the boon of the drifting moon.

Ann reached the pass first, just as the sun crested the snowy pinnacles to the east. Mike was a few minutes behind her. Disheartened by three false summits, I struggled through bouts of nausea for the last half hour of the ascent. Goman shadowed me, offering periodically to carry my pack, but determination and recollections of Mom's courage pushed me on.

At the true summit of Thorung La, Ann smothered me with a welcome hug, and then the amphitheater of snowcapped peaks enveloped me, too. Like me, these glaciated massifs seemed to shiver in anticipation of the sun's first rays. Was it clouds or blowing snow that circled the jagged, fractured mountains on either side of the pass?

Within minutes my exposed hands were numb, as I attempted to capture everything on film. The water bottle I had filled with boiling water at the start of the ascent was iced over. Suki Ram danced around happily in only a T-shirt. Sanu was content in a cotton sweatshirt and wool hat. I felt silly, shivering in my layers of Capilene, fleece, and Gore-Tex, as Suki Ram and Sanu rubbed my hands until gradually I could feel my fingertips again beneath their strong, coarse hands. I managed a laugh as Basu ambled up the pass. He looked like a cartoon character wrapped in Hildy's blue rain suit, capped in a floppy white Gilligan hat that was dwarfed by his 70-pound pack, and flanked, as always, by his trusty guitar. These guys continually bewildered me with the enormous loads they carry, their endurance, their tolerance for cold, and their good humor no matter what adversity they face.

After a few more quick snapshots, Ann and I began adding stones to a collapsed chorten that Buddhists had built at this sacred high pass. In honor of my dad, I placed the saligram from Chubarbu and a wishing stone from the Kaligandaki valley on top of the chorten, and Ann draped a string of prayer flags across from an adjacent chorten. For five minutes I fumbled with two lighters, trying to light a candle. Mike, thinking more clearly than me, suggested that maybe the lack of oxygen was the problem and not the lighters, but, despite my numb hands, I was determined to light the candle. Success. Flame. Gust. Smoke. I placed the smoldering candle inside the chorten.

Weeping uncontrollably from the exhaustion of our ascent, the pain in my numb hands, the exhilaration of reaching the pass, and the act of purging my grief for Dad's untimely death, I became momentarily confused by a spiritual dilemma. Why did I build this Buddhist chorten to honor my Methodist father?

My thoughts, though slow in coming, began to crystallize. My attraction to Buddhism and the concept of universal compassion was a natural extension of my upbringing, not a rejection of my Christian roots. I didn't inherit a compassion gene. I learned compassion from my parents. Love and compassion: isn't this what life is really about?

Mom and Dad's lives exemplified love and compassion. I just hadn't ever fully grasped this truth. I realized Mom's courage, faith, and compassion throughout Dad's torturous struggle with alcoholism could serve as a landmark, a beacon for me on my own spiritual journey.

Reflecting now on the Thorung La experience, my spirituality seems clearer. Having faith isn't about choosing between Buddhism, Christianity, or any other belief system. It's about love. Embracing love. Honoring love. Spreading love. Now, as I write of this revelation, echoes from my past swirl through my head, like the spindrift snow in those dawn gusts on Thorung La:

Kahlil Gibran, *The Prophet*: "Love one another, but make not a bond of love . . ."

First Corinthians: "Love bears all things, believes all things, hopes all things, endures all things."

Dad's best man wedding toast: "You are both so deeply committed to each other and the environment. We wish you a life full of joy, accomplishment, and hopefully grandkids."

My wedding vows to Ann: "I ask you, Ann, to be my friend, my wife, my soul mate . . . I solemnly vow to dwell harmoniously with you, in the hope that the love and harmony we create together will spread to others . . ."

Why have I complicated my life with guilt and confusion about the need to choose one religion? Won't my life be richer if I draw upon many world religions and philosophies? Can't my spirituality revolve around the variety of belief systems that resonate for me?

I know now what I didn't know standing in wonder at 17,755 feet. Nature is my church. Mountains, forests, rivers, islands—these are the places I feel most free to worship and celebrate the blessings of life. Wilderness is where I experience epiphanies, not church pews. In the rarefied Himalayan air, I was closer to my God than ever before.

I knelt, rested my forehead against the memorial, and said a silent prayer:

> *Dad, we built this chorten as a symbol*
> *of our undying love for you.*
>
> *Peace be with you.*

As we made our gradual descent from Thorung La, I bounced along with nascent energy. Traversing the pass was both a physical and spiritual passage for me—a physical transition from the western to the eastern flanks of the Annapurna Himal; a spiritual transition from western beliefs to greater understanding and appreciation of eastern beliefs. And the chorten we left behind was much more than a memorial to my dad; it was a cairn on my meandering spiritual path—a path that would take me another 18 days through the Annapurna Himal and ever deeper into my own heart and soul.

12

Solu Khumbu Sojourn

> *The secret of the mountains is that the mountains simply exist, as I do myself: the mountains exist simply, which I do not . . . I understand all this, not in my mind but in my heart, knowing how meaningless it is to try and capture what cannot be expressed, knowing that mere words will remain when I read it all again, another day.*
>
> -Peter Matthiessen, *The Snow Leopard*

The day started with the *whir* of helicopter blades shredding the mountain air, and a takeoff so smooth that I didn't even realize we had lifted off the ground. The terraced hillsides of the Kathmandu Valley rippled into low mountains, then taller, steeper ones flanking precipitous gorges. Forty-five minutes later we landed at Syangboche, the portal to the Solu Khumbu region of the Nepalese Himalayas, and a common departure point for trekkers and climbers headed toward Mount Everest.

Although we had already spent more than a month trekking in the Himalayas, we were still concerned about adjusting to the thin air at such high altitude, and we wisely decided to descend 1,000 feet to Namche Bazaar ("Namche") for the night. Along the way, we stopped at the Sagarmatha National Park Pollution Control Office, and we were pleased to learn of the many active environmental projects in the Everest area. Rubbish dumps with incinerators, solar toilets, education programs, tree planting, and increasingly higher Everest expedition fees to cover the costs of hauling out garbage were just a few of the innovative environmental stewardship programs. We were disappointed, however, that we were unable to find a single lodge in Namche with solar heating or solar showers. Deforestation appeared to be as big a problem here as in the Annapurna region. After asking around, we learned that frequent clouds and high winds make solar impractical in Namche, which sits at 11,287 feet.

Just past sunrise the morning after we arrived, I set out alone to explore the village while Ann caught up on badly needed sleep. The houses in Namche were strikingly modern and well kept, and I saw none of the prevalent poverty that left such a deep impression on me near the end of our Annapurna trek. Anxious for a higher view, I ascended the eastern slope of Namche toward the Sagarmatha National Park Visitors Center, where I caught my first glimpse of Mount Everest. *Sagarmatha* is the Nepali name for the world's highest peak, but from this vantage point, I cannot honestly say that Everest wowed me. She was a tall, picturesque peak with no outstanding features I could discern, and she looked much like many other pyramid-shaped peaks I had seen in New Zealand and the Swiss Alps. Ama Dablam, on the other hand, held me spellbound. I found myself pondering how she stayed upright with her hooked, gravity-defying summit. Towering in isolation from any surrounding peaks, Ama Dablam (22,494 ft) was the stuff of dreams.

From this ridgeline, I realized that the village of Namche is shaped like an amphitheater, with houses perched on three sides of a u-shaped valley carved between two staggering ridges. The open end of this valley plunges nearly 3,000 feet down to the Bohte Kosi River. Each Saturday, people come to the bazaar at Namche from all the neighboring Sherpa villages in Solu Khumbu, and some from as far away as Tibet. Set amidst the backdrop of the world's highest mountains, this has to be one of the world's most colorful and frenetic open-air markets. At this early hour, I could already see Sherpa and Tibetan buyers and sellers beginning to congregate.

The name *Sherpa* means easterner, because these people originally came to Nepal roughly 600 years ago from Kham, in eastern Tibet. The cultural and religious ties to Tibet and Tibetan Buddhism remain especially strong in the main Sherpa villages of Solu Khumbu at Namche Bazaar, Khumjung, Khunde, Thame, Pangboche, and Phortse. Daily life in Solu Khumbu revolves around each village monastery called a *gompa*, and Buddhism for these people is more than a religion; it is the unifying principle of all aspects of their lives. Sherpa Buddhism—an offshoot of Nyingmapa, the oldest sect of Tibetan Buddhism—aims to generate spiritual energy for the benefit of all sentient beings.

I wandered around the Namche market for nearly an hour before finally mustering the courage to ask a middle-aged, bald monk whether I could take his picture. He grinned and held up a painted, aluminum tea decanter he had been admiring. His head, the decanter, and his saffron sleeved robe all seemed to glow in the vibrant morning sun. Nearby, I ran into Ann talking with a handsome Tibetan trader with a red hair braid characteristic of the Kham region of eastern Tibet. He agreed to let her take his picture in exchange for her ballpoint pen. With limited success, we attempted to learn more about where he was from and how far he had traveled to get to the market. He motioned north up the Bohte Kosi River valley, and we could only infer that he had crossed into Nepal from Tibet over Nangpa La, a treacherous pass and historic trade route commonly used in the last 40 years by Tibetans escaping from Chinese oppression in Tibet.

The Namche bazaar was a cornucopia of colors, smells, people, and interactions. Household goods, chickens, jewelry, sides of beef, produce, grains, electronics, butter candles, prayer scarves, blankets, clothes off people's backs . . . virtually everything was for sale for the right price. Most of these people seemed uplifted by the sunny day and the give and take of vigorous bartering that is a trademark of the Sherpa culture. Only the listless cows, soon to be sides of beef, seemed oblivious to the pace of activity, as they munched on discarded cardboard and gazed down from a rocky promontory above the market.

Caught up in the frenzy, I tried to capture my sensory overload on film, before realizing what I really wanted was to connect with some of these people—to understand more about them, to participate in the moment rather than being a detached observer hidden behind a camera lens. I wanted to grasp the juxtaposition of old and new that lent an air of the bizarre to this bazaar, and be able to explain to friends back home the irony of observing these weathered Sherpas and Tibetans bartering in front of the shiny metal roof and satellite dish of Namche's newest tourist lodge.

After a day and a half in Namche, the differences between the Everest Region and the Annapurna Region were increasingly apparent. These Sherpa people, the dominant ethnic group of Solu Khumbu, seem to have a much higher standard of living than most other Nepalese people. Since the 1950s, Sherpas have gained a reputation as some of the best mountain climbers in the world, and they are famous for their indomitable strength and courage at high altitudes. They are often the unrecognized support team for high-profile, international mountaineers attempting ascents of Everest, Makalu, Lhotse, and hundreds of lesser-known peaks. On these expeditions, Sherpas typically do all the grunt work with none of the glory—they carry supplies, establish routes, fix ropes, set up camps, save climber's lives, and sometimes die in the process. Many Sherpas derive their only income from the growing parade of wealthy foreign trekkers and climbers who visit the Everest region each year.

I was surprised and amused to see so many Sherpa women wearing their traditional ankle-length woolen robes (*chubas*) and colorful, striped aprons (*mahtil*) with running shoes made by Nike, Adidas, and New Balance. While the women's clothing, with the exception of their shoes, appeared to be fairly traditional, the men wore mostly foreign clothing. I noticed many Sherpa men wearing jeans and T-shirts instead of the traditional chuba and high-collared shirt called a *todung*, and many wore expensive watches and leather hiking boots, as compared to the bare feet, flip-flops, and cheap Chinese tennis shoes we saw throughout our Annapurna trek. By Nepalese standards, Namche and its Sherpa residents appeared to be thriving.

From Namche, we made our way slowly up the Dudh Kosi River valley toward Gokyo, being careful to drink plenty of fluids, get plenty of sleep, and not climb more than 1,000-2,000 feet in elevation each day. We reminded ourselves daily that we were embarking on a trek that would take us from a little less than 12,000 feet up to nearly 18,000 feet. Unlike our trek in the Annapurna region with multiple porters, cooks, and guides, Ann and I ventured into the Everest region alone in mid-May, 1996. We carried our own packs and slept in Sherpa tea houses, which offered accommodations ranging from a blanket on the floor of a shack, to a bed in a private room of a well-furnished lodge. We spent many frigid nights huddled close to whatever source of heat, if any, was available, typically a wood stove with a smoky, yak-dung fire that reddened our eyes and filled our throats with phlegm. Within a few days, we had both developed the hacking cough so prevalent among these Sherpa people, who spend their lives breathing thick smoke in unventilated rooms.

In contrast to our Annapurna trek, where seemingly every day was enlivened by contact with a new ethnic group, we saw few other people in Solu Khumbu. As the monsoon season neared, the trails emptied. At times, it felt as if we had the magnificent Dudh Kosi River valley and surrounding mountains to ourselves. This solitude was both a blessing and a curse, for while we relished the opportunity for silent reflection and uninterrupted, intimate conversation, we also longed for the camaraderie, dancing, and singing of our Annapurna trek.

My belly was full with a piping hot dinner of fried noodles and eggs, as I savored my last cup of hot cocoa and reflected on the day. I was thankful I had begun this day before the sun had crested the peaks, and ventured out on a morning walk that was frigid but serene. In the subtle glow of the sun's first rays, I took photos of stoic, wooly yaks—bison-like mounds of muscle and fur braced against the incessant wind, snow, and ice of their high-altitude home. Three hundred yards down a gravel outwash bank I saw two musk deer, one of the most endangered species in the Himalayas, and nearby, two pink and white blood pheasants.

On the way back to the lodge, I spooked a different kind of pheasant, a male that displayed his brilliant blue body flecked with iridescent colors, green face, turquoise eye mascara, yellow- and red-tipped tail feathers, and a regal crest of red, green, and yellow. I learned from our *sauni* (proprietress) that this pheasant is the national bird of Nepal, which the Sherpas admiringly call *danphe*.

Bubbling with enthusiasm, I rejoined Ann for a quick breakfast of freshly baked cinnamon rolls, before hitting the trail to Maccherma. Staggering views of peaks buoyed our spirits and made the third straight day of steep climbing seem worth the effort. Looking back toward Dole, our previous night's stop, we were greeted by two of the most beautiful mountains I had seen in Nepal: Thamserku (22,336 ft) and Kangtega (22,250 ft), twin sculpted towers of ice and snow. Winding our way through one stone-enclosed yak pasture (*kharka*) after another, we reached a high point next to a Buddhist chorten where soaring pinnacles spanned the skyline to the east. Tawoche (21,463 ft) and Cholatse (21,128 ft) were especially imposing, because they seemed to hover within reach, just across the river. To the north, directly up the Dudh Kosi valley, was the grandest peak of them all: Cho Oyu, a stunning massif so smothered in glacial ice and snow that little exposed rock was visible. She loomed high above everything else in sight. At 26,906 feet, Cho Oyu is the sixth highest mountain in the world, a fact that only heightened my sense of awe.

We arrived in Maccherma shortly before noon and devoured a hearty lunch of noodle soup with dried yak meat. After several hours of reading in the dim, smoky hut, we braved the cold and wind to play in the yak pasture with Pemba, a little girl whom we guessed was four or five. We played tag and chase, and she shrieked in delight as I tossed her spinning into the air. But her greatest glee came from watching me chase a white fluffy dog with a black face around and around in circles. Whenever the dog came too close, Pemba would clutch Ann's leg in fear, and Ann would cradle Pemba in her arms, cooing, "It's ok, it's ok," while they watched me exhaust myself.

In the late afternoon, snow wafted like feathers released from a down pillow, and the levity of our earlier frolicking with Pemba was soon blanketed by stillness that was both beautiful and eerie. We played cards, drank hot cocoa, and gobbled up crispy coconut biscuits. Near dusk, the snow stopped and the clouds lifted. Through the one small sooty window in the hut, I could see sunlight on Thamserku, and we emerged to see the first really colorful sunset we had witnessed in Nepal. As the sun's last rays pulsed along the snowy peaks, pink billowy cumulus clouds danced across the blue sky. For an encore, the mountains glowed in waves of fuchsia and lavender, as if they were releasing stored heat. While the sky slowly darkened, we watched as a crescent moon skittered over Kyajo Ri. I shivered as the wind lashed my cheeks.

For two days, we had been unable to get warm, despite each wearing every layer of clothing we had: polypro top and bottom, fleece jacket, down coat, fleece hat, and gloves. It was so cold that my camera's light meter only worked if I removed the batteries and warmed one under each armpit for several minutes. During those two days, I also endured a mild headache that simply wouldn't go away. That night at Maccherma, I took my first dose of Diamox, a prescription drug used by climbers to make breathing easier at high elevation. I slept fitfully, and slunk shoeless outside to pee three times during the night.

We started our final push to Gokyo just after dawn, hoping to take advantage of clear skies. The consistent weather pattern continued: crystal clear until about mid-morning when the clouds rolled in and stayed until mid-afternoon winds whisked them away. The most memorable part of this ascent was following the upper Dudh Kosi River to the terminus of the Ngozumba Glacier moraine. The Dudh Kosi ("milk river") was appropriately named, as the river here looked like powdered, frothy milk, and the massive boulders cast aside looked whitewashed. At the snout of the glacier, a superb view of a group of needle peaks to the west reminded us of pictures we had seen of the Torres del Paine in Chile. We also had unobstructed views downriver toward Kangtega and Thamserku, rigid sentinels at the valley's entrance.

We kicked steps into a soft bank of snow and crested what appeared to be the lip of a waterfall, where a clear creek, slightly wider than jumping distance, flowed out of Taoche Lake. Colorful white-capped river chats declared their name as they flitted from rock to rock chattering incessantly, their flight a blur of red bodies and blue wings. A solitary blue whistling thrush preened in mid creek on a water-smoothed boulder. The glint of its iridescent purple tail was the color of alpine lupine covered in morning dew.

Enchanted by the diaphanous, glacier-fed creek, the colorful birds, and the sculpted snow banks, and invigorated by the taste and feel of the high mountain air, we waltzed into Gokyo half expecting to have the place to ourselves. For five days, we had seen no other trekkers, and although we had heard in advance of the Gokyo "Resort," we were initially aghast at how much it looked and felt like an American ski resort.

Bronzed, exceedingly fit young men and women lounged in T-shirts, shorts, and bare feet inside a glass solarium while worshipping the unpredictable sun. The initial shock of this hedonistic scene passed quickly. The solarium thermometer proclaimed 70°F and I was already forming a mental "to-do" list: sew up hole in fly of pants, trim toenails, clean camera body and lenses, organize and label exposed rolls of film, play cribbage with Ann, catch up on journal entries, nap, eat, buy chocolate, eat, buy more chocolate. As I looked around the room, I saw backpacks, wool socks, water bottles, hiking boots, novels, decks of cards, and various other accoutrements of the twenty or so reptilian sun-worshippers haphazardly strewn about, shed like unneeded skin.

In bed asleep by sunset, we awoke before 5 am, and a half-hour later we were hiking toward the fifth lake north of the Gokyo solarium. The morning was vacant of any wildlife or perceptible sound, other than the patterned *c-r-u-n-c-h, c-r-u-n-c-h* of our Vibram soles on frozen snow. By 8 am, the cloak of clouds parted and daggers of sun pierced through. On a ridgeline above the unnamed Lake 5, we stopped for the day, unable to imagine that a finer panoramic view existed anywhere in the world. Cho Oyu now seemed incomprehensibly high, and neighboring Gyachung Kang must surely have been created as the archetypal Himalayan mountain. Cha Kung, Pumori, Everest, Lhotse, Kangtega, Thamserku, and countless other unnamed peaks tattooed the flawless blue skin of sky.

It was like sitting inside one of the "top of the world" posters I had seen for sale everywhere in Kathmandu. Ann stretched out in the sun-warmed divot of a boulder larger than our house, and began to sketch Mount Everest. I wandered off to record every degree of the 360-degree view on film, guessing at proper exposures thanks to a light meter that no longer functioned properly on spent batteries. Among all these peaks, Gyachung Kang (26,089 ft) gave me the greatest pause, for according to our map its summit was on the border between Nepal and Tibet. I imagined myself ascending its formidable glacier, then crossing over the pass between Gyachung Kang and Cho Oyu into Tibet, a place I'd dreamed of visiting ever since reading *Seven Years in Tibet* in the mid-1980s.

Roiling clouds and an icy wind blowing north across the top of Ngozumba Glacier roused me from my reverie. We descended to Gokyo in less than half the time it took us to get to Lake 5. Back at the resort, I replaced my two dead camera batteries for the exorbitant price of 500 Rupiah ($20 US). I was surprised and relieved that the backpacker's store had the size I needed, but wondered, at that price, how long they had gathered dust on the shelves, and whether they had any charge left.

The ground was dusted with frost as we began our ascent of Gokyo Ri at 5:15 am the next morning. It was eerily silent — no wind, no birds, no water, only the rhythm of our sluggish footsteps and labored breathing. The one glimmer of daybreak was a patch of golden sunlight illuminating the southeast face of Cho Oyu. Yet, minutes later, as we crossed the stream that drains the lateral moraine of Ngozumba Glacier, sunlight also grazed the sawtooth ridge to our west. Gokyo Lake reflected the gleaming teeth until a white duck, the size and shape of a bufflehead, slowly paddled across the lake, scattering the ridgeline reflection in its wake.

We paused for a brief, chilled hug, already sensing the promise in this breathtaking start to the day. For the next two hours, we plodded straight up. We were half expecting to feel nauseous or dizzy, or experience blurred vision or some of the other myriad symptoms of altitude sickness. I never felt anything more than some minor gas, a few burps, and a slight pain in my right ear, which didn't want to pop easily. I experienced none of the nausea or throbbing headaches that plagued me on our slightly higher Thorung La crossing in the Annapurnas. Perhaps our slow pace and careful acclimation over the previous week were paying off, or maybe the Diamox was beneficial. In hindsight, I only recall feeling buoyant, as if some external force was lifting me up this precipice.

At the 17,519-foot summit of Gokyo Ri, we were blessed with another 360-degree panorama that encompassed four of the world's highest peaks—Everest, Lhotse, Makalu, Cho Oyu—and many more unnamed, and likely unclimbed, peaks over 23,000 feet. Is it possible anywhere else in the world, besides Solu Khumbu, to capture three 26,000-foot peaks in one photo? Without a doubt, this was the finest mountain view I had seen anywhere.

We knew as we took four rolls of slides that these could never do the view justice, but still we couldn't resist attempting to capture images of this view of a lifetime. I took one complete panorama in color, and then Ann took another in black and white. The third roll we took together, laughing as we alternated setting the self-timer and running to the appointed rock, so that Everest or Cho Oyu or some other divine peak loomed over our shoulders. The fourth roll was dedicated to mountain faces shot with a long zoom lens: the yellow stripe on Everest, the hanging glaciers on Gyachung Kang, the ice-cream dome of Cho Oyu, the perfect pyramid of Pumori, and a ridge of unnamed needle pinnacles. Afterwards, we simply sat and stared—for five hours.

The summit was a garden of rock cairns draped with Tibetan prayer flags and silk scarves, fluttering in the occasional puff of breeze. It was still early morning, but the low sun already provided ample warmth to sit comfortably in one place. We nibbled on coconut cookies and savored a fruit and nut Cadbury chocolate bar, talking idly.

Equatorial Crossings

But this felt to me like a place for reverence, not talk, and before I could express this to Ann, I knew from her distant gaze that she had already journeyed within.

Overlooking Ngozumba Glacier from Gokyo Ri reminded me of peering down at Grand Pacific Glacier on our Glacier Bay, Alaska kayaking trip five years before. Upon seeing Grand Pacific for the first time, I recall thinking there could be no other glacier of such raw power and beauty. Now, Ngozumba Glacier, miles longer, wider, and higher, seemed larger than life. This crawling river of ice, rock, and snow spanned my peripheral vision from left to right. Yet, the difference in scale between the two glaciers was insignificant compared to the magic place both hold in my heart. I smiled as I recalled how full and rich my life had been since meeting Ann and undertaking that first wilderness trip together in Alaska; the corners of my mouth collected the slow trickle of salty tears—tears of thanks, and joy, and disbelief that a mere three months earlier, my life had nearly ended in an Indonesian hospital.

In 1989, more than two years before we were married and during the height of our passionate courting, Ann gave me a copy of Peter Matthiessen's *The Snow Leopard* with the inscription, "For Dave, my soul mate—a book that inspired me greatly, and influenced who I am." I read *The Snow Leopard* while traveling with my buddy, Mike, in the Swiss Alps. I had just completed my Master's thesis and was feeling a compelling urge to travel, but, at the same time, I was struggling to decide whether a long-term relationship with Ann was what I wanted. I earmarked a page of Matthiessen's masterpiece and underlined the following passage:

> *Snow mountains, more than sea or sky, serve as a mirror to one's own true being, utterly still, utterly clear, a void, an Emptiness without life or sound that carries in Itself all life, all sound.*

Seven years later in the stillness of that dawn on Gokyo Ri, amidst the greatest snow mountains on earth and snuggled comfortably next to my wife and soul mate, I understood what Matthiessen meant, for as I sat on bare rock, stripped of ego, expectations, and desire, life and sound seeped into the emptiness within me.

※

For the next three days, as we descended the Dudh Kosi River valley back toward Namche Bazaar and then up the Bohte Kosi River valley toward Thame, our conversations focused on how and where to spend our remaining four months before returning home. In Kathmandu we had several indications that our destiny might be the Buddhist teachings the Dalai Lama was giving in Spiti, India in mid-June. Ann was lobbying hard for attending these Kalachakra initiation teachings, and then continuing on into Pakistan and western China. She pointed out that when we left Australia, New Zealand, and Indonesia, each time we left feeling as though we might have moved on too soon. She was inclined to continue exploring the Himalayan region more, and more thoroughly, until satiated.

My own thoughts were entirely focused on getting into Tibet however possible, legally or illegally, and then possibly heading to Africa. We agreed to continue thinking and talking about the choices until we returned to Kathmandu, both of us acknowledging the importance of leaving space and time for serendipity to play its hand.

We planned our arrival in Thame for the beginning of the annual *Mani Rimdu* festival, the most significant Sherpa festival of the year. Also known as the "lama dance festival," Mani Rimdu originated in Tibet, and the festival is a celebration marking the completion of ten days of prayers that bring peace and good fortune to all sentient beings. As we neared Thame, we walked for a quarter mile along the longest wall of weathered prayer stones we had seen in Nepal. Bearing intricately carved prayers, these mani stones can only be placed by designated Buddhist monks and lamas. Walking within arm's reach of the sloughing wall, I had the distinct sensation these sacred stones were chanting the Tibetan Buddhist mantra OM MANE PADME HUM. Once again, I was surprised by Tibetan Buddhism's growing grasp on my intellect and emotions. My fascination with Buddhism, which began nearly a month earlier on the Annapurna circuit, seemed suddenly deeper than I could comprehend.

All the way to Thame, Ann and I had been discussing whether or not to hire a guide to interpret the Mani Rimdu ceremonies for us, and to help us find accommodations with a Sherpa family. We were both admittedly nervous about venturing alone into this remote high village, off the beaten trekkers' circuit, but we consciously made a decision to relax and accept that we couldn't predict or control what would happen once we reached the monastery settlement.

As we entered the settlement, the first sizeable building we saw was the Tashi Delek Lodge. We laughed and started to walk past, still thinking it would be more interesting and rewarding to stay with a family, but we decided to buy lunch there and leave our packs while we investigated other options for accommodations. Our search eventually and circuitously led us back to the lodge, the only one in Thame, where we were given a private room, just off the kitchen.

The next morning, the first day of Mani Rimdu, I awoke well before sunrise and quietly left our lodge, hoping to take some photos of the village and monastery in the dramatic light of dawn. I managed to compose five images before ominous clouds blanketed the valley. The last photo, taken from a window in a covered area at the perimeter of the Thame Monastery's courtyard, was of the ramshackle houses of upper Thame village, which cling perilously to a vertical rock face like limpets at low tide. Perched high above the Thame Kola River along an ancient Tibetan trade route, the Thame Monastery appears to jut directly out of the rock face it abuts. Built in 1667, the monastery is one of the oldest and most dramatic in all of Solu Khumbu.

I wandered through the monastery's empty, cobblestone courtyard and poked my head through the embroidered curtain hanging over the entrance to the monastery. In the several seconds it took for my eyes to adjust to the dim candlelight, I realized more than twenty monks and the *rinpoche* (head lama) were assembled in meditation. Mortified that I had just interrupted a sacred ceremony, I squatted to make myself as compact and unnoticeable as possible and began slinking backwards toward the curtain. A monk opened his eyes and smiled at me, motioning vigorously for me to sit near him on the floor. Torn between my western sensibility of not wanting to feel conspicuous and my emerging traveler's sensibility to follow the path of serendipity, I awkwardly removed my hiking boots and sat where the monk had motioned. I watched and listened, sitting cross-legged on the carpet, hesitant to move and scarcely breathing.

I let my eyes wander, pausing on each monk's face, the low wooden ceiling, the resplendent altar, the cracked timbers, and the cold, damp, dirt floor. Each monk wore a maroon robe the color of Merlot with a matching shawl that went over his left shoulder and under his bare right arm. Seated on raised platforms in two rows facing each other and perpendicular to the altar, the monks, eyes closed, appeared to be in deep meditation, led by the guttural, other-worldly vocalizations of the rinpoche.

I understood little of what was taking place, but, even so, the mesmerizing chants and periodic ringing of bells resonated with me, as did the smell of incense, the colorful masks and robes, the butter lamps, and the framed portrait of the 14th Dalai Lama on the altar. I unzipped my waist pack, tooth by tooth, and studied a postcard of the Dalai Lama that I had been carrying with me throughout our travels in Solu Khumbu. A young monk, who looked to be twelve or thirteen at most, noticed the card on my lap and approached me. He indicated with silent body language that he was curious why I had this image. I motioned that I wanted to leave the Dalai Lama postcard on the altar to indicate my respect. He whispered, "OK" in my right ear, in English, and I tread with bowed head, eyes on the floor the whole way to the altar. My hand visibly fluttered as I carefully placed the card behind the first of many rows of burning candles, next to a pyramid-shaped sculpture made of butter with alternating tiers of red, blue, and yellow, each bearing the carved icon of a different Buddhist deity. Stepping slowly toward my spot on the floor, I looked up and was relieved, invigorated actually, by the smiling eyes and nods of several approving monks. I sat down and breathed what seemed like my first breath in five minutes.

Over the next hour, I was guided through a ceremony that left me captivated and speechless: an incense lamp was waved under my chin so that a cloud of juniper smoke enveloped me; two little red beads about the size of a pin head were placed into my right palm and I swallowed them, following the lead of the glowing monk who initially invited me into the monastery; I drank a bitter, fermented liquid that was poured into my cupped palms; I ate four sweet, doughy balls slightly smaller than doughnut holes; a brass pitcher of water with peacock feathers in the spout was first touched to my forehead and then water was poured into my cupped hands; mimicking the monks, I drank the water and then rubbed my wet hands across the crown of my head; a red spot was painted on my throat just above the Adam's apple; and finally, a brass bowl with a cake sculpture and sticks of burning incense inside was briefly placed on top of my head.

When the ceremony was over, I continued to sit, partly in awe, but mostly because I didn't want the joyous feelings upwelling from within me to end. I was as profoundly moved and spiritually uplifted as ever before in my life. Serendipity had once again led me to the right place at the right time, and I was brimming with feelings of honor and gratitude. Why was I welcomed into a ceremony so intricate, so steeped in tradition that to this day I don't know the full significance?

I don't really know why I was invited inside, or why I was allowed to approach the altar. Nor do I know why I was encouraged to take photos after the ceremony was finished. What I do know is I followed my heart into the monastery, when my head was saying "leave," and I emerged enriched because of that decision.

Equatorial Crossings

After breakfast at the lodge, Ann and I returned to the monastery courtyard to observe the day's events. Hundreds of Sherpas and dozens of travelers were now gathered, and the whole village was bustling with activity and anticipation. The day unfolded into a mass blessing ceremony, similar in many respects to what I had experienced earlier that morning inside the monastery. As I watched each Sherpa man, woman, child, and baby file past the monks to receive the rinpoche's blessing and then the same sequence of red pellets, fermented beverage, dough balls, and holy water, I understood that the morning ceremony I had stumbled upon was intended for the monks only. Realizing this made me feel even more privileged and simultaneously more puzzled about why the smiling monk had so readily welcomed me into the monastery.

Ann and I both made a donation to the monastery and received *kata* (prayer scarves) and blessings from the rinpoche. By mid-afternoon, we were so tired and overwhelmed by the day's events that we returned to our lodge only to discover that every available space, including our room, was being used to make *momos*—dumpling-like, traditional Tibetan dough pastries filled with dried buffalo or yak meat, pickled radishes, and vegetables. We joined the assembly line and were treated as family, evoking laughter and smiles when we began singing *Ray Sum Phee Ree Ree* and other Nepalese folk songs we had learned on our Annapurna trek. Eventually our room was cleared of momos and people, and we collapsed into what, for me, had to be one of the deepest, most contented sleeps of our entire world trip.

Early the following morning, prior to the start of the dancing, I took photos of a temporary altar that had been erected in the courtyard, several drums and horns, the expectant crowd of Sherpas and travelers, and several close-up portraits of monks. I couldn't resist taking a photo of the incongruous scene of the rinpoche, sitting stoically in his Ray Ban sunglasses while his daughter, in her pink Converse high tops, tugged impatiently at the sleeve of his robe.

In Namche, Ann had read that the sixteen ritual dances of the Mani Rimdu festival are really a series of teachings about the fundamentals of Buddhism. The spectators, both Sherpas and travelers, learn that through the betterment of themselves the world itself will become a better place. The name Mani Rimdu comes from: *mani*—prayers to Pawa Chenrezig, the God of compassion; *ril*—little red long-life pellets; and *du*—the blessing on the ril.

The ceremony began when two monks blasted deep, hoarse notes through *dun chen*, long horns made of human bones. From the perilously steep rooftop the notes reverberated down through the swelling crowd, as older monks in maroon robes and yellow hats encircled the altar with colorful flags, followed by younger monks clashing cymbals and beating drums. As the din diminished, a group of lamas in ornate costumes and black hats slowly weaved across the cobbled dance floor. I later learned from an English-speaking Sherpa that this dance is an offering to the gods, who are capable of improving one's longevity, appearance, health, and intelligence. In the second dance, a group of monks in colorful, striped costumes and smiling papier-maché masks spun, twirled, and leapt in a high-energy performance that riveted the crowd. Their sheer athleticism filled me with wonder, as simultaneously the symbolic meanings of each synchronous movement filled me with questions.

After the third dance, I grew tired of being smashed into the window frame through which I was trying to take pictures. I moved down to a spot in the courtyard, which provided me with an unobstructed view of the dancers, as well as the buzzing crowd. Finally free to move around, I was startled when a visiting lama from the Tengboche Monastery invited me to stand next to him on his raised platform. I was unwilling at first, because the Thame rinpoche had given this lama a place of honor to sit. But he was very persistent and once I moved next to him, I realized he was simply anxious to talk to someone. He told me in nearly incomprehensible English the name and purpose of each new dance, which I scrawled in my photo log. As best as I could determine, each of the dances was somehow related to the prayers in the preceding ten days. By the seventh dance, I was weak from hunger. I caught Ann's eye and mimed that I needed to eat something. I placed my hands together, bowed to the lama, and said "*namaste.*"

We returned after a satisfying meal of hot momos and tea to discover that the crowd had thinned a bit. During our lunch break, I lost track of the individual dances, but the one that received the largest crowd response was the final dance of the day, involving two characters in a comic routine: a tall monk in a Tibetan costume with no mask, and a hyperactive dancer in a leather, disfigured mask and yak-skin pants. This was the only dance that involved any speaking, and the Tibetan character made everyone laugh hysterically. Periodically, he would stop telling jokes and drink *chang* (beer made from fermented barley or millet) out of a glass flask on the altar. While all the attention was on the Tibetan, the disfigured character came running into the courtyard and, amidst shrieks and gasps, he dived into the crowd and rolled around on top of people. The response was a strange mixture of laughter and terror. The kids seemed particularly frightened by this character, but everyone still laughed at his physical antics: sitting on people's laps, stumbling, and tripping. The two characters then began dancing around and poking fun at various Buddhist rituals we had observed: receiving kata from the rinpoche, drinking chang, eating dough balls, and spinning prayer wheels. The puzzling routine ended when the Tibetan character prostrated three times in front of the rinpoche and then pulled out a sword from inside his costume and pretended to impale himself. The crowd erupted and money rained down onto the dance floor, as people threw rolled and wadded bills. The Tibetan character arose, and he and the disfigured man began carrying off their props. Monks came out with silver trays and scooped up the money.

On the final day of the festival, all but one other tourist had left, and no Sherpas gathered to witness the closing ritual, a fire *puja*. We were graced with the first sun in four days, and Ann and I were allowed to wander freely around the grounds of the monastery. We watched four crouching monks in the early stages of creating an intricate four-foot square painting called a mandala out of brightly colored sand grains. Mandalas (*kyil-khor*) symbolize the order and harmony of the enlightened mind, and are often used by Tibetan Buddhists as aids in the practice of meditation. For four hours, these monks patiently designed an exquisite sand painting with a square cross in the middle surrounded by multiple circles, each with a different deity as the central focal point. During that time, Ann and I helped peel hundreds of potatoes that were to be part of a feast for the monks following the final ritual.

An hour later, the meticulously created mandala went up in flames, when the monks heaped yak dung on top and lit a fire. The mandala, as well as all of the butter sculptures (*thorma*) from the monastery's altar, was burned to remind people to let go of material values: the ultimate Buddhist expression of the impermanence of all things. We were told by an American student who was studying Tibetan Buddhism that several hours later, after the raging fire burned out, the monks would carry the remaining sand and ashes to the Thame Kola River and pour them into the river to symbolize "the continual flow of life, unencumbered with desires that distract us from a good and loving life."

The significance and symbolism of the Mani Rimdu festival remains largely a mystery to us. Yet, the lasting feeling I have is one of privilege. It was such an improbable honor to be allowed to observe the festival in its entire splendor; not knowing all the details of the dancing or the rituals adds to their allure and continues to fuel my imagination. Not knowing also inspires me to return again someday to learn more.

Following our remarkable four and a half days in Thame, we debated whether to continue trekking as planned or return to Kathmandu. We decided to head back into Namche Bazaar, and reassess. The night we arrived in Namche, we took our first showers in twelve days, and we enjoyed the simple pleasure of sleeping curled up next to each other with clean skin and hair. The next morning, feeling fully recharged, we decided to proceed up the Imja Khola River valley to Chukkung; the prospect of close views of Ama Dablam, the Lhotse-Nuptse Wall, Everest, and countless glaciers proved too enticing to leave Solu Khumbu yet.

Masks of Nepal · ASmale 5/96

Three days later, we arrived in Chukkung, after nearly continuous low clouds, gloomy, wet, clinging fog, and no views worth mentioning. We spent two days in Chukkung, hoping for a break in the weather that never came. Visibility was approximately 25 feet, roughly the distance from the door of the guesthouse to the outhouse. We huddled next to a yak dung fire, shivering. The one and only time I saw any mountains was in the middle of the second night when I got up for one of my multiple Diamox-induced pees. Illuminated by the nearly full moon and framed in a circle of fog that created a halo around her flanks, Ama Damblam was stunning. Down the valley, Khumbila, the guardian mountain and sacred protector of the Khumbu Valley, appeared to glow beneath the backdrop of fog. I dashed inside to wake Ann, but she didn't stir even with repeated forceful shaking. I re-emerged with camera and mini-tripod in hand, and within twenty minutes the fog window snapped shut and I was again immersed in a total whiteout. I shuffled toward the guesthouse, thankful that my full bladder had awakened me.

The next morning we awoke to find that the weather had worsened. In addition to the ominous fog, gusty winds and sleet lashed the windows of the guesthouse. We packed and left, deciding there was no point waiting in Chukkung for majestic mountain views.

At Pangboche, we stopped for lunch at a guesthouse and asked about visiting the local gompa. To our surprise, we were told this was the second day of a two-day festival at the monastery. We left our backpacks at the guesthouse and hiked up the hill through a lovely juniper forest to the monastery. Once inside, the rinpoche immediately captivated us; his smile radiated warmth and his face beamed wisdom. His frequent laugh was contagious and kept the mood of the ceremony light and fun, as he interacted and joked with the people. At one point, a nun with an enormous brass pot full of rice came around and gave us each a ladle full of steaming rice in our cupped hands, followed by another who served us butter tea in small brass cups.

After finishing our rice and tea, we went outside to try and track down a Sherpa man who I recognized from our helicopter flight to Syangboche two weeks earlier. He immediately recognized us, and we learned that he was in charge of planning this ceremony, known as *Nyungnay*, a Tibetan Buddhist practice designed to get rid of negative karma and accumulate merit and wisdom. For one and a half days everyone fasts and drinks only water, meditates, and tries to generate a "Bodhisattva attitude;" then on the afternoon of the second day (when we arrived totally by chance) everyone feasts and drinks chang. Each family received a package with cookies, Tibetan bread, sticky rice cones called *tso*, wrapped hard candies, and other items we couldn't identify.

Tsering, our new Sherpa acquaintance, gave me two bananas and Ann a tso. He then asked the monastery's caretaker to open the upstairs and give us a tour. The caretaker described, as best he could with limited English, the various deities represented by statues, and he opened locked drawers containing the bones and possessions of former lamas. He also showed us statues of deceased lamas who had been reincarnated. After the second reincarnation, life-like statues were carved in their honor. Ann and I lit several butter candles and gave donations to the monastery and to the caretaker.

Intrigued by yet another glimpse of the richness of Buddhist culture, we decided to spend the night at a lodge right next to the monastery. As we were descending the hill to retrieve our backpacks, we saw Ama Dablam, Kangtega, and Thamserku clearly for the first time on this leg of our trek. There was a window in the pinkening clouds and Ann pronounced with a smile, "Those mountains look like gods the way they're illuminated by the setting sun."

At the lodge, we discovered that five Tibetan nuns were also spending the night, and we spent the next several hours trying to converse with them using Nepali and body language. We all laughed when one of the nuns perfectly pantomimed a photo dropping out of a Polaroid camera. We explained that we didn't have one, but they were still excited to have us take pictures of them. We gave each of them a postcard of the Dalai Lama and promised to send copies of the photo Ann had just taken of them holding the cards. The oldest and most conversant nun explained that she had come to Nepal 33 years previously; another nun had come 20 years earlier. We were able to discern that they had each escaped from Tibet with the assistance of yaks, but we were unable to learn exactly why each had left. All five nuns now live at the Junbesi Monastery in Nepal, about half way between Lukla and Jiri.

What began as a dismal, bitterly cold hike through fog and sleet, ended serendipitously with a traditional Buddhist festival, sunset over the mountains, and the laughter of five new friends. Radiating inner and outer warmth, I drifted off to sleep, gazing out at the full moon.

Two days later, we flew out of Lukla with a Russian climbing expedition just back from successfully climbing 27,805-foot Makalu. As our helicopter whisked us out of the mountains and back into the smoggy, bustling Kathmandu Valley, I was attempting, above the deafening roar of the churning blades, to explain to one of the Russian climbers how much our time in Solu Khumbu had meant to me. Beyond a sense of unparalleled reward and irrepressible joy, our trek into the Everest region left me feeling humbled: physically humbled by the high elevation and impossibly steep terrain, spiritually humbled by the Sherpa people and their compelling Buddhist way of life, and mentally humbled by my ever deepening journey inward. I came away from our travels at precipitous heights with one lofty revelation: the insight to stop simply existing, and start existing simply. *Live simply Dave*, urged the Himalayas, *don't simply live.*

Lhasa to Little Lhasa

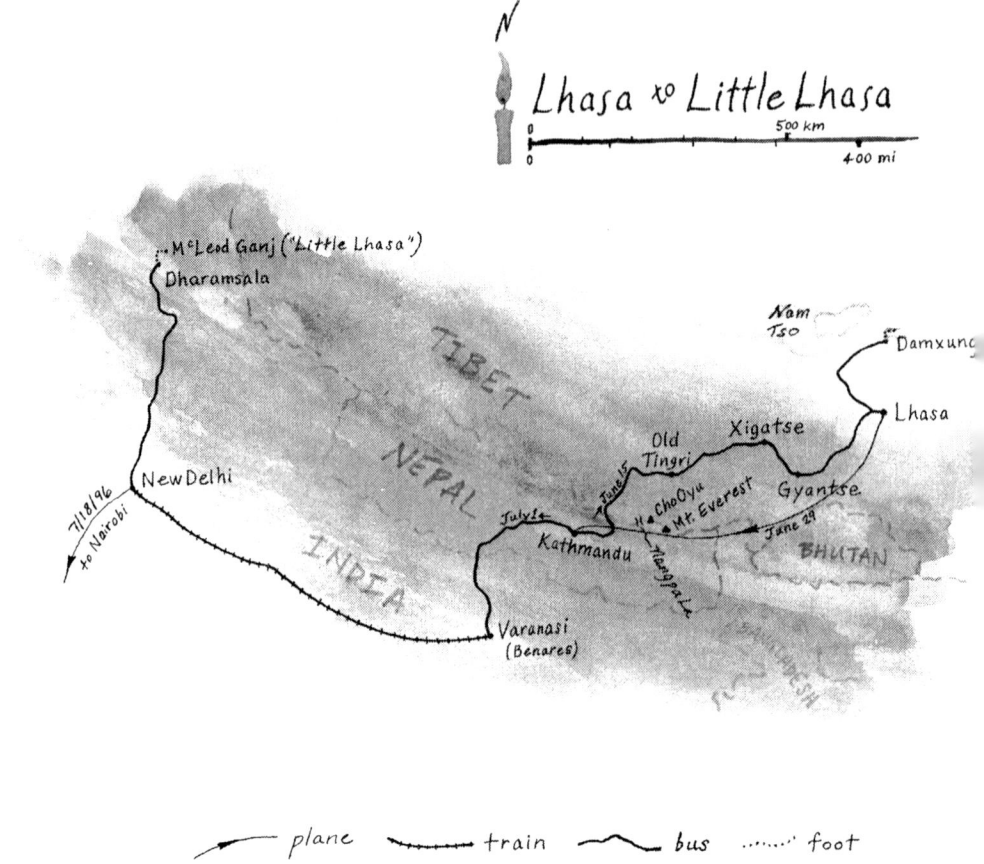

N

500 km
400 mi

McLeod Ganj ("Little Lhasa")
Dharamsala

TIBET

NEPAL

Nam Tso
Damxung
Lhasa

Old Tingri
Xigatse
Gyantse

7/18/96 to Nairobi
New Delhi

INDIA

June 15
Cho Oyu
Mt. Everest
June 29

July 1
Kathmandu
Thangla La

BHUTAN

Varanasi (Benares)

BANGLADESH

→ plane —•—•— train ⌒ bus ⋯⋯ foot

13

The Friendship Highway

> *The antidote to hatred in the heart, the source of violence, is tolerance. Tolerance is an important virtue of Bodhisattvas—it enables you to refrain from reacting angrily to the harm inflicted on you by others. You could call this practice 'inner disarmament,' in that a well-developed tolerance makes you free from the compulsion to counterattack.*
>
> -The 14th Dalai Lama,
> "The Dalai Lama on China, Hatred, And Optimism,"
> *Mother Jones*, December 1997

I was born into an overly consumptive culture in which material gain for one individual or group usually necessitates loss or suffering for another; a culture so bent on compulsive growth that "well-being" seems increasingly equated with gluttony—insatiable desires for more food, land, money, and possessions, and the thirst for more comfort, when less would do. Left unrestrained, our culture has the capacity to expand our numbers and extend our influence over every last inch of the earth.

Indeed, mounting evidence suggests that we are depleting the very natural resources upon which our survival depends far more quickly than the earth's natural processes can replenish them. I worry where this path is leading us, and ponder more each day how we, as individuals or a community of human beings, can honor

Equatorial Crossings

Thoreau's memorable plea to "Simplify." It seems this route of headlong greed, of always rushing into the future as if time were just another commodity to exploit, has shuttled American society not only to alarming environmental degradation, but also greater unhappiness, less time for family and friends, and growing intolerance of others' religious beliefs, sexuality, values, or simple need for space and quiet.

For these reasons among many, Tibetan Buddhism, with its tenets of tolerance, inner disarmament, and universal compassion for all life forms, has long been intuitively appealing to me. At this stage of my life, inner disarmament especially intrigues me because of the growing frequency and intensity of violence, terrorism, and warfare around the world. As espoused by the Dalai Lama, inner disarmament is a simple concept that should have universal appeal, but doesn't. Perhaps nations won't disarm militarily until individuals do internally. If so, then lasting world peace can only come about through internal transformation — world peace through inner peace, inner peace through universal compassion. We are, after all, the only species on the planet endowed with the capacity for reason, and the inherent ability to choose to preserve, rather than destroy, our fellow creatures — and each other.

Our journey to Tibet began in Kathmandu, Nepal, on June 15, 1996. For five days, we traveled overland by minibus along the Friendship Highway from Kathmandu to Lhasa. This "highway" — nothing more than a steep, rutted, yak-trail converted to a road — took us through some of the most spectacular scenery in the world: from the lush, almost tropical-looking forests and precipitous river gorge near the Tibetan border checkpoint at Zhangmu, over three towering mountain passes above 17,000 feet, and up onto the arid, nearly treeless Tibetan Plateau.

We were joined by eleven other travelers from Japan, Belgium, Wales, Israel, Denmark, and the U.S., as well as a Tibetan driver (Tsering Dorje), a Tibetan guide (Cham Chong), and a Chinese guide (Miss Lu), whom many of us believed was along as an informant, not a "guide-in-training," as she professed. Accustomed to traveling independently for the previous eight months, Ann and I were delighted to discover how well this diverse group of people coalesced into a temporary family. We laughed easily together, engaged in spirited debates, explored similarities and differences between our respective cultures, and nursed each other through altitude sickness.

The Friendship Highway

One afternoon we stopped in a place called Old Tingri, from where we could see Mt. Everest (29,035 ft) and Cho Oyu (26,906 ft), and just below Cho Oyu, Nangpa La — the 18,000+ foot pass where many Tibetans have died trying to escape into Nepal. At sunset and sunrise, I spent hours trying to photograph the subtle patterns of light that painted the mountains and clouds into the watercolor grandeur of a Thomas Moran masterpiece. Stretched out before me was a vast and fragile landscape unlike any other place on earth: a landscape still graced with pockets of undisturbed wilderness, which shelter wild horses, kiang, blue sheep, and snow leopards — endemic species I sensed were out there, but never saw; and a landscape increasingly scarred by Chinese military encampments, bulldozed rivers, and obliterated monasteries that I saw far too often.

From the crest of a hill near a demolished former monastery, I watched in silence as Tibetan men, women, and children toiled. They were busy digging up 2-foot x 2-foot plots of sod, loading them on horse-drawn, wooden carts, and then stacking the sod blocks, like bricks, to dry in the sun. I surmised these were the building blocks for future homes. I descended the hill to get a closer look, and I was instantly overwhelmed by five snotty-nosed, earth-caked Tibetan kids, who rubbed the hair on my bare arms, poked skinny, candy-grubbing fingers into my pockets, and grappled to determine who would hold my hands. This was my first physical contact with Tibetan children, and their filth and overt begging initially dismayed me. Now, however, through the lens of time and distance, I chuckle at the experience, and draw on it as a reminder to leave my western sensibilities and judgmental inclinations behind when I travel.

That night, the few of us not overcome by altitude-induced nausea stood on the roof of our guesthouse and gazed at the endless stars. It was cold, still, and moonless. Without any artificial lights to obscure our vision, the night sky was brilliant. The snow on Cho Oyu glistened in the starlight. I closed my eyes and tried to imagine how arduous the journey must be from where I stood to Nangpa La, the most distant landform on the horizon. The escape route to Nangpa La takes up to one month, and Tibetans often travel at night in the middle of winter to avoid detection by Chinese border guards. The escapees must travel fast and light, with very little food, and wearing shoes and clothing that are woefully inadequate for the severe weather, ice, and high altitude. Those who struggle to keep up are often, out of necessity, left behind.

Equatorial Crossings

Yet, every year, more than 3,000 Tibetans arrive in McLeod Ganj, the Tibetan community in exile in northern India. What drives so many Tibetans, many of them children sent by their parents, to risk their lives crossing Nangpa La? To leave their homeland, not knowing when, or if, they will ever return? Some may be driven by the hope of a better education in Nepal or India than what they can receive in the Chinese schools in Tibet. Others may be driven by the desire to escape Chinese oppression, and the lure of a new life or perhaps a better rebirth in freedom. All are driven by the desire to receive a blessing from their exiled spiritual leader, the Dalai Lama, who personally greets all new refugees who survive the journey to McLeod Ganj.

Standing on that rooftop and staring into the flickering expanse of sky, the gravity of the Tibetans' plight sunk in. The realities of Chinese occupation that I had read so much about in *Tibet Information Network* news updates and the *Tibetan Monitor* newsletter suddenly seemed far grimmer, far more chilling than the night air in Old Tingri:

- An estimated 1.5 million Tibetans have died of execution, torture, starvation, and suicide since the Chinese Red Army invaded Tibet in 1949.

- More Chinese now live in Tibet than Tibetans (5.5 million Chinese [250,000 of these military personnel] compared with 4.2 million Tibetans).

- As an incentive to resettle in Tibet, the Chinese government offers Chinese citizens wages up to 87% higher than in China.

- In 1979 the Chinese government introduced a one-child policy in Tibet, and Tibetan women are often coerced or physically forced into having abortions.

- There are hundreds of known political prisoners in Tibet (and thousands more suspected), and more than 50% of the known prisoners were arrested while minors.

- More than 5,000 monasteries were looted or destroyed in Tibet during Chairman Mao's Cultural Revolution (1966-1976).

- China has felled half of Tibet's forests and extracted more than a quarter of Tibet's mineral resources since 1949.

The Friendship Highway

- China admitted in an official *Xinhua* news report on July 19, 1995 to dumping nuclear waste on the Tibetan Plateau near the shores of Lake Kokonor, the most sacred of all Tibetan lakes.

And the list of atrocities goes on and on.

The next day our minibus was flagged to a halt at a military check post. I watched in both anger and fascination as Chinese guards ransacked all of our possessions, looking (presumably) for images of the Dalai Lama. Several weeks earlier at Ganden Monastery, Chinese security forces shot several monks who refused to remove photos of the Dalai Lama from their monastery. Tibetans are routinely imprisoned, tortured, or even killed for simply possessing a picture of their God-King.

Cham Chong had warned us in advance that somewhere along the route to Lhasa we would likely be searched, and that he would be in grave danger if any of us were caught with photos or postcards of the Dalai Lama. The only photo we had was a Dalai Lama image in our Tibet guidebook, which Cham Chong assured us we didn't need to tear out. I realized, as I watched the guards rifle through our belongings and toss them to the ground, that this was the latest perplexing form of Chinese control and intimidation. I searched the guards' faces for emotion that wasn't there. They were robots performing as programmed. One at a time, we were called forward to claim a pack and unveil its contents. Toothpaste tubes were squeezed. Journals were scrutinized. Every stuff sack, plastic bag, and container was emptied onto the dirt. How one could hide a photo in a toothpaste tube still baffles me. If one picture is worth a thousand words, what is one picture of the Dalai Lama worth? 1.5 million Tibetan lives?

The central tenet of Tibetan Buddhism is universal compassion. For Tibetans, the path to happiness and inner peace is elimination of suffering for *all* sentient beings. In contrast, for the Chinese government, the perceived path to happiness is economic growth and centralized power. Tibetan Buddhism is called "poison," and the Tibetan people are viewed as mere road bumps on the imperial highway. This revelation jolted me as we sputtered away from the check post back onto the well-traveled path ironically called the Friendship Highway.

On the floor underneath my seat was my journal full of scathing indictments of the Chinese government, and a coverless copy of *A Stranger in Tibet*, the riveting story of a Japanese Zen Monk who illegally entered Tibet in July 1900 to search for original Mahayana Buddhist manuscripts. The robots hadn't bothered to search our minibus.

⇒·⇐

Three long days after leaving Kathmandu, we finally visited our first Tibetan monastery in Xigatse, the second largest city in Tibet. Xigatse's Tashi Lhunpo Monastery is one of the most famous monasteries in Tibet, because it is the historical seat of the Panchen Lama, the second most revered Tibetan spiritual leader next to the Dalai Lama. I asked Cham Chong what he knew about Gedhun Choekyi Nyima, recognized by the Dalai Lama as the reincarnation of the tenth Panchen Lama. Cham Chong's reaction startled me. He became visibly frightened and he didn't, or perhaps couldn't, speak for more than a minute. He withdrew his head into his shoulders, like a turtle seeking the refuge of its hard, exterior shell. Later, he motioned me into a dark hallway away from the tour group, where he pleaded that I not ask any more questions about the Panchen Lama.

According to news reports in the western media, the Chinese government kidnapped 6-year-old Gedhun and his entire family in late 1995 and subsequently named their own puppet, a Chinese boy, as the eleventh Panchen Lama. No event since the Cultural Revolution has caused such heightened tension between Tibet and China. Tibetans view Chinese meddling in the selection of the Panchen Lama, the most sacred of Tibetan Buddhist rituals, as a heinous, politically-motivated crime. Since the 15th century, the Dalai Lama has recognized the reincarnation of the Panchen Lama, and vice versa. Thus, the current Panchen Lama has the authority to recognize a successor to the current Dalai Lama upon his death. Within the Tibetan community, there is growing concern about the fate of their homeland. The 14th Dalai Lama is in exile in India and the 11th Panchen Lama is in prison in Beijing, or perhaps even dead. What will happen to Tibet when Tenzin Gyatso, the 14th Dalai Lama, dies?

In the days to follow, Cham Chong would several more times express his fear of reprisal if he were to answer my probing questions about Chinese policies and activities in Tibet. I longed to converse with him, as he was my sole source of information regarding the Tibetan perspective on Chinese oppression. I trusted him and wanted him to trust me. But I quickly learned that I must be far more careful, for imprudent words and actions on my part could have severe repercussions for him and other Tibetans.

The Friendship Highway

Tashi Lhunpo, the largest monastery on our tour, was constructed in 1447 AD by the first Dalai Lama, Gendun Drub, and served for more than five centuries as one of the major monastic universities in Tibet. During the Cultural Revolution, China partially destroyed Tashi Lhunpo, along with an estimated 5,000 other monasteries the Red Guard looted and razed. In the early 1990s, the Chinese government decided Tashi Lhunpo was one of several remaining monasteries they would restore, in the hope that western tourists would spend money to come here.

I stood on the same sacred ground as thousands of monks before me, in a building centuries older than any in my native America. What mystery, what wisdom was stored in these hallowed walls? Dim light filtered through the small, overhead windows of the main assembly hall, highlighting rows of purple and saffron robes left behind by monks. One room of the monastery was cluttered with white silk prayer scarves, large drums on long wooden handles (*nga*), pellet drums (*damaru*), cymbals (*rolmo*), conch shell horns (*dungkar*), and exactly 108 frayed and yellowed prayer books. In the palace of the tenth Panchen Lama, we saw literally hundreds of statues of Buddhist deities, including a stunning 100-foot tall statue of Buddha Champa, the future Buddha, plated with gold, and the jeweled throne of the tenth Panchen Lama, his robe poised as if awaiting his return.

The visual feast was too rich to digest: yak butter candles provided minimal light, but enough to make out the soot-stained walls with original, blackened murals from the 15th century depicting Buddha's teachings; *thangkas*, sacred paintings on silk that are visualization aids for meditation, hung from wooden rafters; and a small turquoise swastika was embedded in the floor.

"A swastika?" I whispered incredulously to Ann. I crouched to touch the stones, fixated on the symbol and wanting to verify its meaning. Sensing my discomfort, Cham Chong explained, "The swastika is a Tibetan symbol of good luck, not Hitler." After returning home, I learned that the swastika is the oldest emblem in the world. This universal symbol of good luck has been found in ancient Rome, excavations in Grecian cities, on Buddhist idols, and on Chinese coins dated 315 B.C. Native Americans used the swastika as an amulet. My only previous frame of reference for the swastika was its use as a Nazi symbol—a visceral image of horrific carnage.

Cham Chong was exceptional at deciphering for us some of the intricacies of Tibetan Buddhism. We learned from him about many deities and figures: *Chenrezig*, the deity of compassion of whom the Dalai Lama is an incarnation; *Majushiri*, the expression of the Buddha's wisdom; *Sakyamuni*, the historical Buddha; *Padmasambhava*, the tantric master; *Milarepa*, the poet; *Marpa*, the famous translator of Indian Buddhist texts; and *Dolma*, the female manifestation of perfected wisdom and compassion. Mesmerized by Cham Chong's descriptions, I became enmeshed in a culture and belief system that I knew I could never fully grasp.

I sat down on the dirt floor and drifted off to the monotone hum of Cham Chong's voice. I visualized the life of a monk in this monastery: the daily rhythm of prayer, meditation, chanting, prayer, meditation, chanting. And I imagined how vibrant this place must have been at its peak with more than 4,000 monks in residence, compared to the 400 at present. My shoulders slouched forward and my lower back ached, unable to bear the weight of Tibet's troubled history. I leaned against a mud wall and shivered at the cold silence that enveloped me.

Unlike the city of Xigatse, Gyantse has retained much of its Tibetan character. The storefronts and most of the people we saw were Tibetan rather than Chinese. In Gyantse, we ate at our first Tibetan-owned restaurant. Over fried yak meat, vegetable and mutton momos, egg noodle soup, and rice, we bonded with three of our fellow travelers, Liz, Bert, and Hein, who were each traveling for a year or more. The bond we formed that night would sustain us through the remainder of our time together in Tibet. We shared common experiences, the joys and pitfalls of travel, and the serendipity of life on the road. We laughed as heartily as we had in our previous eight months of traveling, but the mood turned more somber as the meal progressed.

For hours we discussed the parallels and contrasts of the Tibetans' plight and that of the Australian Aborigines, New Zealand Maoris, and North American Indians. We pondered what it is about human nature that has fostered and maintained such oppression throughout history? Answers were elusive. There was little refuge in the realization that each of us comes from a dominant white culture, where freedom, education, and opportunity are taken for granted. Yet, we all belong to a larger culture, the family of humankind. For Ann and me, meeting this greater family was a major incentive for traveling.

The most impressive building in Gyantse was the beautiful Kumbum Stupa, built in 1440 AD. The three-tiered *stupa* is several hundred feet high and resembles a giant swirled soft-serve ice cream cone, topped with 13 gold-plated rings and painted on four sides with the "all-seeing" eyes of Buddha. According to Cham Chong, each tier contains many separate shrines—108 in total. As we ascended the stupa, we discovered that each shrine was dimly lit by a yak butter candle, which illuminated the statue of a significant deity, or an original, undamaged mural. These intricate murals are thought to be some of the oldest remaining Buddhist paintings to survive the pillaging of the Cultural Revolution.

From the top of the stupa, we had expansive views of the Nyon Chu valley and the surrounding agriculture. Although Gyantse was fairly lush in comparison to many parts of Tibet we had seen, the view of the small, green agricultural plots, interspersed among huge piles of rock, reminded me again of the hardship of growing anything in this harsh climate with few trees, lashing winds, and little arable soil.

Instead of joining the others on the tour bus, Ann and I walked back to the hotel. Along the way, two gruff-looking Tibetan women stopped and stared at us like we were from another planet. I placed one of my size 10-1/2 sandaled feet next to one woman's felt and yak-skin boots and motioned that I wanted to trade shoes. They both looked shocked, then smiled, and finally erupted in laughter. We laughed, too, and I was tickled that they understood the absurdity of my joke. Cumulatively, such brief contacts with Tibetans helped me to understand just how important humor is in their lives. In retrospect, I realize humor has helped them survive all the horrors of occupation. Tibetans' sense of humor is seemingly an outward manifestation of their inner peace.

The next day the rear axle of our bus broke for the second time that day, and I took advantage of the opportunity to talk one-on-one with Cham Chong, without the fear of being overheard by Chinese informants or the risk of "bugs" in the walls. I was impressed that he had taught himself English so that he could guide trips when he wasn't teaching school. We talked about Tibet's plight and his hopes for the future. I asked if he would ever consider leaving Tibet. "Where would I go?" he replied. "My family and my work are here, and the Dalai Lama has asked us not to leave. By leaving, we only increase the Chinese influence over our country." I was disgusted to learn first hand what I had previously only read: the Chinese government forces most Tibetan students to learn only Chinese in school, and Cham Chong is forbidden to teach his students their own language, history, or religion.

Traditionally, children learned about Tibetan Buddhism and history at the monasteries, where every Tibetan child (male and female) would spend a minimum of one year. The Chinese government has disallowed this practice. I wondered how

Cham Chong could remain so cheerful in the face of such subjugation, and so I asked. He told me he considers himself lucky. His family runs a successful business in Lhasa and his parents are resourceful and well educated. Only 24, he has already been given opportunities for social and intellectual advancement that few Tibetans have in an entire lifetime. Thus, he feels it's his obligation, as a teacher and devout Buddhist, to help Tibetan children—a role he fulfills with great sincerity and compassion. From this conversation, I gained profound respect for Cham Chong's knowledge and commitment to preserving Tibetan culture from within his homeland rather than in exile. I would have chosen exile.

While I was talking with Cham Chong, Ann, Amy, and Limore wandered off to strike up conversations with some Tibetan laborers, two men and one woman, who were digging sand and loading it into dump trucks at a nearby Chinese gold mine. Unable to do much more than exchange names, Ann decided to show them how her point-and-shoot camera works. Miss Lu emerged from out of nowhere and emphatically scolded Ann, "No photo here."

After five long days on this yak trail called a highway, a broken axle, several other bus breakdowns, and a search by armed Chinese guards, we arrived in Lhasa at 1:30 am on June 20th, my 33rd birthday. Our hair, clothes, and backpacks were permeated with a thin layer of fine road dust. We were exhausted, but thrilled to finally be in the "forbidden city," which for centuries was isolated from the outside world. Being here felt like a gift, especially after learning in Kathmandu, via the travelers' grapevine, that China was preventing any independent travel into Tibet. Ann and I briefly reveled in the realization that we would celebrate not only my birthday, but also our fifth wedding anniversary and her 35th birthday, here in Lhasa. Punchy giddiness gave way to deep sleep.

Stiff and tired, we arose early the next morning anxious to explore this holy city, and we spent my birthday at two monasteries on the outskirts of Lhasa. Drepung Monastery, established in 1416 AD, was once the largest monastic institution in the world, housing about 15,000 Buddhist monks at its zenith, up until the Chinese invasion of Tibet in 1959. Following the invasion and destruction of an estimated 70 percent of the monastery, 250 monks managed to escape the holocaust and rebuild their monastery in southern India. The Drepung Monastery in India has grown to about 2,500 monks, mostly young spiritual aspirants who have fled Chinese-occupied Tibet. The Drepung Monastery in Lhasa has been partially rebuilt and there we had the privilege of watching the resident monks debate Buddhist philosophy.

Monks in Tibet are highly respected for their wisdom and intelligence, and debating, we were told, helps keep the monks stimulated. These daily debates, called *tsen-nyi* ("reflective inquiry"), are an elaborate form of both physical and mental exercise, in which monks are encouraged to challenge each other's understanding of Buddhist philosophy. In a courtyard setting underneath clumps of shade trees, we watched as the most animated of the debaters threw his whole body into directing a question at his opponent. Like a baseball pitcher firing a fastball, the inquirer would wind up and hurl his question, punctuated by abruptly smacking his hands together in a loud *CLAP*. Instantly, the respondent, the catcher within this baseball metaphor, would snap back his reply with a resounding *CLAP* of his own, as if he were saying, "Come on, throw strikes." The pitcher would then frame a new question, a curve ball or change-up, designed to expose flaws in the catcher's stance. The occasional wild pitch was greeted with a boisterous "you must be joking" laugh from the catcher.

From a distance, the clapping sounds of the pairs of monks debating reminded me of a strand of firecrackers exploding sequentially. The monks, both the active debaters and the observers, appeared to genuinely enjoy this vigorous activity. I imagined that the debates were a refreshing change from long days of solitary meditation and prayer.

Later that same day, we arrived at Sera Monastery at the start of an elaborate welcoming ceremony for a new monk. In the main Assembly Hall, more than 600 resident monks gathered to welcome the young boy. A wrinkled Tibetan woman with dark, sparkling eyes patted the ground, inviting me to sit down next to her. I bowed my head and smiled, accepting her offer. From this prime spot, I could peer over a railing at the monks 30 feet below us. I watched and listened as the monks chanted in unison, led by the deep, guttural voice of the rinpoche. When I closed my eyes, the rhythmic chanting felt like it was emanating from within me, and, for a fleeting moment, I was a chanting monk, rather than an awed observer.

The chants of the monks carried me back in time, through the corridors of Tibetan history: a history woven with strife, hardship, and turmoil; a history of hope and survival. I imagined I was the poet, Milarepa, meditating in a cave for six years in search of nirvana and subsisting on only berries and leaves:

> *Having meditated on love and compassion*
> *I forgot the difference between myself and others.*
> *Having meditated on my lama,*
> *I forgot those who are influential and powerful.*
> *Having maintained pure awareness,*
> *I forgot the illusions of ignorance.*
> *Having meditated on this life and the life beyond,*
>   *I forgot the fear of birth and death.*

What was this strange grip Buddhism was gaining on me? What did it all mean? In the midst of this Buddhist ritual was I rejecting my own Christian upbringing? "Dave . . . DAVE, time to go." Cham Chong was shaking my shoulder.

That's the problem with group tours: tour leaders always seem in a hurry to get to the next stop on the itinerary, right when you're approaching some crystalline insight about the significance of the present stop. Later, Cham Chong told us he had learned that the young monk's father had bribed Chinese officials with an unbelievable sum of money (the equivalent of $7,500 US) to ensure that his son got into the monastery. Everyone in attendance, even lucky tourists like us, received white silk prayer scarves (*kata*) blessed by the rinpoche for good luck. We were surprised to be so openly welcomed and included in this Buddhist ritual, and delighted that serendipity had found us once again. My Sera prayer scarf is now draped around a framed image of the Tibetan Plateau in the living room of our home. I cherish the scarf as an uplifting reminder of the resonant experience of attending this young monk's blessing ceremony, and a symbol of my ongoing attraction to Tibetan Buddhism.

The Friendship Highway

Late afternoon, Ann and I parted from the tour group and explored Lhasa on our own. The streets were a noisy, dirty, smelly snarl of Chinese bicycles, motorcycles, rickshaws, cars, buses, trucks, and motorized three-wheel tractors. Most of the businesses were Chinese-owned and had either neon lights or wooden signs, hand-painted with Chinese characters. Most of the people we saw on the streets looked Chinese rather than Tibetan, and it seemed as though we were witnessing first hand the dilution of Tibetan culture; Tibetans in Lhasa were merely grains of salt suspended in the sea of Chinese immigrants.

Ann and I had plans to go out for a special birthday dinner, but instead she surprised me by taking me to the hotel restaurant, where our whole tour group was assembled. We laughed and joked into the early hours of the morning. The Tibetan cook at the Banakshol Hotel made an outstanding chocolate cake, even though birthdays are not celebrated in Tibet. In this culture, where reincarnation is an accepted truth, the day of death is far more significant than the day of birth. Nevertheless, the whole restaurant sang happy birthday to me, and the kitchen staff gave me a prayer scarf for good luck, my second kata that day.

On June 21st, our fifth wedding anniversary, we toured the world famous Potala Palace. Completed in the mid-1600s, the palace served as the winter home of every Dalai Lama from the fifth through the fourteenth, until the fourteenth and current Dalai Lama fled in 1959 when China invaded Tibet. Perched on the side of a steep mountain high above Lhasa, the red and white Potala commands attention. From the outside, the Potala is the most astounding architectural masterpiece I have ever seen. Soaring more than 350 feet, the palace is comprised of thirteen stories of wood, earth, and stone, and, according to Cham Chong, more than 1,000 rooms, now mostly empty. Formerly the home of thousands of monks, the Potala is no longer inhabited by Tibetans — only Chinese guards.

Inside, the sacred palace felt like a morgue, nothing more than a macabre museum filled with surveillance cameras. Some Tibetan pilgrims still do daily circumambulations or prostrations around the perimeter of the Potala, but Cham Chong told us that most Tibetans refuse to set foot inside until the Dalai Lama returns from exile in India and Tibet is once again a free country. The Potala miraculously survived the Cultural Revolution and has, thus far, survived Chinese occupation. Tibet may not.

At the base of the Potala, Chinese vendors hawk imported fruits and vegetables, as well as butchered meat, live fish, and various housewares in a sprawling open-air market. Nowhere in the market did I see any Tibetans. Tibetan homes, many of them centuries old, were razed here and neighborhoods were uprooted to make way for a Tiananmen-style square. Looking across this square from the main facade of the Potala, one sees an immense, concrete-block Chinese disco, which throbs into the night with blaring music and gyrating spotlights that puree the once luminous sky into a lifeless pulp. In a scene too surreal to believe had I not witnessed it in person, Chinese couples circle around an artificial pond in neon-lit paddleboats, while Chinese prostitutes roam the square.

With excessive pride, Chinese residents in Lhasa point to the concrete square, the artificial pond, and the nightlife as shining examples of how the Chinese government is improving life for Tibetans. It's true, from what I've read, that modern plumbing, telecommunications, electricity, and a multitude of other so called "improvements" were non-existent in Tibet prior to the arrival of the Chinese. Yet, the Chinese government neglects to mention, despite world outrage, that it has killed more than a million Tibetans and outlawed the teaching of Tibetan language and culture in schools, or that the grounds of the Potala, once a place of spiritual pilgrimage for all Tibetans, are now paved for Chinese whores—sacred paths of devotion now cemented in lechery. Tibetan *prostration* to Chinese *prostitution* to world *protestation*: this precipitous skid of words and ideologies left me deflated at the end of the "friendship" highway.

14

Beyond Lhasa

With truth, courage, and determination Tibet will be liberated.

-The 14th Dalai Lama, *1989 Nobel Prize acceptance speech*

Frustrated and dumbfounded by the rampant Chinese oppression that we experienced along the friendship highway, Ann and I left Lhasa to search for "un-Chinafied" Tibetan culture. Along with our new friend David, a fellow American from the tour group, we boarded a public bus that took us about 75 miles north of Lhasa to a small, roadside settlement called Damxung. There, we hoped to hitchhike another 40 miles or so to a remote lake called Nam Tso, a pilgrimage destination for some devout Tibetans. In Lhasa, we had learned that Nam Tso was one of the few places the Chinese government was allowing foreigners to go in Tibet without hiring Chinese guides and applying for outrageously expensive permits.

The bus lurched along a raging, muddy river for several hours, before climbing up and over a mountain pass at which all the Tibetans on the bus whooped and threw stacks of 2-inch x 2-inch papers printed with Buddhist scriptures out the windows. We descended back down into the greenest, most fertile-looking river valley we had seen in Tibet. Yellow, mustard-like flowers lined the banks of the river. Rock-strewn goat and yak pastures, interspersed with fields of barley, dominated the surrounding landscape. I remembered reading in Namche Bazaar that these prehistoric-looking yaks are absolutely essential to the survival of Tibetans, who depend on these rugged animals for meat, butter, milk, hair for blankets, hide for clothing and tents, dung for fuel, fertilizer, and most importantly, transportation.

After eating lunch at a roadside stall near where the bus dropped us, we hiked to the junction of the road to Nam Tso. We dropped our backpacks at a bridge and tried for five hours to hitchhike. Only three vehicles passed. None stopped. Late in the afternoon, as we were debating what to do, a Tibetan woman named Kaysang and her two daughters stopped to talk to us. She didn't speak any English, but motioned for us to follow her.

And follow we did, although I stopped often to photograph this idyllic valley. The sky was a vivid blue, scattered with white-rimmed but otherwise black cumulus clouds, through which the sun periodically crept, illuminating the valley in golden light. At the head of the valley, as far as I could see on the horizon, was a perfectly formed rainbow. I ran a short distance to a stone wall, where I could get a wide-angle shot of a nomad's tent next to a small creek in the foreground, and a backdrop of the mountains, the clouds, and the rainbow. From the tent emerged a young couple and their daughter, who approached me with big smiles. Using hand signals, they invited me into their tent for tea. Reluctantly, I declined, motioning off in the distance toward Ann and David and gesturing how I needed to run and catch up with them.

It was nearly dark when Kaysang led us to a windowless, rectangular, concrete-block house, where the tenants agreed to let us spend the night. We gave Kaysang three oranges and some coins and thanked her for helping us; she and her daughters kept walking. Although the house was very warm, thanks to a well-stoked wood stove, we felt uncomfortable under the unblinking stares of the two men and one woman who intently watched our every move. One of the men wore a green military-style jacket and dark sunglasses, even at night when candles provided the only light. Our repeated efforts to communicate met with silence and more stares—cold stares that suggested their silence wasn't solely attributable to the language barrier. We weren't even certain that these were Tibetans; the concrete-block house and their style of dress looked Chinese. Were they planning to report us to Chinese guards in Damxung in the morning? Too intimidated to even ask for hot water, we ate a cold meal of apples, yak cheese, and cookies, then Ann and I immediately curled up together in our one sleeping bag. I faced the wall and pulled the bag over my head in a conscious attempt to shut out the stares.

The next morning, after a nearly sleepless night, we decided not to try and get to Nam Tso. We were concerned that even if we did make it to the lake, we might get stuck there, and we didn't want to risk missing our flight back to Nepal in three days or overstaying our visa. We opted instead to investigate a small village with eight or ten houses, which we had noticed to the west the previous evening when Kaysang departed with her daughters. After approximately two miles of walking, four Tibetan children ran up to greet us. Throughout our travels, it was always the children who were the most curious, and the least inhibited about trying to communicate. I was pulling some stamps out of my pack to give them, when a young man appeared. "*Tashi Delek, mero nom* David," I fumbled in a crude mix of Tibetan and Nepali, which he somehow understood. He responded by pointing to his chest and telling us his name was Nima Pinza. He motioned toward the village and invited us to follow him to his house for tea.

There we met his mother, Chookoe, whose smile and relaxed manner immediately made us feel right at home. We called her *Ama* (a term of endearment that is the English equivalent of "mama"), and she chuckled. She made us butter tea, the traditional Tibetan beverage of black tea mixed with rancid yak butter inside a 4-foot tall wooden churn with brass fittings. Upon trying my first sip, I had to suppress a gag reflex, as the hot, liquid butter became lodged in the back of my throat. But after several smaller sips, I began to like the warm, buttery sensation in my throat and belly, and I better understood why the Tibetans drink cup after cup of this calorie-rich concoction. Drinking our butter tea turned into a game of sorts. If we emptied our cups, Ama immediately refilled them. But if we left a full or partially full cup sitting for too long, she would motion for us to drink. Ann found the taste of the butter tea revolting, and she finally resorted to gestures to indicate that the tea bothered her stomach. I eventually learned, after six cups, that covering my cup with one hand was the proper signal for no more.

The simple, square house consisted of two rooms: the main room, approximately 100 square feet that served as the kitchen, living area, and sleeping area, and a second room that we never saw inside, whose opening was covered with a yak skin. The house was constructed primarily of rock and mud with very little structural wood, presumably because wood is a rare resource in this mostly treeless region above 12,000 feet. A yak-dung fire burned continuously, keeping the house comfortably warm, but the fire inside the microwave-size, metal stove gave no light, and even in mid-day the interior of the house felt like the inside of a cave. There was only one 24 inch x 36 inch wood-framed window facing north, and the sill was nearly 2-feet deep, suggesting that the walls must be at least as thick. The only other sources of light were from around the edges of the yak skin hanging over the entrance, and a yak-butter candle illuminating a picture of the Dalai Lama. During the time we were there, this candle never went out, and I never saw the family add more yak butter or a new wick.

Ama Chookoe and Nima Pinza watched us with curiosity as our eyes wandered around the room. I was bursting inside with questions that I didn't know how to ask. How long have you lived here? What are those white, paste dots all over the kitchen wall? Do you worry about having a Dalai Lama photo displayed? How much yak dung do you burn in a year? Where do you go to the bathroom? I wanted to jump up and offer to churn the butter tea, or put more yak dung on the fire, or run my fingers across the intricate, blue and red yak-wool rug. I've never been good at communicating with strangers, and I'm even worse at sitting still.

The father of the family, Tseten Dhondup, returned in the early afternoon and all focus shifted to him. Despite our language barrier, "Papa" kept us entertained for hours. His most precious performance was acting out how we should speak to a truck driver if we attempted to hitchhike to Nam Tso. First, he pretended to be us waving down the driver. He taught us to say, *Paysha monga mindu* and *cuchee, cuchee*, which we interpreted to mean, respectively, "I don't have any money" and "please, please." Then, he glared at us and acted out the truck driver's response and we were in complete hysterics. Whenever we didn't understand something, Papa found three or four ways to say or act out the same idea until we finally understood.

During Papa's antics, Ama made us *tsampa* balls, the Tibetan dietary staple made with barley flour, sugar, and yak butter. She gave us each a ball the size of a softball, and showed us how to break pieces off and dip it in our yak-butter tea. While we were eating, a neighbor woman stopped by. Apparently the word had spread that some American visitors were in the village, and we would periodically see curious new faces pop in the door to catch a glimpse of us. The neighbor had her hair braided in the traditional Tibetan style with long, colored strands of yarn woven into two braids of hair and then tied together in the back. Ann asked the woman to braid her hair in the same style with the turquoise and brown Tibetan yarn that I had given her for her birthday. The beaming expression on this woman's face still remains one of my favorite mental images from our travels.

With the aid of our English-Tibetan dictionary, we determined from Papa that Nima Pinza was 24, Ama was a youthful 45, and that he was a very spry 55. This was the archetypal Tibetan family I had read so much about—simple, hearty, gracious beyond any American standard, good-humored, and anxious to learn about the world outside of Tibet. Nima was fairly quiet and reserved around his parents, but once we went outside he quickly became the ringleader around the younger village kids, who all seemed to idolize him. At a creek meandering through a nearby yak pasture, Nima initiated a creek-jumping contest when he launched into a tremendous leap of such grace and power that I was left shaking my head in disbelief. I was further astonished by the jumping ability of all the Tibetan children; even the smallest, only four or five years old, were able to jump two feet or more across the creek. On my first attempt, I soaked both boots.

None of the children had manufactured toys. Instead they played with each other or made toys out of rocks, pieces of yak wool and yarn, dried yak dung, flowers, and any other natural materials they could find. They used the rocks in throwing contests, but also to play a game very much like jacks. The girls in particular liked to play games with the yak yarn, and Ann was able to join right in, because they were similar to games like cat's cradle that she had played as a child. The boys liked to heave chunks of the dried yak dung like a discus, and everyone, except me, could make a shrill whistle by blowing into a conical flower. It was like blowing into a balloon that simply wouldn't inflate. They laughed as I turned purple trying.

One shy little girl led me around by the hand, stopping to pick wild plants for us that tasted like chives. Her hand felt small and coarse in mine, and the leathery skin of her fingers reminded me of her yak-skin garment. She bent to pick wildflowers and then smiled up at me, her striking eyes sweet and wide with innocence. I nearly melted as she nimbly threaded two flowers, one purple and one yellow, through my jacket zipper and wove the stems together. Her hand curled again in mine and she led us to meet her mother, who was milking naks (female yaks) in a pasture by their home. Her mother invited us into their house for butter tea, but, having already consumed at least a dozen cups that day, we politely refused.

The young boy who had limped along behind us all day clung to the colorful apron hanging over his mother's yak-skin chuba. I pointed to his left foot, asking what was wrong with it. I had noticed earlier that the injured boy didn't participate in the jumping contest, and was very careful to walk only on his left heel. She shrugged, but his sister very clearly demonstrated that he had punctured his little toe. David carried him piggyback to a neighbor's house, while I went to retrieve my headlamp, soap, and first-aid kit from my pack at Ama and Papa's.

Equatorial Crossings

In the dim light from a candle, I carefully removed the boy's shoe and examined his foot. His two little toes and the whole top and outside edge of his foot were grotesquely contorted from swelling. His foot was badly infected and caked with dirt. Before a growing audience of villagers, I did the best I could to relieve the boy's suffering. With Ann and David's assistance, I started by soaking the boy's foot in boiled water and washing it with soap. Once the caked dirt was removed, I could see a scab between his two little toes, which I presumed marked the location of the puncture. I sterilized a sewing needle and the tweezers from my Swiss Army knife in a candle flame and carefully probed the scab, while Ann gently spread his toes apart and David held his shoulders. The hot water had loosened the scab enough that it peeled off easily. Pus and blood squirted out, and his toes shrank in size before our eyes. I removed a wood splinter half the length of a toothpick and three times the circumference.

After multiple soakings and squeezings, there was no longer any pus draining out, and despite the boy's stoic resolve not to cry, I knew he was at the limit of his pain threshold. I soaked his whole foot in clean, boiled water one last time and then dressed the wound with antibiotic and a sterile bandage. I looked up into his eyes and asked if he was "OK." He smiled for an instant and limped away as fast as he could. In that fleeting smile, I saw gratitude and savored the warm glow of satisfaction that must sustain those in the medical profession.

By western standards, these were among the dirtiest children we met during our travels, but probably the happiest and certainly the most affectionate toward us. In contrast to my first exposure to Tibetan kids near Old Tingri, I didn't find the dirtiness of these newfound friends repugnant; I simply appreciated these children for what they are: simple beings living a simple existence in harmony with a harsh environment and their Buddhist beliefs. We felt completely comfortable with these Tibetans and they seemed endlessly curious about us.

As the day drew to a close, one young girl adopted Ann. She called herself Saathi (in Nepali, Saathi means "friend") and we soon learned she was the daughter of the woman who had braided Ann's hair earlier in the day. At Saathi's request, Ann ended up staying with this family. David and I spent the night with Ama, Papa, and Nima.

Papa was clearly the head of our household, but not in a domineering way. His family showed him such obvious love and respect, and who wouldn't — the smile rarely left his face. He was funny, compassionate, and reverent. He was a gifted communicator and simply a joy to be around. I wondered if this is what it feels like to be in the presence of the Dalai Lama, the special type of person who lights up a room just by being there.

After my second bowl of rice piled 6-inches high and smothered with yak butter and sugar, Papa surprised us once again, by emerging from the back room with a radio. We listened to the Voice of Tibet (VOT), which broadcasts news in the Tibetan language for 30 minutes every day. The gist of the news, as best as David and I could discern from the few words we understood, was that China had just dropped bombs on Taiwan, and the U.S. was going to Taiwan's aid. It was three days before we learned the actual details, but Papa, acting as an interpreter, indicated that the U.S. was strong (flexed bicep) and good (thumb's up) for standing up (waving fist) to the Chinese (gun to his head).

I was stunned by the fact that Papa even had a radio, and more stunned by the broadcast we had just heard. I slumped onto one of the mud benches, curled into a fetal position, and threw my down coat over me for extra warmth. Less than a minute later, Ama rushed over with a thick wool blanket, which she carefully placed on top of me and then tucked under my feet and between my back and the wall. On top of the blanket she put a yak-skin chuba, and smiled, as if to let me know everything would be all right. Despite the depressing radio broadcast, I fell asleep feeling surprisingly comfortable and at peace, thanks to Ama and Papa. I lay there thinking this was the Tibet we came looking for, and marveling at our good fortune to have stumbled upon it.

I awoke the next morning to the sleepy grin of Papa, and started the day with a good laugh, when he motioned that I should roll over, pull the yak-skin chuba over my head, and go back to sleep. This is exactly what he did for another hour or so, while Ama made us tsampa softballs, dried yak jerky, and butter tea. Later that morning, as I was asking Papa about the previous night's radio broadcast, I was devastated to learn that even in this fairly remote village, the people live in fear of the Chinese. Every time Papa wanted us to know he was referring to the Chinese, he grimaced and shaped his fingers into a gun and menacingly shook it at us.

Our two days in this yak-herders village were really a capsule of our whole Tibetan experience. I suppose in retrospect it is easy to romanticize, and yet, our brief time with the villagers was precious beyond words. The whole scene is still so vivid for me: the frolicking kids, the green pastures, the surreal mountains, the yaks and goats, the acrid smell of yak dung fires, the taste of tsampa and butter tea, and the smiling faces and tears of our generous hosts. On June 25, 1996, I wrote in my journal:

> *I have little doubt that my snapshot into their lives and homes will be one of my most cherished trip memories. I haven't even left yet and I'm already dreaming of returning . . . hopefully during a time when travel in Tibet is less restricted and the ominous specter of Chinese oppression has dissolved.*

As we packed to leave, Saathi's mother sobbed and clutched Ann's arm, reluctant to let her go. She rose and unearthed a small, ragged cardboard box, which she had cleverly hidden in the mud wall. Exiled in the box was her collection of Dalai Lama photos. She touched each photo to her forehead carefully, with reverence, before passing it to us. Tears streamed down the furrows in her weathered cheeks as she formed her trembling thumb and index finger into a gun. She pantomimed how the Chinese would shoot her in the head if they discovered a Dalai Lama picture displayed on her wall. As her whole body shook then tensed, I sensed she had witnessed such an execution. When she pulled the trigger, I recoiled. With my limited Tibetan vocabulary, all I could think to say was "China very bad," and cry for these peaceful, compassionate people.

In several monasteries in Lhasa, and now in this home, I had seen empty picture frames on display. Suddenly, in the aftermath of this woman's painful drama, the magnitude of the empty frame symbolism became clear. The Dalai Lama is missing from Tibet, but not forgotten.

Ann cut out the English-Tibetan language pages and the only photo of the Dalai Lama from our guidebook, and she gave them to her new friend Ani, a nun who was Saathi's older sister. Ani silently accepted the gift with an initial reaction of shock, followed by a meek, touchingly beautiful smile. She put the pages and photo in a small notebook, where she also had a collection of five loose photos of the young Panchen Lama and the Dalai Lama. Ann later wondered and worried if she had in any way placed Ani at risk, given the close watch the Chinese keep on all monks and nuns in Tibet.

Ani shouldered Ann's pack and insisted on walking with us the five miles to the main road. After parting with Ann's host family, Ann, David, and I returned to Ama and Papa's home, where they resolutely refused our offers of money, food, or clothing. I wanted so badly to give Chookoe and Tseten Dhondup something in return for all they had given us, and I was as persistent as I thought I could be without offending them. Ann, David, and I each gave them one of our extra passport photos, and we all signed a single postcard of Olympic National Park with a thank you message that I wrote, as best I could, in both English and Tibetan. To our mutual amazement, Ama placed the photos and postcard on the same shelf as the yak butter candles, next to their Dalai Lama photo. Why was this family willing to openly display the Dalai Lama photo, but Ani and Saathi's family hid theirs in fear, leaving only the empty frame on their altar?

I stashed my pen and secured the last cinch strap on my backpack. The tears started flowing even before I fumbled for the right words to express my profound gratitude. Papa flashed me a reassuring smile and then cradled a dried yak flank in my arms. I opened my mouth to protest, but didn't, couldn't. And I wonder to this day if Papa knows how much our two days together changed my outlook on Tibetan and Chinese relations, magnified my adoration of Tibetan people and their culture, and gave me a sense of hope for world peace.

I strapped the yak flank to the outside of my backpack and hugged Ama and Papa both at once, one last time. "*Tukuche*," I whispered, overwhelmed by their generosity and this selfless gift of one of their most prized possessions. After several minutes, I turned for one last glimpse over my shoulder. Our new friends had parted, except for Papa. He stood next to his meticulously constructed pile of dried yak-dung, smiling, and still waving.

Within a half hour of leaving the village, Ani waved down an enormous truck with wheels half my height, and we pushed and pulled each other into the back. Ani persuaded the driver not to charge us. We thanked her and said our final farewells. For the next 40 minutes, we were tossed around along with eight Tibetans as the truck traversed the deeply rutted road. I gave up trying to stand and sprawled on top of my pack, next to an old man who was balancing tenuously on a tire and leaning against the truck cab. I untied the yak flank from my backpack and offered the sinewy man my pocketknife to cut himself a piece. He burst out laughing, as he bumped his gums together and pointed into his toothless mouth. We all laughed, and I carved a handful of the dried yak meat and offered it to his friend, who was braced in the corner atop a pile of burlap bags filled with grain. He declined, too, knuckling the one remaining tooth suspended like a hangnail from his upper jaw.

The two men stared at each other for an instant, then clutched in writhing hilarity. Spontaneous laughter is the national anthem of Tibet.

※

On the Chinese-run public bus back to Lhasa, I was sitting in an aisle seat, behind and to the left of a Chinese man seated by the window. As we crested a hill, I noticed a lone Tibetan yak-herder who was standing by the side of the road smiling at our passing bus. The Chinese man in front of me leaned out his window and made a gesture at the Tibetan with his little finger. His two friends laughed. I was horrified.

Three days earlier, we had learned from an American studying Buddhism in Lhasa, that the Chinese often use this gesture towards Tibetans. It is somewhat analogous to giving someone the finger in the western world, but far more severe: the connotation is roughly, "I hope you die, scum." Several times we had heard from Cham Chong and other English-speaking Tibetans in Lhasa that the Chinese government indoctrinates Chinese emigrants before sending them to resettle in Tibet. These emigrants are taught that they are inherently superior to Tibetans, who are backwards, dirty, and primitive.

I would like to simply dismiss this regrettable bus incident as a churlish Chinese man acting out his brainwashed delusions. But my journal entry captures the ferocity of the moment better, more accurately, than any after-the-fact relaying of the details through the filter of time and distance:

> 'What are you doing,' I roared. For a brief moment, our eyes locked. I struggled to keep my face expressionless, but my eyes had to have betrayed my rage. Never before had I felt such raw hatred for a fellow human being. It scared me that I was even capable of such vitriolic emotions. Then and there I gained a new and profound respect for Tibetans. Despite such hateful treatment by vermin like this Chinese man, Tibetans remain peaceful people. I realized that universal compassion isn't just a doctrine for Tibetan Buddhists; it's a way of life. I felt suddenly inadequate and riddled with guilt because of my overwhelming desire to spit in this loathsome Chinese man's face. At that instant, he represented for me everything evil in the world.

Until that day, I had never hated anyone. My hands trembled. Rage coursed through me. Fighting the urge to lash out with my fists, I sat on my hands and stared

Beyond Lhasa

at the floor, over and over again repeating a mantra: "Think compassion not violence; think compassion not violence." Perhaps this was a test of my own capacity for inner disarmament. I obviously had a long way to go.

Before visiting Tibet, I was troubled by what I read about the Chinese occupation of this autonomous nation, but no amount of reading could have prepared me for the roller coaster of emotional highs and lows we would experience in Tibet. I formerly believed "cultural genocide" was sensationalistic jargon relished by the news media. Our travels in Tibet taught me what cultural genocide really means, and I am deeply burdened by this knowledge. Captives in the homeland they call *Po*, Tibetans are struggling just to survive under Chinese occupation and the Chinese government's systematic policies designed to obliterate Tibetans and their culture.

An hour later, as we walked back into Lhasa, my mind was still cluttered with a mixture of anger and regret. The bus trip back to Lhasa had shattered the calm we found in the yak-herders' village. Despite my funk, Ann had the foresight to pause and snap a picture that remains one of the more telling images of our travels in Tibet. The photo shows me in mid-stride on the wide, shoulder-less, main street of Lhasa. A motorized, go-cart like vehicle is crossing directly in front of me. On the opposite side of the street are bicycles, pedestrians, and motorcycles, which all look like stage props. Signs written in Chinese characters are visible on every building. My head and torso aren't visible beneath my towering backpack. I'm reduced to blue legs sticking out beneath a red pack. But there, hanging from the pack is Papa's dried yak leg.

I spent the following morning interacting with Tibetans in the Barkhor, my favorite place in Lhasa and the one remaining part of the old Tibetan Lhasa that has survived Chinese occupation. Here the faces are predominantly Tibetan, and the businesses are mostly Tibetan-owned. But armed Chinese guards patrol the area, and I saw many surveillance cameras permanently mounted on rooftops. Twice Chinese guards forced me to break off conversations, when I lingered too long talking to Tibetan vendors. Because of its sprawling market and the lure of the ancient Jokhang Temple, the Barkhor is the heart of Lhasa and probably the busiest place in Tibet. I wandered among the maze of stalls, where venders were selling raw yak meat and produce, prayer flags, incense, jewelry, clothing, shoes, housewares, hardware, and more. The constant stream of worshippers, spinning their prayer wheels, counting their prayer beads, and doing their clockwise circuits around the Jokhang Temple added to the excitement of the atmosphere. It hurt to see all this alone, knowing that Ann was flattened by a second straight day of nausea and painful cramps.

Jokhang Temple, built in 647 AD, draws worshippers from all over Tibet who hope to achieve a better rebirth and salvation in future lives by doing their daily circumambulations here. This temple remains the heart and soul of the Tibetan community living in Lhasa. From the roof of the golden-topped temple, I watched the concentration of worshippers doing their inchworm-like prostrations in front of the temple entrance. Juniper smoke billowed out of two large mud ovens. In the distance, beyond the ebbing tide of Tibetan bodies below me, I could see the imposing Potala, an uninhabited island awash in the occupied Chinese sea. As I admired the devoted worshippers, I shuddered at the bleak thought that one day the Chinese government could overrun the Jokhang Temple, the Barkhor, and, indeed, all of Tibet.

That afternoon, our last in Tibet, Ann rebounded, and together we explored the maze of narrow Barkhor streets. We bought wedding gifts for two newly married couples, souvenirs for our Nepal trekking companion Mike, and a few keepsakes of our own. Our most significant purchase was a Tibetan dzi bead necklace.

When Ann agreed to marry me in 1990, I gave her a wooden ring I carved out of a piece of walnut that I had picked up years before at the Shreffler family farm, homesteaded by my great grandparents in the late 1800s. Ann wore the hand-carved ring for only a week before it cracked in half. For a while afterwards she wore the glued pieces on a necklace, but stopped for fear of losing the ring. In Tibet, I decided I wanted her to have a dzi bead necklace as a fifth wedding anniversary gift—a daily reminder of Tibet and our many world adventures.

Unique to Tibet, intricate black and white dzi beads with oval "eyes" are a rare and precious form of etched agate. Among Himalayan peoples, the dzi is a powerful charm that protects the wearer and holds secrets to be revealed in the future. Cham Chong learned from his grandmother that a person who thinks good thoughts and does good deeds would receive "eternal good luck and health" from a dzi bead. If worn by a bad person, the dzi bead would fly away.

According to Lois Dubin's *History of Beads*, knowledge of the dzi bead is derived from oral traditions and thus there is much controversy concerning their source, method of manufacture, and even precise definition. In Tibetan culture, there is a rich and varied mythology associated with how dzi beads are formed. Some Tibetans say dzi's fall from heaven; others say they are formed underground. One legend suggests dzi beads are created when lightning strikes the ground, and the only way to find a dzi bead is to look for one in barley fields on the Tibetan Plateau. If you see one, you must throw a blanket over it, before it flies away. Another legend teaches that to find a dzi bead you must go to the Amdo region of Tibet, where there are black and white caterpillars that look just like dzi beads. Then, you must strip and throw your dirty clothes over the caterpillars and return in the morning after the caterpillars have turned to stone.

There were a variety of dzi beads available from vendors in the Barkhor, but these imitation dzi beads were made from plastic and mass produced for the tourist trade. We really wanted to find Ann an authentic, stone dzi bead, which meant finding a Tibetan who was wearing one and was willing to part with it. This was a tricky process, because Tibetan custom holds that dzi beads should be passed from one generation to the next within a family. Yet, many savvy Tibetan traders have realized the economic value of dzi beads, and thus, a thriving market exists both in Tibet and Nepal for these beautiful and mysterious beads. Our dilemma was whether we would feel ok about buying a dzi bead necklace that might otherwise have been passed on to the wearer's children.

After hours of searching and nearly giving up, we finally found a Tibetan vendor wearing a two-eyed dzi bead, which he was willing to sell. He took his necklace off and scraped the dzi bead with his pocketknife, showing us that the dzi was stone and not plastic. His opening price was three times higher than we were capable of paying. Nevertheless, after prolonged bartering under the watchful eyes of a growing crowd of Tibetans, we finally agreed on a price and spent all our remaining Chinese currency. Because of the customs and mythology associated with dzi beads, Ann was still hesitant about acquiring a dzi bead in this way. But when she removed the plastic dzi bead necklace from the Annapurna trek and put the new necklace on, an elderly Tibetan woman, who had keenly watched the whole transaction, approached Ann and rolled the dzi stone between her thumb and index finger. She patted Ann on the shoulder and smiled. This simple smile was the reassurance Ann needed, and she didn't remove the necklace for the remainder of our travels.

At dusk we returned to the Jokhang Temple, hoping to watch the resident monks debate, but a sudden, violent downpour squelched any outside activity. The evening debates were canceled. We offered, instead, to help a group of Tibetan pilgrims clean and polish butter lamps. They were incredulous that we wanted to help, as if we were the first visitors ever to offer. I helped polish lamps and cut new wicks. Ann was given the special job of pouring hot yak butter over the wicks. Fittingly, we finished our Tibetan sojourn, working side by side with Tibetans at the Jokhang Temple, the one place in Lhasa where the strength and vitality of the Tibetan community overshadows the Chinese oppression.

This simple moment continues to remind me that Po is a magical place, where the beauty of the Tibetan people eclipses even the splendor of the Himalayas. Yet, the Tibet we discovered was hardly the remote civilization sequestered from the ravages of time that Heinrich Harrar so vividly depicts in his epic book *Seven Years in Tibet*; nor was Tibet the Shangri-La of James Hilton's *Lost Horizon*—hidden, secret, forbidden, a heaven on earth. The Tibet we visited was a haven on earth, an enclave where inner disarmament is possible, and the currency that matters most is spiritual not economic.

15

The Power of Compassion

Compassion is not religious business, it is human business, it is not a luxury, it is essential for our own peace and mental stability, it is essential for human survival.

-The 14th Dalai Lama, *Tibetan Portrait*

*R*ecurring images of Old Tingri, Lhasa, and Damxung spun like prayer wheels across my closed eyelids as we boarded the plane for Kathmandu. Leaving Tibet was like trying to swim against an incoming tide with a leaden body and even heavier mind. When I opened my teary eyes, we were at 30,000 feet, winging along at 500 miles an hour. Yet, time stood still.

Below us loomed Mount Everest at 29,035 feet, so high that she generates her own weather. Lhotse, Nuptse, and Makalu, all spectacular 25,000-plus feet massifs, paled in comparison to Everest, the mountain Tibetans call *Chomolungma*, Goddess Mother of the Earth. From the aerial perspective, our views of the Goddess Mother were even more arresting than from the Solu Khumbu region of Nepal, or from the Tibetan Plateau. I gazed upon her in reverence, as snow blasted horizontally from her summit.

One month earlier, eleven people died on Everest's icy slopes, more than any season in history: experienced guides and their paying clients, solo climbers, and Sherpas. Never before had the ascent of Everest been such a public spectacle. Three different websites provided real-time, cyberspace links to the climbers, while the towering peak became a headstone. The day that we finished our Annapurna trek—May 11, 1996—was the day that finished Scott Fischer, Rob Hall, and nine other Everest climbers for good.

I took a few quick snapshots and became lost in thought. Closing my eyes again, I discovered a collage of faces: Tseten Dhondup ("Papa"), the hateful man on the Chinese bus, Cham Chong, the Dalai Lama, and Rob Hall, somehow summoning the fortitude to name his unborn child (via satellite phone) as he lay dying below the summit of Everest. I tried desperately to make sense of the tragedy on Everest and our many unsettling experiences in Tibet. I longed for some sort of closure.

Closure came, nearly one month later, in McLeod Ganj, India, the home-in-exile of the Dalai Lama and the Tibetan government. We went there hoping to be granted an audience with His Holiness. On the morning we arrived, the Dalai Lama left for Australia on a world tour of his own. Just two hours earlier, there had been a grand procession, during which the Dalai Lama handed out good luck necklaces made by Tibetan monks in exile. Several travelers proudly showed us theirs—handmade of twisted, colored threads.

We had our own necklaces—braids of colorful memories and long, twisted strands of unanswered questions about our experiences in Tibet. We spent hours reading Tibetan journals and newsletters in the Library of Tibetan Works and Archives, until we couldn't stomach any more evidence of Chinese oppression, torture, and genocide. On the way back to our hotel, we stopped at the Namgyal Monastery, which faces the Dalai Lama's residence. Inside the monastery, we discovered the most intricate Buddhist painting I have seen, an exquisite Kalachakra mural that depicts how the universe is reflected in every human being. As I was studying the English description of the mural's significance, a stooped Tibetan man handed me a magazine opened to an article entitled, "The Mission of the Warrior Monk." I read the title out loud, thinking this elderly Tibetan wanted to hear how the words sounded in English. Then, he flipped to a picture on the next page. His picture.

I sat down on the floor beneath the vibrant mural, with the Tibetan to my right, his hand clutching my knee, and Ann to my left, her hands circling my bicep. I read the whole article, swiping at tears and snuffling nose drips, before passing the article to Ann.

This skeletal monk, Jampa Phuntsok, led other monks in armed resistance, when the communist Chinese army stormed the Potala in 1959. Although taking up arms was against his Buddhist beliefs, Jampa prayed for forgiveness and fought for survival. He was thirty at the time, and he spent more than thirty years in Chinese prisons in Tibet—

The Power of Compassion

three decades of physical and psychological terror too brutal to comprehend. He was tortured, beaten, and interrogated so many times that the Chinese didn't know what to do with him and finally turned him loose. In 1991, at the age of 62, Jampa escaped from Tibet into Nepal over 18,753-foot Nangpa La. With assistance from the Tibetan refugee community in Kathmandu, Jampa eventually found his way to McLeod Ganj, where the Dalai Lama has given him the special mission of helping the Tibetan cause by telling his story. Jampa is revered in McLeod Ganj as a national hero. He has inspired hundreds of political prisoners in Tibet, teaching them by example to keep hope alive.

Although he could speak no English, Jampa indicated that he badly wanted to communicate with us. He kept squeezing my hand and patting my arm in an affectionate, paternalistic manner. He pointed with surprising vigor at the Kalachakra mural. I simply nodded and smiled. With the help of another monk who could speak a little English, we made arrangements to meet Jampa the next morning at his room in the monastery. Jampa's whole face lit up when the monk explained to him that we had slides from our recent visit to Tibet.

The next morning, in better light, Jampa's bent body seemed burdened, but his face looked free. With trembling fingers, he carefully held each slide from Tibet up to the window. He studied postcards from our home in Washington, and photos of our families. Jampa showed us photos of himself with other tourists whom he has met while serving as caretaker of the Namgyal Monastery. Jampa's friend, Tse So—a monk in his early thirties who met Jampa in prison in Lhasa—served as an interpreter. Jampa smiled warmly and thanked us again and again for visiting Tibet and for America's help in Tibet's freedom movement. We didn't have the heart to explain that the U.S. government had once again given China "most favored nation" trade status; that money and access to the world's largest market matter more to the U.S. government than the sanctity of human life.

Jampa was a gentle man with bright eyes and a warm smile, hardly the "warrior monk" he was portrayed to be in the magazine article. Yet, he moved his withered 67-year-old body in a tortuous way that made my soul ache. How could anyone, I asked myself, violate this decent man with an electric cattle prod? The proud look in Jampa's eyes will forever remind me that his body was relentlessly beaten but his spirit was never broken.

Like our Tibetan friends outside of Damxung, Jampa was also an extremely gracious and generous host. He served us yak-butter tea and sugar cookies, a surprising blend of salt and sugar on the taste buds. He even showed us how he liked to make tsampa balls by mixing yak butter, hot water, sugar, and barley flour with his fingers, and then molding little doughnut hole-size balls that we could easily pop into our mouths. This process released a pleasant odor reminiscent of hot oatmeal with melted butter on top.

We noticed that Jampa wasn't eating any tsampa. According to Tse So, Jampa eats very little and suffers from constant headaches, nightmares, and nausea. Tea and traditional Tibetan herbs are his sustenance. Tsampa makes him vomit. Thankfully, Jampa has many friends who take care of him, like Tse So and Phurbu, a shy Tibetan refugee who cooks and cleans for Jampa and supports herself by weaving yak-wool rugs. These rugs were remarkable for their artistry and striking colors, as well as the Tibetan history and symbols hand-woven into each piece.

Jampa stood with difficulty and removed a photograph from one wall of his 14-foot square room. His face glowed, as he handed it to Ann. The photo was taken in the Barkhor at a March 5, 1988 peace demonstration. Jampa, standing rigid in his monk's robe in front of the Jokhang temple, raised a fist and cried out, "Free Tibet!" An American journalist captured the priceless image just seconds before Chinese security forces stormed the Barkhor with bullets and tear gas. The peaceful demonstration erupted into a full-scale riot involving 2,000 Tibetans. An estimated 16 Tibetans were killed — some were shot, some were beaten to death with iron bars, and at least two monks were hurled from the roof of the Jokhang Temple. Several days later, at one of the McLeod Ganj guesthouses, we saw a haunting documentary that captured their horrific freefall on film. Eight hundred Tibetans were arrested and thrown in prison. Official Chinese reports put the death toll at one, a Chinese soldier.

I asked Jampa, through Tse So, how Ann and I could best help Tibet's cause. Both seemed uncertain how to answer. Tse So disappeared and returned ten minutes later with a smiling monk named Lobsang, who spoke fluent English, as well as Tibetan, Nepali, and Chinese. We told Lobsang about our sojourn in Tibet: the Chinese guards who searched us for photos of the Dalai Lama; the reported murder of four monks at the Ganden Monastery for refusing to remove photos of the Dalai Lama from the altar; the arrest, at Sera Monastery, of several monks who spoke out following the murders at Ganden; our journey to the yak-herders village outside of Damxung; the Tiananmen-style square, disco, and prostitutes across from the Potala; and our gut-wrenching exposure to the ubiquitous Chinese oppression. As we ranted on and on, he listened calmly, patiently, and then responded with great wisdom.

The Power of Compassion

"Compassion," he said soothingly, "is always better than anger." None of what we told Lobsang shocked or even surprised him. Like the Dalai Lama, Lobsang is filled with unwavering hope. He shares the Dalai Lama's belief that anger is not productive.

Not all Tibetans in exile agree. The Dalai Lama's youngest brother, Tendzin Choegyal, and a growing group of Tibetan intellectuals in McLeod Ganj, claim that a non-violent approach won't work with China, because the Chinese have no conscience, only contempt.

Lobsang advised us to pressure the U.S. government for economic sanctions against China and to personally boycott Chinese products. He urged us to return someday to McLeod Ganj to learn the Tibetan language, so that the next time we visit Tibet we can have an even richer experience communicating with the people. He spoke of how anxious the Dalai Lama is for westerners to meet Tibetans and exchange ideas. According to Lobsang, such exposure will ultimately assist the Tibetan cause. Awareness fosters compassion. And compassion has the power to heal both the giver and the receiver.

Lobsang also translated the address of our yak-herder friends into both English and Chinese characters. He became quite concerned, though, when we explained our hopes of sending pictures and letters to Ama and Papa. He explained that staying in the home of a Tibetan family anywhere in Tibet was illegal, and that our friends could be imprisoned or even shot if the Chinese government intercepted pictures of us with them. We knew we had placed ourselves at risk by visiting them, but this was our first realization that we had put them at risk. This knowledge made the memory of our time together even more poignant. As we parted company, Lobsang whispered that, if we sent the letters and photos to him in McLeod Ganj, he would do his best to get them to the yak herders via their underground network.

Underground network? Had I heard him correctly? I was reminded of the Underground Railroad during the time of slavery in the U.S., and the network of Europeans hiding Jewish refugees during World War II. We profusely thanked Lobsang, Jampa, Tse So, and Phurbu for making us feel so welcome in their home in exile. And for the third time in two days, words turned to tears.

The precious dream of freedom is being kept alive in more than 50 Tibetan refugee settlements in Nepal, Burma, and India. Tibetan culture is flourishing in exile in McLeod Ganj, India, which is sometimes referred to as "Little Lhasa" because in many ways it is more Tibetan than the Lhasa in Tibet. We learned that under the guidance of the Dalai Lama, Tibetans in McLeod Ganj have formed their first democratic government. As we watched hundreds of clean, professional-looking Tibetans in traditional dress cheerfully doing their business around town, Ann remarked, "It's much easier now for me to imagine modern Lhasa had China not invaded. "

In Little Lhasa we visited Tibetan schools, a children's village, a performing arts institute, the library, and several monasteries. By good fortune, we stumbled upon a performance at a local school, where we watched in fascination as four-to-ten-year-old Tibetan refugees sang traditional Tibetan songs, and then, dressed as ethnic groups from around the world (including Chinese), sang in English, "We are the world, we are the children." The melding of these innocent voices still resonates for me, as an uplifting chorus of hope.

Years later, I am still discovering how deeply Tibet penetrated my core. I am burdened by the knowledge that the atrocities I had read so much about are real and ongoing. I am troubled by the guilt associated with discovering my own capacity for hatred on a Chinese bus outside of Lhasa. I am humbled by the realization that, despite everything they have endured, most Tibetan people feel only compassion for their Chinese oppressors, not anger. And yet, upon writing this, I think what arrogance for me to presume I understand Tibetans or their plight after only two short weeks. What I'm really attempting to understand is my own poignant emotions, which haven't faded with time and distance from these experiences.

I know I am profoundly grateful for my brief exposure to new sources of inspiration: the Dalai Lama, ocean of wisdom; Chomolungma, Goddess Mother of the earth; and Jampa Phuntsok, the embodiment of hope ... all lofty company for a wide-eyed traveler. And I trust that Tibetans' Buddhist faith will ensure that their culture survives. With each new Tibetan we met, it became clearer that the Tibetan people as a whole radiate an inner light. I have felt their power of compassion. In all my travels, I have never met people so at peace as Tibetans. They exude humor and compassion. Chinese oppression cannot prevail.

Or can it? Jesus, Mahatma Ghandi, Martin Luther King, Jr., and Yitzhak Rabin all preached non-violence, and each was brutally murdered by fanatics. Is the Dalai Lama next?

"Many times I am asked if I am angry at the Chinese for what has happened," the Dalai Lama writes.[1] "Sometimes I lose some temper, but afterwards I get more concern, more

---

[1] P. Borges. 1996. *Tibetan Portrait: The Power of Compassion*. Rizzoli International Publications, Inc., New York, New York.

compassion towards them. In my daily prayer, I take in their suffering, their anger, and ignorance ... and give back compassion. This kind of practice I continue. Brute force, no matter how strongly applied, can never subdue the basic human desire for freedom."

I hope we may one day return to a free Tibet to visit our yak-herder friends, without fear for their lives or ours, and that I can retell the story of Jampa Phuntsok with a new ending about his return to his homeland, a magical place called Po. Until then, I will cling to my vivid memories. And one image. One image among four thousand slides from our travels:

> It's early morning. Juniper smoke fills the air. Prayer flags flutter. Prayer wheels spin. Tibetan pilgrims walk, limp, and crawl in circuits around the Jokhang Temple, as they have for 1500 years. Young. Old. Men. Women. Crippled. One man among the sea of pilgrims stands out. It's not his tan felt hat with a wide black band, the gray tuft of his billy-goat goatee, his worn beige jacket, or his methodical gait. It's his eyes — that look of utter peace.
>
> I click the shutter, as he rounds a pillar draped with prayer flags. The ball of his prayer wheel is frozen in mid-air, suspended against the muted backdrop of the quivering flags. The blurred bodies of the other pilgrims provide a sense of perpetual motion. He alone is in sharp focus. He is gazing forward and slightly down, his eyes half-squinted yet resolved.

This image visually defines for me the power of compassion: loving kindness is the key to opening one's inner door to happiness. But only now, by defining the image in words, have I discovered its deeper meaning. The ten-letter word compassion is the fortuitous union of seven letter compass and seven letter passion, and more than the sum of its parts. Like the Tibetan's prayer wheel, my spiritual compass may oscillate as I circle through life. The world around me may, at times, seem out of focus, like the backdrop of the slide. And like this man, resolute in the face of all life's troubles, I can still live life with passion. For within compassion, I have found the compass to guide me and the passion to feed my soul.

Southeastern Africa

0 — 800 km
0 — 400 mi

7/19/96 from Delhi

Marich Pass
Kakamega Rainforest
L. Baringo + Bogoria
Masai Mara
L. Naivasha
Nairobi
Serengeti
Ngorongoro
Lake Manyara
Tarangire
Arusha
Mombasa
Wasini Island
Dar es Salaam

KENYA
Equator
TANZANIA

Kapiri Mposhi
ZAMBIA
Lusaka
10/1/96 to Paris
Harare
Nyanga N.P.
Chimanimani N.P.
ZIMBABWE
MOZAMBIQUE

Indian Ocean

plane ······· train ······· bus, "matatu" ······· foot

16

Jupiter's Moons

Be glad of Life!
Because it gives you the chance to love and work,
to play and to look up at the stars.

-Henry VanDyke

We entered the Masai Mara National Reserve as the amber July sun crested the seemingly endless horizon and the undulating grass plains sprung to life in the golden glow of sunrise. Just before dawn, on our way into the Reserve, we had spotted a large, black-maned lion, whose pendulous stomach swung from side to side as he slowly sauntered down the dirt track in front of our jeep. The scene was like something out of a Gary Larson *Far Side* cartoon. Noting the two hoof-like protrusions when his stomach swung to the right, I joked, "He must have swallowed a *whole* zebra for breakfast."

Within thirty minutes of passing through the Olaimutiek gate, we saw hundreds of zebras, scurrying guinea fowl, three browsing elephants, many grazing—but ever alert—impala, and a lethargic herd of more than 500 Cape buffalo, including one massive, overzealous male who repeatedly tried to mount various disinterested females. In every direction I looked, a new animal appeared, and before I had a chance to fully grasp what I was seeing, my attention was diverted to the gasp or "wow" of one of my safari-mates.

Yet, the proximity of the wildlife was even more astounding than the outrageous abundance and diversity. With the aid of binoculars or my 200-mm zoom lens, I had the eerie sensation of being eyeball-to-eyeball with a ten-ton male elephant. I could see the breath of a buffalo and the nervous forelimb twitches of an impala. By zooming in on a zebra's back, I saw the magnificent colored landscape become suddenly and entirely black and white. When I switched to a wide-angle lens, the scene expanded into an impressionist's painting—a study of texture and color over form and detail. In that first thirty minutes, I blazed through three rolls of film, trying futilely to record what my eyes were seeing but my mind couldn't register.

In the language of the indigenous, cattle-keeping Maasai people, *mara* means spotted, a reference to the patchy mosaic of bushes and trees on the grassy plains. Our guide, Njau, surveyed the habitat mosaic with binoculars and then excitedly directed Ken, our jeep driver, to a water hole beneath a group of circling vultures. There, in the golden, creek-side grasses of the Ngama Hills, we discovered a pride of 18 lions devouring a recently killed buffalo. In an adjacent upstream pool was a second buffalo, dead and uneaten. Several hours earlier, under the cover of darkness, this group of three females and 15 cubs must have ambushed the two buffalo as they were drinking.

Ken edged the jeep to within several feet of the feeding frenzy—close enough to hear the crunching of bones and see the ripping of flesh. Two cubs with red muzzles and blood-spattered paws played tug of war with a buffalo rib bone. Fresh blood dripped from the jaws of one female, who was greedily chomping the buffalo's heart and snarling at any cub that dared to come close. I dubbed her "slash-nose" because of the gaping crimson gash on her snout. Njau suspected that this female had led the assault and sustained the injury from the slashing saber tip of a panicked buffalo's horn.

The annual movement of herds of zebras and wildebeests from the Tanzanian Serengeti to Masai Mara is one of the world's most breathtaking wildlife spectacles, known locally as "*The* Migration." It is this migration that maintains the delicate ecological balance of the Serengeti-Masai Mara ecosystem. The Masai Mara's extensive grasslands, opened up by fire and elephants, attract huge herds of grazing herbivores during the Serengeti's dry season. Moderate to heavy grazing of the Mara's grasslands actually stimulates grass growth and results in a greater variety of low-growing palatable species that support the enormous biomass and diversity of these grazers. The abundance of grazers, in turn, provides a ready food supply for the Reserve's many large predators. And the annual July to October tourist pilgrimage mirrors The Migration.

Driving west toward the Central Plains, we saw a herd of elk-like topi, a female elephant romping with her baby in a mud pool, and a listless lioness sprawled with a suckling cub beneath the shade of a nearby acacia tree. At the Mara River, we got out of the jeep and walked around, shaking life back into cramped arms and legs and struggling to fill our lungs with the still, hot air. The shallow, muddy riverbed and sloughing banks were littered with the carcasses of hundreds of rotting wildebeests that had drowned or been trampled during the mass migration. Hooded vultures and marabou storks scavenged the remains. Hippos snorted and belched in the deeper pools, and, although we saw no crocodiles, Njau assured us that they were abundant along this stretch of the river. With such a glut of food, he surmised that the crocs just weren't actively feeding.

After a sack lunch replete with vervet monkeys aggressively pestering us for food, we drove past the hippo pools and up a hill with a commanding view over the Central Plains of the Reserve to the north, and south across the Tanzanian border into the brown grasslands of the Serengeti. We could see hundreds of thousands of wildebeests, zebras, and Thompson's gazelles dotting the Central Plains; the Serengeti looked empty, as if the earth had tilted on its axis, tipping all the Serengeti wildlife into Masai Mara.

Late that afternoon, we saw our first spotted hyenas, a herd of sleek Grant's gazelles, and one of the estimated ten remaining black rhinos in the Reserve. Within fifteen minutes, a dozen other safari vehicles had completely encircled the rhino, each driver continuously jockeying for position to get his passengers the closest possible look. Njau was beside himself, because he was the first safari guide to spot this rhino, and he hadn't seen one in his previous three months of guiding trips into the Reserve. Because of Njau's enthusiasm, Ken was overzealous in trying to get us close to the rhino, too close. The rhino repeatedly raised its head, sniffed the air, and walked 50 feet in one direction, before turning and running in the opposite direction. There was no clear path through the wall of vehicles.

I was furious that we were directly contributing to the stress of one of the last remaining rhinos in the Reserve. Poaching may be the number one threat facing black rhinos, but tourist harassment can't be helping them any. When I voiced my anger, Njau loudly rebuked me. The other passengers remained silent, leaving me uncertain whether they agreed with Njau.

Equatorial Crossings

I didn't travel to Africa to watch a cornered, wild animal panic. Yet, in other vehicles, crazed tourists, who were overly anxious to photograph the rhino and check it off their list of the "big five" (lion, elephant, rhino, buffalo, and leopard), encouraged their drivers to get ever closer. After forty minutes, the safari vehicles pulled away one by one, and the frenzy slowly dissipated. Amidst the choking cloud of dust, I looked back through binoculars and I saw that the dazed rhino hadn't moved.

The memorable day was crowned with an archetypal African sunset and another swaggering male lion ambling down the road—a regal King of the savanna. As the magnified orange orb sank below a horizon framed with acacia trees, Ann laughed, "It feels like we're in Africa." Our safari-mates grinned in silent affirmation.

When we returned from our three-day safari, we discovered, to our unrestrained delight, that two friends were in Nairobi. We had first met Lee and Jean at a cramped book shack on one of the many nameless back streets of McLeod Ganj, India. For several days thereafter, we enjoyed Tibetan and Indian meals with them and developed an easy, comfortable friendship, born of mutual respect, the camaraderie unique to world travelers, and hours of stimulating conversations. In this short period, we connected with Lee and Jean on a deeper level than most other travelers we had encountered. They had "cashed out," selling their house and most of their possessions after reading the landmark book *Your Money or Your Life* and choosing life. When we left for Nairobi, there was no sadness in our embraces, because we all sensed that serendipity had brought us together and our paths would cross again.

We tracked down Lee and Jean at their hotel and made a plan to go together to the Rift Valley by *matatu*, the unnerving, jam-packed, mini-van-like deathtraps of Kenya's public transportation system. For four days we camped together on the shore of Lake Navaisha and savored the opportunity to stay in one place and slow the pace of our wanderings. I read two books, photographed the remarkable diversity of birds each dawn, took afternoon naps, and filled my journal with thoughts and images of our journey to that point.

I also spent a lot of time mulling over the wisdom that Lee and Jean shared with us about materialism, self-verification, and stress. They pointed out that, "For most Americans, material wealth and mental health are opposing forces—as wealth increases, health and happiness decrease." They had realized in their mid-50s that happiness cannot be purchased, and they sold their house, cars, furniture, and most of their material possessions. What little was left they put in storage, so that they could travel without the hindrance of a mortgage, insurance, and too much stuff. They chose a simpler life over money and materialism, a decision few Americans ever have the insight or courage to make.

We all agreed that traveling had changed our perspective on what is important in life. For Ann and me, traveling had diminished the desire to return home to our former 40 to 60 hour-per-week careers and too-frantic lifestyle. We recognized, thanks to our serendipitous meeting of Lee and Jean, that, like many Americans, we had fallen into the trap of consumerism — an endless cycle of working more to earn more money to buy more things, while increasingly neglecting our family, friends, and spiritual needs. We were "dinks" (double income no kids) slowly being lured into the seductive trap of accumulating material wealth at the expense of our physical and mental health.

Jean, a former hospital administrator, referred to this vicious cycle as "affluenza," a highly contagious disease that had likely afflicted me ever since I landed my first paying job after graduate school. Lee explained how he and Jean had come to this understanding: "We re-examined our relationship with money, and the power it had over us. By determining exactly how much money we needed to live the lifestyle we wanted, we intentionally chose to work only enough to achieve that precise income." Ann and I knew that our travels would give us the opportunity to rethink our consumer ways, but I never imagined that this trip would be necessary therapy to bring our early stage affluenza into remission.

Following dinner on our last evening together, Lee looked up at the shimmering sky and inquired, "Have you ever seen Jupiter's moons?"

"No," I replied.

"Once," Ann said, "when I was in grad school in Arizona."

"Well, you're in for a real treat," Lee beamed.

He demonstrated how, by lying on his back and using a pair of binoculars, he could clearly focus on two of Jupiter's visible moons. An avid astronomy buff and former science teacher, Lee explained that Jupiter has four planet-sized moons, called the Galilean Satellites, plus twelve other smaller satellites. As he described each moon, I heard only fragments of what he was saying: "ice crust" ... "volcanically active"..."Callisto's craters." My mind was far more focused on the immensities than the particularities. Spellbound, I peered through binoculars into a distant universe, and I knew intuitively that sprawled before me was a whole new way of visualizing my place in the world.

I was born into the "me generation," an era of rugged individualism in America in which I was constantly bombarded by TV and radio slogans: "Believe in yourself;" "Be all that you can be;" and "Just do it." My high school football coach urged me to "Show your intestinal fortitude." Teachers encouraged me to "Be the brightest star." Yet, the pervasive emphasis on the individual in American culture exists in direct contrast to the emphasis on others we had observed in Indonesia, Nepal, and Tibet. In Tibetan Buddhism the path to enlightenment requires elimination of suffering for *all* sentient beings, and thus inner focus must shift from oneself to others. As I lay there, gazing up at Jupiter's moons, I realized our travels had taught me to reject the "Just Me" mindset and adopt the much richer mantra of "Just Be."

During the last few months of our journey, I tried to be ever more cognizant of this mantra, even though my natural inclination is toward spending my time as a human *doing* rather than a human *being*. Ann and I tried to slow down, stay longer in each new place we visited, and reflect more on the richness of our adventures. After more than ten months of traveling, we had nearly reached satiation and we needed to digest everything we had experienced before embarking on new adventures.

We spent nearly three more weeks slowly exploring Kenya's Rift Valley and tent camping in or near villages not listed in any of the popular traveler's guides—desperately poor villages where nearly everyone greeted us with welcoming smiles, and Ann remarked, "I feel so alive here."

She had been reading a book by Daisy Waugh called *Small Town*, which chronicles a year of the teenage author's life spent as the only white person in a rural African farming community. Because of this book, Ann was increasingly wishing we would stay put in one place. She longed to learn the names of everyone in an entire village, and to know who cooked the best *ugali*, and whose chickens laid the tastiest eggs. She wanted to sip tea and savor lengthy conversations with rural Africans.

The further we ventured from guidebook destinations, the more we knew we stood out. But we felt more enlivened by this slower pace of travel off the beaten tourist path, and the more meaningful human contact that such a pace allowed. We didn't expect and didn't receive special treatment. As we met more and more people outside of Nairobi, we began to see the warmth and resilience in the human face of Africa. We chatted, explored, and ate on our own volition, without a tour schedule or a guide interpreting for us. We moved to a new place when inspired to by our collective mood, rather than some predetermined schedule. One day in the Kakamega Rainforest, I took two naps in the same afternoon, and Ann teased me that these were my fourth and fifth naps of the entire trip.

The Africa that tourists, and certainly most Americans, know and expect to experience is the diverse "wild kingdom" one discovers on safari. The other side of Africa that we were slowly discovering was the human face of an ancient land; therein lies the real story of our brief foray into the Rift Valley. And one individual, in particular, still comes to mind after all these years.

Near dawn one morning, on the shores of Lake Baringo, we met Julius. He was a tall, stringy man in his early 20s, with a dashing but slightly nervous smile and muscled calves that suggested a life spent walking. He moved with the long, graceful strides of a gazelle and the silent agility of a cheetah stalking prey.

Our prey that morning was birds. Renowned as the bird-watching center of Kenya, Lake Baringo supports more than 450 of the 1,200 different bird species in Kenya. We had hired Julius, a respected local bird expert, to take us on a guided walk. For the next several hours, we traversed open bushland, scoured the woodland fringe beneath 300-foot tall eroding red sandstone bluffs, and tiptoed like herons through the tall marsh grasses by the lake. By noon, we had seen more than 75 different bird species and heard dozens more that Julius identified by call alone. Ann and I were bewildered to have seen and heard so many. Julius apologized in his gentle manner, "Not a good day for birds, sorry."

That afternoon, I purchased *Checklist of the Birds of Lake Baringo* and languished in the shade as I checked off as many as I could remember. The checklist made reference to a record for the greatest number of different species seen in a 24-hour period at Lake Baringo by one individual—a remarkable 351 species, more than twice the total number my local Audubon chapter counts in their annual Christmas bird count, which typically involves 50 or more skilled birders.

Julius found us again in the late afternoon, "You like another walk, for free? I like birds, you like birds ... let's go." I jumped at the chance, but Ann was content to continue reading her novel in the shade. By 6 pm, dark clouds blew in from the south over the lake, turning the water a muddy crimson color. A spectacular rainbow formed to the west. Periodically the sun burst through cloud breaks, illuminating the tips of the marsh grasses like millions of tapered candles. In an hour's time, Julius and I added seven new species to our morning tally, including one of his favorites, a double-banded courser, roughly the size and shape of a North American nighthawk. Keen-eyed Julius also pointed out a hummingbird-sized, striped kingfisher, whose metallic, indigo plumage shimmered in the low sun as it skittered for cover, and a larger, virtually camouflaged, brown-hooded kingfisher perched in the crook of a tree—two species he had rarely seen before. Excited by these sightings, Julius said twice, "Many thanks, David."

"No, Julius, thank you," I replied with glee. "You're the best birder I've ever met."

That evening Ann and I bought Julius dinner at Mama Lena's, the only restaurant in the nearby village, and we expanded our conversation beyond birds. Ann asked, "Have you ever been to Masai Mara?"

"No," Julius replied, "I going to Nairobi one time, and Lake Bogoria two time."

Otherwise, he had spent his whole life at Lake Baringo. He talked of his "great hope" of visiting other parts of Kenya and Africa, but not being able to afford to travel. He mentioned the names of nine family members he was responsible for supporting.

"I want to see every bird in Kenya," he went on enthusiastically.

"Would you like to go to Kakamega Rainforest Reserve?" I inquired.

He replied, "Yes! Very much I like to go, but no money."

Ann chimed in, "How much would a matatu to Kakamega cost?"

"I think maybe $250 KSH ($4 US)," Julius estimated.

Ann and I looked at each other in a way that I knew she was thinking precisely the same thing as me. Before leaving Kenya, we mailed Julius a letter and enough money to visit Kakamega, Kenya's only remaining protected rainforest. We also included extra, with the suggestion that he should use the money to further his dream of seeing every bird in Kenya.

For two years after we returned home, Julius wrote us letters telling us of his ongoing dream of becoming an ornithologist. One of these letters contained a collection of beautiful stamps depicting the ornate birds of Kenya. The last time we heard from Julius, he sent us a letter with a humble request for bus money so that he could participate in a birding competition in Nairobi. We sent money, but suspect he never got it. We haven't heard from Julius since, but I haven't given up hope that our paths may one day cross again. I am, after all, a firm believer in serendipity and suspect that our chance meeting of Julius may foreshadow more than just our one memorable day of bird watching together. But even if we never meet again, thanks to Julius and our many other newfound friends in the Rift Valley, we learned the rewards of a "just be" mindset; a corollary to the "live simply" message of the Himalayas and the "power of compassion" we discovered in Tibet.

❖·❖

After another ambitious three-day wildlife odyssey, consisting of one whirlwind day in each of three Tanzanian preserves—Ngorongoro Crater, Tarangire National Reserve, and Lake Manyara National Reserve—we decided we really needed what Ann termed, "a vacation from our vacation." This decision was precipitated by a string of unsettling events: a death-defying jeep ride down the rim of the Ngorongoro Crater with a driver turned maniac (Ann later told me she had shoved a note in her pocket saying, "If I die on this road, it was our driver's fault. He's wacko!!"); repeated encounters with rude or aggressive vendors and touts; and a counterfeit US $100.00 bill passed off on us by a major, international bank. So, we returned to Kenya and spent a week on Wasini Island, a tropical paradise off the Kenyan coast, with no power, phones, or roads. Free from these supposed "necessities," we were able to relax more and enjoy the laid-back lifestyle of this island fishing community of roughly 500 people. We stayed with the Muslim family of Masood Abdullah, who operated a small lodge and restaurant in the quaint village of Mpunguti.

We were immediately charmed by the idyllic, freshly-painted cottages overlooking the water; the groomed walking paths lined with sun-bleached corals and magnificent blooming bougainvilleas; the stunning sun birds; enormous drooping Baobab trees; and the beaches covered with many varieties of traditional wooden dhows, dugouts, and catamarans. From the shaded porch of our cottage, we looked out across a fringe of mangroves toward a coral reef that demanded exploration.

Masood and his large, always-smiling family also charmed us. They have made it their mission to get folks like Ann and me to slow down and live more simply. Each day at breakfast Masood reminded us "*polay, polay*" (slowly, slowly). Concerned about squeezing in sailing, snorkeling, and village explorations on a rapidly dwindling budget, I peppered Masood with questions. "*Hakuna matata*" (no problem), he said. "Let life come to you. Do not worry. We will talk about money later. Now you enjoy your meal."

After only one day here, we developed a comfortable routine that included a morning stroll into the village to barter for bananas and fried doughnut-like *mandazi*, followed by snorkeling, reading, writing, daydreaming about our 11 months of adventures, bird watching, napping, and talking for hours on end. Our evenings revolved around the splendid, multi-course dinners cooked by Masood's wives and daughters. Among the many savory Swahili foods we tried, a few in particular can still make me salivate by remembrance alone: fresh grilled fish called *taffi* in coconut sauce; spongy rice bread hot from the oven; flaky fried *samosas*; seaweed marinated in vinaigrette; octopus with a tangy red-chili salsa; a snapper-like fish baked in a fragrant sauce of tomatoes, onions, and cilantro; and the ever present rice, beans, and tortilla-like *chapattis*. All of our meals were served on a hand-woven, linen tablecloth artfully sprinkled with bougainvillea blossoms: five star cuisine and service, with no pretension, for about five bucks a day for two of us.

Because there were no lights to interfere with stargazing, we witnessed some of the most stunningly clear night skies of the entire trip. The Milky Way felt touchable as I squinted my eyes and stretched my fingers toward the sky. Jupiter shone so brightly I envisioned it as the sun of the night sky. In conjunction with the savory food, tropical setting, and the relaxed pace of life, these luminous nights inspired some of the greatest reveries of our journey. We nurtured our tired bodies and spiced our marriage with liberal sprinklings of insights and wisdom we had gained during our travels. We snorkeled at the Kisite Marine Reserve, a Kenyan national treasure every bit as diverse as Masai Mara, and we sailed one of Masood's catamarans. Periodically, we attempted to photograph the people and capture the essence of this place that moved us so deeply. Mostly, though, I remember the value of learning to move less and reflect more.

Had we not previously arranged to spend time in Harare, Zimbabwe with Phebion and Nancy, friends of Ann's from graduate school days, I think we could easily have spent a month on Wasini Island. Perhaps as much as the place itself, it was the timing of our arrival there—the fact that serendipity had led us to a place of calm, at a time when quiet reflection was what we needed most. But the Wasini sojourn ended abruptly with a wavy trip on a dhow to the Kenyan mainland, followed by a kidney-jarring, rooftop ride to the Tanzanian border on an overloaded bus. For the next 3-1/2 hours, Ann could ponder nothing else but the thought of what would happen to us, the other 25+ people on the roof, and the fifty folks crammed inside, if the bus was in a collision or strayed off the road and rolled. Once again, we had thrust ourselves back into traveler mode.

One week after leaving Wasini Island, we arrived in Harare after dark, following a frustrating and seemingly interminable day on three broken-down buses. On the final bus, we had decided to splurge on a guesthouse, which included breakfast, a swimming pool, and a phone in every room.

Along an unlit block lined with overhanging trees, Ann sensed we were being followed, and we ducked into a dimly lit place called Backpacker's Rest. The rate was more than we wanted to pay, so we continued walking toward City Inn, our original destination, which was still a fifteen-minute walk away. One block past Backpacker's Rest, a security guard at an apartment complex warned us that two "street kids" were following us. We dismissed the warning, still fixated on clean sheets, homemade breakfast, and the promise of a pool.

Two blocks later, we realized, beyond any doubt, that not only were these two street kids stalking us, six more teens were converging, in three pairs, from every other direction. My instinct was flight. By the time I grabbed Ann's hand, they had closed to within twenty feet, and we turned around and sprinted back toward Backpacker's Rest and a lighted intersection. Fifty yards later, just before we reached the intersection, a car turned onto our street. We flagged it down and jumped in headfirst, packs still on our backs. The street thugs were nowhere in sight. The driver, an Indian man, dropped us back at Backpacker's Rest, and we offered him sheepish thanks, still reeling from his troubling advice to "carry a very big knife" if we planned to do any more walking at night.

Davis, the clerk at Backpacker's Rest, informed us that earlier in the week two German women were nearly beaten to death when they resisted street thugs who wanted their cameras. Just an hour earlier, I had remarked to Ann how much Harare reminded me of Seattle, and how comfortable it felt to be walking along clean streets with curbs, sidewalks, traffic lights, and garbage bins. We had walked past a downtown park, a fast-food joint called the Chicken Inn, and well-lit department stores that reminded us of home. Harare was the closest we had come to familiar civilization since leaving the U.S., and, by letting down our guard, we nearly lost everything.

We paid for a dorm room and each collapsed on separate single beds. I woke up the next morning still in my clothes, feeling like I'd slept surprisingly well given the previous night's trauma. I rolled over and saw Ann sitting upright in bed, writing in her journal. "How are you doing?" I asked, stretching my arms over my head and yawning.

She didn't answer for a long time, then finally replied, "I'm tired . . . I'm tired of traveling. I'm tired of feeling vulnerable. I'm tired of making every decision together, of *being* together 24 hours/day for eleven months."

I sat up and looked at her, but before I could respond, she added in tears, "I want to separate for awhile."

Dumbfounded, I said, "You're joking, right?"

"No, I mean it," she replied.

"We just about got mugged," I stammered, "and now you want to venture out on your own?"

"Yes," she murmured.

"Well that's pretty damn selfish isn't it?" I retorted. "All you have to do is hook up with Phebion and Nancy. What am I supposed to do, go make friends with the street thugs?"

Riled by my outburst, she said "I'm fed up with you snapping at me; I don't feel respected. I've been wanting time to myself more and more . . . I don't want to have to agree on every single meal, destination, and means of transportation . . . I'm tired of making decisions when you're unable to . . . and . . ."

I listened for ten minutes without saying a word. When she was finished, I got up, went to the bathroom, and slammed the door behind me.

I stared in the mirror in shock, asking myself how she could make such a rash decision. I splashed cold water on my face, followed by a shave with scalding hot water. How could she contemplate separating after everything we'd been through over the past eleven months, not to mention the past 24 hours?

In the shower, my anger dissipated a little and I realized all my thinking centered on her, and not on my own inadequacies that could be driving her away. Yet, despite this brief moment of logic, I emerged from the bathroom and began packing my things, without looking at her or speaking. It was only after I was fully packed and lacing up my hiking boots to leave that Ann forced the issue, and said, "Let's talk."

"What's there to talk about?" I sighed. "Sounds like your mind is made up."

"Yes, but I don't want to separate when you're filled with such anger," she offered, coaxing me to start talking.

We began by reviewing the multiple stresses of the previous week. Since leaving Wasini Island, we had faced some of the greatest adversity of our travels. The 1,100-mile journey from Wasini to Harare was a blur of matatus, buses, and trains. We had endured threats, heat, cramped legs, aching backs, and stagnant air. About the only moment of laughter we shared was when we passed a butcher shop near the Kenya-Tanzania border called the *New Tourist Butchery*. Little did we know at the time that street thugs often have the last laugh.

In Kenya, we had been told at the High Commission that a 5-day Zambian transit visa would cost $5 US/person. Yet, on the train from Dar es Salaam, Tanzania to Kapiri Mposhi, Zambia, a Zambian immigration officer threatened to kick us off the train unless we paid him $25 US each for a transit visa. Knowing that this was extortion, I refused to pay and he took our passports. I followed him for the next 45 minutes, as he checked the passport of every passenger on the train. I wasn't about to let our passports out of my sight. I appealed to him repeatedly, but he was rude, stubborn, and unwilling to listen. He was also a good 100 pounds heavier than me, with hands that looked like he could snap my neck like a twig.

I plead my case to the conductor, who was sympathetic but said he was powerless to do anything. His suggestion, in hushed tones, was to "offer a bribe." So, Ann and I offered the immigration officer $20 US and the equivalent of $12 US in Zambian money — the sum total of our remaining cash. He hesitated and seemed on the verge of refusing, when I said, "Look, we will pay you $50 US in Kapiri Mposhi, after we cash a traveler's check, but we don't have that much cash on us."

"OK," he relented with a grunt, hurling us back our passports.

Once we were out of hearing range, I cursed, "I'm so fucking tired of dealing with people who make their living cheating tourists."

The next day in Kapiri Mposhi, a Sunday, all the banks were closed. Fortunately, there was no sign of the hulking immigration officer. So, after all our stress, we ended up not paying any bribe. But we still didn't have transit visas, leaving us vulnerable to future fines or extortion, at minimum, and possibly time in jail. We wanted out of Zambia as fast as possible.

Two days later, after multiple torturous bus rides in searing heat, a life-threatening flat tire at high speed, a bout of explosive diarrhea, and frequent sniping between Ann and me, we arrived, still without visas, at the Zambezi River—the last hurdle in our epic journey to get out of Zambia. Our objective was to cross the river into Zimbabwe. It was mid-morning and the equatorial sun was unmerciful. The only available shade was in the slim shadow of parked buses.

For more than an hour, while Ann pretended to be in the exit visa line, I studied the massive metal bridge at the border crossing, trying to detect whether there were any guards. From my vantage point 100 yards away in the shadow of a parked bus, there appeared to be four armed guards on the Zambia side of the bridge, and none on the Zimbabwe side; people only seemed to be crossing one way, from Zambia into Zimbabwe. I noted that whenever a bus arrived the guards left their post at the bridge and moved to the nearby thatched-roof building to observe the visa line. So, we timed our bridge crossing to coincide with the next bus arrival. It was a simple strategy that worked. We simply walked across the bridge like we knew what we were doing. No one stopped us. My only regret is that we were too nervous to stop and take a photo from the Zimbabwe side of the bridge, looking back toward Zambia.

Once on Zimbabwe soil, we briefly hugged in relief and disbelief, and then quickly moved to the entry visa line. The entry process took about an hour, with no hassles and no fees. We were legally in Zimbabwe, but still hundreds of miles from our ultimate destination. Eight hours and three bus breakdowns later, we arrived in Harare, after dark. That same night, we were nearly mugged.

As we relived these misadventures in our dorm room, it became obvious that even though we never ended up paying bribes to obtain Zambia transit visas, we paid plenty in emotional capital. No wonder there were heightened tensions between us.

We delved deeper than we ever had into our innermost feelings about one another—the good and the bad. Four hours later, after intense, often painful, but brutally honest dialogue, we made love. Afterwards, we decided not to separate. We left open the possibility of spending time apart, but only if we did so willingly and on good terms, rather than bad.

In the end, we surmised that our recent pattern of impatience, criticism, and resentment was directly tied to our stress and exhaustion from the arduous journey to get to Harare. This unhealthy pattern, which had characterized our week since leaving Wasini Island, was a clear signal that we needed to return to the respect, admiration, and gentleness that have characterized our marriage.

At the Holiday Inn in downtown Harare, we treated ourselves to an all-you-can-eat lunch buffet. We spent the afternoon wandering around the city and getting oriented, in full daylight. We debated about going to see a movie, but instead decided to go back to our room and make love again. Several days later, Ann would write,

> *In the tender afterglow of this day, I won't soon forget that buoyant feeling — the power love has to lift your spirit, passion, awareness, self-image, and outlook on the world!*

When we finally connected with Ann's friends, Phebion and Nancy, the next day, we were still emotionally fragile, and we needed nearly a week of family life to regain a sense of balance and direction. Phebion and Nancy opened their hearts and home to us and welcomed us like beloved family members. Phebion is a gifted artist and art history professor at the University of Zimbabwe. Nancy taught at a local elementary school, but she was at home on maternity leave during our visit. Both are natives of Zimbabwe and dearly love their country and their culture. But times were hard, and they seemed to be barely scraping by. Their vehicle sat in the driveway unused, because a needed repair part would have to be ordered from Japan at a price more than Phebion's monthly paycheck.

Equatorial Crossings

Phebion and Nancy were both gentle and caring, and Nancy, in particular, loved to laugh, so being around them was easy and fun. We both were craving the opportunity to have meaningful conversations with anyone but each other, and Phebion and Nancy both loved to talk. Without knowing it, they rescued us at a time when our traveling rapport—our relationship—badly needed new vigor and renewed commitment.

We shared cooking and meals with Phebion and Nancy, and went on several occasions to hear traditional *mbira* music. We also traveled to an agricultural fair, visited a relative's farm, and had a cookout with the family of Nancy's sister. But my fondest memory of our time together is of playing with their spirited daughter, Kudzie, and their newborn son, Munya. Our daily romps with their children helped me realize how much we would have to offer children of our own and how badly I wanted to be a father. Seeing Ann's natural, maternal instincts, I knew that parenthood was increasingly likely to be our next grand adventure. I remember waking one morning to Kudzie's squeals of delight. I arose and watched from the doorway as Ann and Kudzie played "pat-a-cake," with some improvisational dancing mixed in for good measure. Within two days, she bonded with bubbly Kudzie so beautifully, so passionately, that I felt once again like the luckiest man alive.

After spending two weeks with the Kangai family, Ann and I decided to make one last backpacking trip to Chimanimani National Park in eastern Zimbabwe, before flying home via Europe. Similar to Wasini Island, our few days in the Park were a time of individual and joint reflection. We spent much of each day simply talking. At night, we slept under the stars, lulled to sleep by the babble of cascading water and the hum of circling bats. We found ourselves wanting the world trip to be over, but not really wanting to end it. On our last night camping, we basked in the magical light of the full moon, staring wordlessly as it crested crag after crag. The full moon seemed a reassuring sign that everything was going to be ok between us, and that it was time for our journey to end.

The next morning, still riding the highs of the previous night's full moon and its soft light that bathed our camp in lavender, we loaded our backpacks for the trip back to Harare. All morning we followed the gradual descent of the Bundi River, through a grove of trees I called "leopard hollow" and along a series of riffles and pools that reflected the towering ridgeline south of Mount Binga, the second highest peak in Zimbabwe. We knew, as we dropped our packs next to the trail and wandered through ancient red rock formations up to a saddle, that this day in Chimanimani would mark the last hiking of our world journey.

As we gazed across the open expanse of rolling green toward the Mozambique border, a flood of emotions and memories swept over me. The grass was literally greener on the other side of the border, but I had no desire to go there. The magnitude of what we had experienced and the many gifts we had received over the past year overwhelmed me. I felt a sense of debt, a powerful sense that we had received so much more than we had given.

In expressing this to Ann, she pointed out that the first questions friends would ask us when we returned home were: "What is your most memorable story? What was your favorite place? What was your favorite meal, or animal, or ...?"

"Ann," I asked, "What is the greatest gift you have received during our travels?" She sat for a long time quietly sorting through her cache of memories. "There's no *one* gift that rises above the rest," she answered. "Our *whole* journey feels like a priceless gift to me." I knew what she meant, because I couldn't point to any one gift, either. I simply knew that our travels had changed me too profoundly to understand there and then, without the benefit of distance and reflection.

"What is the greatest gift you have given?" I asked.

"An open mind," she replied without hesitation, as if she had anticipated the question.

I loved this answer for many of the same reasons I so deeply love Ann—her succinct answer spoke volumes about her ability to give of herself so readily, her willingness to be open and honest, and the depth of her thinking and caring about others. Years later, I discovered in Ann's Africa journal, the following passage:

> *I have learned in our travels that people everywhere value a warm heart, sincerity, generosity, and imagination. You can communicate these qualities incredibly easily if you want to — no need to have a common language, as body language, gestures, and acts of kindness will express these values perfectly. I have found that I am drawn to people who exhibit these qualities — in fact, I am ready to put my trust in such people ...*

At the time, my answer to the "greatest gift" question would have been a material one: the Swiss Army knife that I gave to Tindatu for helping to save my life, or the gift of my down parka to one of our Nepalese porters, or the money that we gave to a woman in Sulawesi for her children's education, or the donation we made to the nun's at the Bitung Hospital. Ann's answer helped me to understand a simple truth: the greatest gifts a traveler has to give are an open mind and a smile.

We laughed as we tried to imagine what our many new friends might be saying about us: the villagers of Kaleleng; our Tibetan Ama and Papa; the guide in Sulawesi who, upon seeing my bare, hairy chest, warned me not to go in public without a shirt because the locals would call me "monkey;" our Nepalese porters; the Kenyan men in Nakuru who, because we were childless, thought we needed their help reproducing; and the hundreds of others we had met in the course of our journey. Would the memories of these encounters that still burn so brightly for us quickly fade for these people?

In reading the last few pages of Ann's final trip journal, I discovered an unfinished poem:

> A thousand looks. Ten-thousand.
> No need for a common language—
> Their dark, staring eyes convey fear and curiosity, at once.
> I always try to respond with a benevolent gaze.
>
> I may be one of the first whites they have seen,
> and I feel the need to reassure them
> that my people can be warm-hearted.
>
> What else have I to give?

We had touched the lives of many people in a way that, while charming and enlightening for us, is probably even more profound for them. Had we intruded on innocent lives with our Western ways of dress, manners, and thinking, satisfying our curiosity and then leaving behind qualified promises about returning to visit someday? Would we be remembered fondly, enviously, sadly, with disgust or pity, or perhaps not at all?

Reflecting on the beginning of our African adventures more than two months earlier, I pondered the diverse faces of Africa we had witnessed: the violent, cruel face of the streets of Nairobi and Harare; the unimaginably beautiful, but also violent face of the wildlife reserves; and the striking and storied faces of the African people. I recalled how seeing Jupiter's moons filled me with so much joy and reverence and humility that I could barely fathom the depth of the discovery. Yet, where I found hyperbole, Ann found a simple metaphor: "Seeing Jupiter's moons was like discovering hidden beauty within—by looking out we look in." Thanks to Ann, Jupiter's moons will always be a tangible reminder that beauty and mystery exist not only all around us, but also within. We only have to open our eyes and hearts to the possibilities.

    I now see Ann's smile in the arc of the sun, in dew beads at dawn cupped in a cradle of lupine leaves, in my own reflection off the mirror surface of still waters. Ann and Jupiter's moons have become defining spheres of my universe. I'm grateful for both and humbled by the lessons they've taught me: the insight to be glad of life, to play and to look up at the stars. And the courage to just be.

17

Trevelrie

> It is a narrow, difficult path if you really follow the adventure of the impulse system in your life . . . Wherever love takes you, there you go, and that's the adventure—that's a true love marriage . . . Follow your bliss.
>
> -Joseph Campbell,
> *The Wisdom of Joseph Campbell: In Conversation With Michael Toms*

Last night, as I was rubbing circles of calendula oil on Ann's silky, pregnant belly, my mind was a gyre of circle imagery. Life is full of circles: the moon, the earth, the sun, a pregnant belly, a salmon's migration, our wedding rings. Birth-life-death is a cycle, a perpetual circle. Even our world journey was a circle, and although circling the globe wasn't ever our intent, I now cherish the way this knowledge feels wrapped around my head and heart.

Our journey was a circle with many beginnings: the icy wildness of Glacier Bay, the uninhabited desert islands of our Baja honeymoon, and the one-way flight to Australia. There was also our eclectic wedding celebration that brought together separate subsets of friends and family, who joined and encircled us as we exchanged vows—vows that drew upon the many belief systems and cultures that resonated for us in that moment of utter joy; cultures we have now glimpsed in the circle of our travels. Joy now magnified because of our journey. Joy we can share with our unborn child. A new life. A new circle.

Would our journey have felt less whole had we not circled the globe? Isn't every journey a circle? At the end of our world circuit, I find there are no easy answers, only more questions, and the realization, thanks to our travels, that life is truly a short and precious gift—a gift of multiple layers to unwrap slowly and seek the hidden beauty within.

On the surface, our world trip was a temporary separation from loved ones, our newly built home, and the so-called "treasures" stored within. I know now this leaving was something deeper. For the first time in our lives, we individually and jointly embraced Joseph Campbell's "follow your bliss" philosophy. By leaving behind our wants, we discovered our needs were few. For thirteen wondrous months, food, water, shelter, and our evolving love sustained us. We started our journey with too much stuff, material things we thought we couldn't live without, and we returned with nearly empty backpacks and overflowing souls.

The day we started driving toward our Olympic Peninsula home, after several days spent visiting Ann's family in Lake Tahoe, the clutch went out in our truck. A night in a hotel, a towing bill, and nearly $800 later, we were underway again. In paying our clutch-related expenses, I couldn't help but think about how long we could travel in Africa or Nepal or Southeast Asia for that same $800. But even the clutch replacement couldn't shatter the good karma of a year of world travels.

Two days later, we were headed up Hood Canal, near dusk, on a crisp October evening, bathed in low amber light. Mount Rainier loomed on the horizon to the southeast, her snowy cap showing hints of alpenglow. The dappled waters of Hood Canal lulled us into silent reflection. Near the hairpin turn at Lilliwaup, a salmon launched free of the water, twisted, and plunged in a slow, silvery-red arc. I pulled over. Ann looked at me with watery eyes, and said, "We're home."

I feel blessed in so many ways, but most of all to have circled the globe with my soul mate on this prelude to parenthood journey. Traveling with Ann taught me to honor the beauty and mystery of marriage. I now see in her the spontaneous child, the nurturing soul, and the fertile mind that draw others close. I found in myself surprising anger and a hidden capacity for compassion.

As I bring our journey full circle to a close, I'm reminded of the incredible choices we have in the U.S. I'm not talking about the sixty-five brands of cereal on the grocery shelves, or the hundreds of available cable TV channels; I'm talking about the freedom to vote, and choices of education, reproduction, and free speech. Through the expansive experiences of our travels, I now appreciate more fully that the freedom to make choices, which we take for granted as Americans, doesn't exist in many parts of the world. I think that many Americans, perhaps even most, take the relative comfort of our lives for granted. How often is true hardship—basic survival—the focus of our daily discourse or actions?

Hardship was forever redefined for me in India by the lingering image of a man in rags, near death, lying on a New Delhi train platform as maggots squirmed on his limp but breathing body and hundreds of people walked by unfazed. Within the ease of my middle-class life, I have never known crippling hunger, or slept in fetid rags on a filthy street, or lived each day in fear of oppression, torture, or death. Instead, I wander through my days feeling graced by providence, by the ability to accumulate spiritual wealth rather than money and to consciously decide between a simple and a complicated life. I have the luxury to choose whether to travel or to stay at home, whereas most people in the world cannot comprehend even having such a choice.

I once heard an interview of Isabelle Allende on National Public Radio in which she commented that, "Americans are blessed with profound natural and spiritual resources." "What we're lacking," she noted, "is natural and spiritual wisdom." I now wonder if epiphanies such as hers can only be realized through the lens of travel, through the act of leaving behind the familiar. I know I returned home feeling blessed that I was born in this country and questioning, "Why aren't more Americans rejoicing?"

I recall the private rejoicing I did on the plane from Harare to Paris. On the next to last page of my fifth and final trip journal, I wrote:

> *I feel like Harare was the end of our world adventure; the rest is simply our journey home. We're leaving the "third world," where we had grown so comfortable, and are heading back to the materialism of the "first world," which I fear. I know that travel awakened me to compassion, and the realization that suffering is universal. I was able for the first time to understand the struggles of people outside America and to feel true empathy for the starving, the oppressed, the forgotten. Experiencing other cultures also brought me to a greater understanding of my own—an acceptance of who I am and where I come from; a stronger connection to my roots and this place I've chosen to call home. And the ultimate realization that we are all members of the same community. All temporary citizens of one incredible earth. One world. One global family.*

Of all the wonder-full adventures and magical experiences we had, my most vivid memories are of the amazing people we met along the way: brothers who helped me redefine my place in the world, without any words, but with a simple smile, a genuine hug, or the unforgettable gift of a dried yak leg; children who taught me the joys of innocence and wonder; and sisters who shared their homes, their hearts, and their stories, and helped me to appreciate that all humans are storytellers. I know now that stories transcend race, culture, gender, and even language. Indeed, the best stories are universal.

Toward the end of our travels, I kept searching for more evocative words to tell our stories to friends and family back home. I played games with inventing new superlatives: awestounding, stupendorific, gloriful, and splendificent. These concoctions danced into my phone calls and postcards more readily than verbs, and somewhere amidst the tumble of these verbal gymnastics, I discovered the one word that has stuck with me.

Trevelrie is my word for the rapture of travel and the corresponding indelible memories that the inner and outer journeys foster. I like the way trevelrie sounds as it skips carefree along my tongue. I also like the resonant meaning behind the sounds:

> **travel** *vb* [ME *travailen* to travail, journey] 1a: to go on a trip or tour: JOURNEY

> **revel** *vi* [ME *revelen*, fr. MF *reveler*, lit., to rebel, fr. L *rebellare*] 2: to take intense satisfaction

> **revelation** *n* [ME, fr. MF, fr. LL revelation-, *revelatio*, fr. L *revelatus*, pp. of *revelare* to reveal] (14c) 3a: an act of revealing to view or making known

> **reverie** *n* [F *reverie*, fr. MF, delirium, fr. *resver*, *rever* to wander, be delirious] 1: DAYDREAM 2: the condition of being lost in thought

> **reverence** *n* [ME, fr. OF, fr. L *reverentia*, fr. *reverent-*, *reverens*, prp. of *revereri*] (13c) 1: honor or respect felt or shown : DEFFERENCE; esp: profound adoring awed respect.

Trevelrie

The cumulative entwinement of travel-revel-revelation-reverie-reverence is Trevelrie—the agony, ecstasy, and serendipity of leaving behind the familiar and opening one's mind and heart to the new.

Trevelrie is my collage of sacred travel memories, my "river teeth"[1]—cross-grained whorls of memories shaped by the river of time; travel experiences condensed and hardened into tight knots of beauty, wisdom, and emotion. I savor these knotty morsels of memory more than any possession, for these travel memories nourish me and bring me comfort. They also keep me humble.

I remember reading, once, that love empowers memory. Thanks to Ann, I know this to be true. I also believe that the reverse is true, that memory empowers love, for a life fully-lived is overflowing with both love and memory, constantly revitalizing each other. This collection of essays is my attempt to share with you glimpses of my travel memories, and hopefully a few well-chewed shreds of traveler's wisdom. Mostly, though, I hope you feel inspired to go and create your own indelible memories.

All this takes is the courage to leave behind the familiar, and the willingness to surrender to the magic of serendipity. Granted, it's a big world out there, but remember that serendipity is one of the greatest joys of traveling: chance encounters with other travelers, indigenous people, or wildlife; unexpected discoveries; unplanned adventures; and the fortuitous convergence of place and time. One cannot count on serendipity or build up expectations around it. Seren-dip-ity, we discovered, is really just serenity with an unexpected dip inserted in the middle. Serendipity happens. It just seems to happen to travelers more often. So, as my dear mom urged us, "Go, and make memories." You never know, trevelrie just might await you around the next bend.

---

[1] D.J. Duncan 1995. *River Teeth: Stories and Writings*. Doubleday. New York, New York.

Epilogue: A Gift of Time

> Time is
> Too Slow for those who Wait
> Too Swift for those who Fear
> Too Long for those who Rejoice;
> But for those who Love, Time is eternity.
>
> -Henry VanDyke

The voice you hear throughout this book is mine. The harmony — the eloquent chords that resonate like the strings of a guitar — is Ann's. Her love plucked me out of bachelorhood. Her love ignited my passion for foreign travel. Her love infused me with the courage to write. And though I have chosen to carry the melody solo, we always attempt to sing the chorus together.

We returned from our ten equatorial crossings in late October 1996, 13 months after leaving home — 12 months abroad followed by one month visiting family in the U.S. Upon returning to the States, we were anxious to share our joy — our trevelrie — with others. For months we told stories and gave slide shows to family, friends, senior's groups, fellow travelers, photography clubs, each other, co-workers, our dog and cat, anyone with the patience to listen.

On Valentine's Day 1997, we were scheduled to give an evening slide show in Port Angeles, a benefit for the Peninsula Trails Coalition. Only two weeks had passed since the tragic deaths of dear friends of ours from graduate school, their two-year-old son, and their newborn baby. They were all smothered in a mudslide that swept their Bainbridge Island home into Puget Sound. We were not through grieving.

Equatorial Crossings

But that night I heard in Ann's voice something new and exciting. Her closing words gave me comfort and renewed my sense of joy in simply being alive. "Most of all," she lilted, "I feel the trip was a gift we gave each other—a gift of time—the kind of time that's slower because every minute is bursting with wonder, the way time passes for children. In retrospect, I think we were children again, for a whole year ... Like I said in the only love poem I have ever written:

With you
>I am satisfied.

I am at peace
>with myself and the world

Then you say I am amazing—
>what can this mean?
>I don't feel amazing.
>Are you amazed at the feelings
>>I have evoked in you?
>New and improved emotions—
>>I feel them, too.

There is a comfort
>which reinforces my being.

There is an excitement
>because I can't imagine
>a more perfect experience
>>than to share in discovery
>>>with the one you love.

We are kindred spirits
>on the ultimate adventure.

There is much to learn
>from an open soul.

>I pray I have the strength
>>to give you me."

Epilogue: A Gift of Time

When she finished, few eyes were dry. There are moments in life so rare, so sacred, that one hesitates to utter word of them for fear they will diminish in the telling. Ann's closing that night was one of those moments.

Nearly one year later, the gift of time we gave each other fostered the miracle of birth. Waverly Soule Shreffler was born January 17, 1998, more than seven weeks premature. For a ten-day period preceding her birth, I was faced with the greatest challenge of my life. I watched helplessly as Ann's pre-eclampsia worsened, and I feared I would lose both her and the baby. Ann's life was at risk if the baby stayed inside her. The baby's life would be at risk outside her.

This sounds so straightforward now, so clinical. But at the time, my entire being was focused on the endless stream of doctors and nurses, the onslaught of medical information, mortality statistics, tradeoffs and risks, ultrasounds, blood tests, urine samples, medications, fetal heart monitors ... because Ann and Waverly's lives depended on them. Ann and Waverly were on the intervention treadmill, and I was sprinting to keep up. As the medical community pulsed through what seemed like a revolving door, I was desperately trying to jam my foot in the jamb. Everything was spinning out of control, and I realized the irony in the dual meaning of "patient."

It wasn't until an hour before Ann's emergency c-section that I voiced my fears to her and fully acknowledged the gravity of the situation. Tasting the salty cascade of my tears, I whispered, "I could recover if we lost the baby, but I could never recover from losing you."

In the end, Waverly's birth was the grandest possible finale to our prelude to parenthood journey. Our traumatic birth experience wasn't the peaceful home birth we had planned, but Waverly was the improvised solo passage, the cadenza, toward the close of our prelude to parenthood concerto. She was the outgrowth of our trevelrie with a twist of serendipity. She was the missing square in our life quilt, or perhaps the first small scrap in a new one. Four-pound Waverly entered the world with a ballad of life-affirming wails, and I knew that instant that new journeys were beginning ... hers, Ann's, mine ... OURS.

WONDER

(for Waverly, the morning after your birth)

Your first wails
roused a symphony
of cheers   heart music

Your first bath
was my tears   soul water

trickling across pink face, blue hands

Cheek to cheek
I held you
Mom and daughter   ONE

hope, fear, love   united

                         Joy beyond metaphor

Precious gift
I called you
Ann too sick
to help bestow a name

Strength
you gave me
long fingers latched
on trembling pinky
delicate preemie head
cupped in my palm

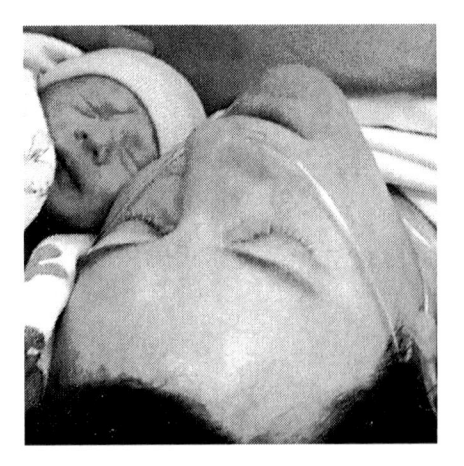

Spirited
said the OB doc
Feisty
reported the NICU nurse
hours old and   already making waves

As Ann lay frail
high on postpartum drugs
I surfed those waves
and you lifted my spirits
with one-armed pushups and frog leaps

Celebrate life!
you implored
with Diva lungs

                        your vigor my solace

Your eyes first opened
in response to Ann's voice
This meeting of eyes

                        a miracle

confirming our choice

Parenthood
our new journey

                        once two, now three

Sing and dance with us, Waverly,
help us see the world anew
through your eyes
with your gift   innocent wonder.

About the Author and Illustrator

Dave Shreffler and Ann Soule have traveled in fifteen countries since 1990, when they did their first expedition together—three weeks of sea kayaking in the icy wildness of Glacier Bay, Alaska. Writing Equatorial Crossings gave Dave the opportunity to mesh his varied interests in travel, natural history, and photography. As a fisheries biologist specializing in ecosystem restoration, Dave derives both personal and professional satisfaction from restoring rivers and estuaries in the Pacific Northwest. He has published more than 40 peer-reviewed reports and journal articles, and he has a life-long zeal for natural history. His photographs have been featured in the Northwest Exhibition of Environmental Photography, *Time*, newspapers, and various scientific journals. Ann has previously done illustrations for the book, *On Celtic Tides*, winner of the 2000 National Outdoor Book Award. *Equatorial Crossings* is their first collaborative book project.

Foreign travel continues to inspire this couple and they relish any opportunity for improved understanding of the world's disappearing cultures. Dave and Ann are also deeply committed to better stewardship of the world's threatened natural resources. They live with their daughter, Waverly, near Sequim, Washington in the foothills bordering Olympic National Park.